Angel
IN A
THORN BUSH

Angel
IN A
THORN BUSH

ROB FYNN

authorHOUSE®

AuthorHouse™
1663 Liberty Drive
Bloomington, IN 47403
www.authorhouse.com
Phone: 1-800-839-8640

Published by AuthorHouse   12/03/2012

ISBN: 978-1-4772-4682-5 (sc)
ISBN: 978-1-4772-4683-2 (e)

This book is dedicated to the memory of Sands, who fought the good fight with such courage and tenacity, always with the time and generous heart to listen and help where she could with others, in spite of her own trials and infirmities.
RIP, dear Gal, 20 June 2012

But those who hope in the Lord will renew their strength.
They will soar on wings like eagles;
they will run and not grow weary,
they will walk and not be faint.

Isaiah 40:31

Foreword

Rob Fynn—a long-standing friend and mentor—is an extraordinary man who has led an extraordinary life, as you will find once you get past this foreword and into his book.

I first met him in 1979 when—as a wet-behind-the-ears immigrant fresh from the UK—I washed up on the shores of Fothergill Island, on Lake Kariba. This was astonishing in itself, as the then Rhodesia was in the final throes of the vicious bush war that resulted in an independent Zimbabwe a couple of years later. The country wasn't exactly flush with tourists, in those days.

Nevertheless, a year or so previously, Rob had successfully completed the building of his Fothergill bush camp—an exercise that involved the acquisition of enormous quantities of sand, cement, gumpoles, thatch, and all other necessary items, their transport across some 30km of open lake, and assembly into what was, in those days, an amazingly luxurious and comfortable safari lodge—all this in the midst of the aforementioned war. This was, I've always felt, a defining achievement. Rob exemplifies the southern African 'can do' mindset.

Not long after, I returned to Fothergill for six weeks and stayed there for three years, during which, through his instruction and example, I was privileged to acquire the basics of wildlife guiding at the hands of one of the finest bushmen in Africa. Rob's knowledge of Zambezi flora and fauna is encyclopaedic; his bushcraft and knowledge of animal behaviour is extraordinary; and his patience with raw Pommies almost (not quite!) inexhaustible—the eruption can be a long time a-coming, but is volcanic when it does.

Since then we have, I like to think, maintained and strengthened our friendship in spite of long absences and sometimes divergent pathways.

But what does one really learn of the "inner man" beneath the youthful Royal Navy officer, the genuinely intrepid aviator, accomplished sailor, dedicated conservationist and totally expert bushman?

I've already noted his "can do, let's make a plan" attitude and should say, in passing, that—coming, as I had, from a feather-bedded environment in which this is almost unheard-of—it also came as a profound revelation and example that I have tried to follow ever since.

But the bedrock, I believe, is Rob the thinker and Rob the seeker. Over the years I have known him Rob has explored many avenues, none—I suspect—fully satisfying, but each contributing a little to his journey towards what some like to label truth, enlightenment, or—maybe more correctly—a personally satisfying philosophy of life. I say this partly because we have, over the years, shared many such discussions; but also because of the way in which he has melded his lifetime of adventure and mental explorations with some priceless—and ageless—attributes: an old-school courtesy and sense of fair play; loyalty to friends and family; and a self-deprecating sense of humour that is never cruel and always at hand.

You will learn vastly more as you read his book. But I think one thing will become obvious to you. Rob is *sui generis;* one of a kind; and—sadly—they don't often make'em like that any more. I've been privileged to enjoy his friendship, and to write this foreword, and I commend him and his book to you.

Dick Pitman
November 2012
Conservationist/Author/Photographer
Founder-chairman, The Zambezi Society

Books:

You Must Be New Around Here (Books of Zimbabwe, 1979)
Wild Places of Zimbabwe (Books of Zimbabwe, 1980)
Rhinos: Past, Present and Future? (Modus Publications, 1989)
A Wild Life (Summersdale, UK, 2007).

Contents

Illustrations

Acknowledgements

To Paul Tingay, Zimbabwean author and script writer, who took my initial writings from an old fashioned 'Richard Burton' prose to this more interesting presentation—you saw, you persevered, and you invigorated—thank you, Pablo.

To John Fynn, my cousin, who sponsored and led the landy trip, and then made his diary and photos available—thank you, Johnno

To Bill Sykes, who laboriously persevered with the final edit that takes men of unlimited patience to achieve—thank you, good friend.

To Paddy Pacey, who generously gave of her time and home to assist in pulling the pictures together into a coherent collage, a herculean work.

To Ant Fynn, good cousin removed, for his fabulous paintings of Fothergill on the cover and Dedication page.

And to all you Rhodesians and Zimbabweans who made this story—I salute you.

Chapter 1

A Safari Too Far

It is September 2008, after a hot, dry, exhilarating day in the Lower Zambezi Valley, Zambia. Evening has come at last. In African fashion, we've cooled off with sun-downers, on the grey green greasy banks of the great river, hippos grunting, water chortling past, and now my guests are sipping liqueurs after a five course dinner under a star-spangled sky, prepared by our Italian chef, Phillipo. They are escorted to their tents by the night watchmen. Phillipo and I make our way along an unlit path to our staff tents upstream, his small flashlight barely illuminating the way ahead. I had forgotten to charge the big light I normally carry.

Nightjars shrill in the still air, distant lions roar, crazed hyenas giggle, and away to our side a leopard coughs.

The night engulfs us.

The crack of a branch up ahead alerts us to elephants quietly browsing in the dense forest. We'd better be careful, some may well be on the path, silently observing us.

"Robeen, you don't have your light tonight," Phillipo says, on reaching his tent. "Shall I escort you further?"

"No thanks Phillipo, I can see myself back safely (*being, after all, the senior guide in camp*). It's only a few metres on. Thank you. Buononotte."

In the pitch darkness I take a few more steps down the path . . . then hear the shuffling of big feet . . . Standing dead still, I listen . . .

1

Nothing.

Probably a hippo making its way to its evening grazing. Is he standing watching me? Or quietly moved on, as they do . . . so nimbly, even for such great lumbering looking animals.

I take a few more steps . . .

Sound of heavy feet fills the black void ahead.

I have no idea what it is. Or which direction it's going. But it's close.

Suddenly, immediately in front of me, white tusks glint in the starlight.

I dive sideways into a vicious *jesse* Woolly Caper bush, aptly named *caparis tormentosa* for its sharp hooked thorns.

I see the light in Phillipo's tent just metres away through the foliage. Hear crushing of branches behind me. And trumpeting.

'Life! She's after me!'

Scrabbling head first, oblivious of the thorns, I make it to Phillipo's tent. He is beckoning furiously, his horrified eyes fixed on the scene behind me.

"Veloce!Veloce!" He shouts.

I dive through the flaps of his tent, landing in a heap. The elephant trips over the step and slides across the concrete base veranda on her tusks and trunk. She rises up, steps back and comes again, this time skewering the step.

And then she is gone.

Silence returns.

"Thanks God!" my Italian friend sighs.

"And His Mister Angel," I quietly remember. Phillipo cracks open his favourite whisky, saved for such special occasions, and we savour the joy of us both still being in one piece.

On surveying the scene in daylight, it seems inconceivable that I was able to break thru the *tormentosa* bush last night, and escape unharmed. Two clear holes in the outer brick-work, a broken tusk and splintered pieces of ivory are all that's left in evidence.

It all started back in 1972 when, as a raw 26-year-old, I was proudly installing my no-frills tented camp on the shores of Zimbabwe's Matusadona National Park on Lake Kariba, the biggest man-made lake of its time, in the great Zambezi River valley.

Friends and family came down to sample my new safari operation. I was trying out my just learned bush tactics on them, a nerve wracking experience as I switched from civil engineer to guide, knowing practically nothing about this unique world I had entered.

My 'practice' photo-safari client is friend and photographer, Peter Jordan. 'Hold it, guys, this is good,' he whispers, leaning against a branch and focusing his bazooka–like camera on a vague grey shape in the dense undergrowth ahead.

'He knows we're here,' I whisper back, watching the big eyelashes flicker on his huge, motionless body, incredibly camouflaged in the dry tangle of branches. I'd come to know this typical posture of an animal on high alert, listening for an intruder disturbing his world.

"Okay to take a picture?" Peter breathes.

I nod, not sure, totally out of my depth, but putting on as brave a front as I can.

Ahead, in the dense *jesse* thorn thicket, naively conceived by us to be good cover for ourselves, stands a large bull elephant. In my mind, it's a most terrifying threat which we should not even be thinking of approaching so close. But then, that's what you do on safari . . . isn't it?

We pick our way stealthily, trying not to breath, and creep, apparently unnoticed, to within an incredible ten metres.

At last Peter is satisfied and ready.

The shutter on his camera reverberates like a rifle shot in the silence.

A cloud of dust whirls and the elephant charges amidst a cacophony of trumpeting and crashing branches.

Looking to our guide, the National Parks ranger, for direction, all I see is a fast-disappearing khaki uniform making a well-planned escape.

"Follow me!" I shout to Peter, aiming to get downwind and lose the charging giant. I know that much.

Peter runs for his life. In the opposite direction. Upwind . . . elephant chasing after him in ground-shaking pursuit.

I watch in horror as Peter trips. He scrambles to his feet but his camera snags on a branch, breaking the strap. This distracts the elephant for a vital few momenta as it destroys his most treasured possession. There are no big trees to be found anywhere. The Parks water tower is the only substantial structure in sight. Peter scales it in one great leap.

Through the dust and commotion I make out the bull standing at its base, trunk raised and trumpeting angrily. Peter is balanced precariously on the tank platform, just out of reach. The battle-worn tusks look ready to turn the whole caboodle upside down.

Finally, it 'harrumpfs' off into the bush, shaking his massive head.

All is quiet again—until our ranger materialises, firing shots in the air—a trifle late.

"Peter, are you all right?" I call.

"Shucks, Robby, thanks for the warning!" He climbs down the rickety tower.

"Sorry about that, old man. Bit of a surprise, huh?" I add lamely.

We head back to camp having retrieved what was left of his camera, hugely relieved that he hadn't suffered the same fate.

An international photo-journalist today, my first safari client remains a good friend, the mangled camera souvenir valued as a memento and centre piece of many a great story.

My purchase of Kazungula Safaris made me the owner of this campsite in Matusadona, and another in Gona-Re-Zhou, the further most National Park at the opposite southeast end of the country.

I had just returned from eight years abroad, having earned a commission in the Royal Navy, followed by a civil engineering degree at Bristol. Failing in an attempt to fly down Africa in a Tiger Moth, the famous WW II biplane trainer, I'd driven in a Land-Rover instead. This latter adventure moulded my decision that if I was going to live in Africa it would be in the bush—the deeper and more remote, the better.

Seduced by the wild beauty of Ethiopia on the overland journey, I had determined to go back there, having planned to earn my start-up capital in civil engineering and then launch a safari business in the most dramatic and romantic land I had ever seen, the isolated Omo River Park on the Kenyan border, above Lake Rudolph.

Then His Royal Highness Haile Selassie was toppled in a revolution and the country fell into chaos.

Rethink time for Rob.

Mum, or Maasie as we now call her, was paging through the adverts in the local Salisbury newspaper, searching for opportunities that might distract her hyper-active son from heading back to Ethiopia. "Have a look at this, Rob—it sounds just the thing," she said.

"I don't know about that, Ma. Kazungula Safaris obviously went under for a reason." I was lethargically unenthusiastic after dropping my biggest and most awesome dream.

"At least have a look?"

The company had been founded at Kazungula, a remote spot on the Zambezi River, upstream from Victoria Falls, where Botswana, Namibia, Zambia and Zimbabwe meet in one of those strange confluences of colonial African mapping.

Kazungula is the name given by the local tribes to the famous 'sausage' tree, *kigelia africana*. I knew of the fruit's healing properties and loved the tree, its name given to that stretch of the Zambezi derived from the sound it made as it gurgled over the rocks.

I decided to have a look.

Taking a boat across the smooth lake, I landed in the 'Matuse' (Ma-tyou-s) on a small wooded peninsula overlooking a tiny natural harbour. Ahead, the magnificent Matusadona mountains rose 400 metres sheer out of the lake and were cut through by the fjord-like Sanyati gorge.

I wondered why we'd never been there before on early family excursions. It was breathtakingly beautiful.

Ozzie, the caretaker of the abandoned camp, met us.

"Welcome, Bwana. Tea? Or mebbe beer? Excepty, velly solly, not quite cold—no flidge."

"Tea would be great, thank you,' I replied, warming to him.

"Velly solly again, Bwana—no milik."

"'Sugar?"

He grinned.

"Excellent."

Three smiling faces, delighted to see somebody, showed me around. The equipment was ramshackle—weather-beaten tents flapped in the breeze; Land-Rovers languished on flat tyres in the beating sun. The centrepiece in the kitchen, a tarpaulin stretched between ant-eaten poles, was an ancient half-drum sink balanced on a wobbly wooden frame next to a collapsed woodstove.

Neatly swept footpaths criss-crossed the camp to the beautifully-sighted tents that peeked out from under the trees onto the panoramic lake and nearby islands. Buffalo grazed nearby on the lush shoreline.

It was a magnificent place.

In the stores tent, carefully stacked out-of-date brochures gathered dust on the shelves, proclaiming the 'luxury' safari camp, along with aging camp furniture and piles of third-hand bedding.

'We'd get back there' I determined.

Safari Operator Rob jumped out of the box. No need for further research, instruction, advice, experience or expertise. None of that seemed to matter. A simple deep-seated confidence that I could make it in this place was the driving force. I had no idea what lay ahead, not that it would have changed anything. The invincibility of youth, a passionate love for life, the wilder and more far-flung the better, and the perseverance and blind assurance of a rhino were the starting blocks.

One night, soon after arriving, I awoke to a strong breeze and the sound of waves crashing outside my tent—I always left the flaps open to enjoy the cool night air—I was startled to see a lion at the entrance, its tail lashing menacingly.

Feeling for my torch, which I couldn't locate, expecting a roaring leap at any moment, I finally managed to strike a match, trusting that the big cat would back off into the dark as it flared.

But there it stood, unmoving, its tail continuing to twitch. Several matches later, and finding my torch at last, amazed I was still intact, I shone the pathetic beam outside. I was staring, not at a lion, but at a configuration of leaves that looked like a lion's head, the swishing tail merely a branch waving in the wind.

Recovering from the adrenalin surge, I lay back on my wooden collapsible stretcher-bed, quite overwhelmed by excitement and exhilaration. I mean, it could easily have been a lion!

This was what I'd thrown everything aside for—I had to be the luckiest guy in the world, doing and living what I loved and dreamed of.

I was keen to be on foot with clients and show them 'the real thing'. I experimented with how close I could get to game, often finding myself up in a tree with an angry wild animal at the base, or in a reckless dash for safety through the undergrowth with a belligerent elephant hot on my heels.

Scary fun. A bit too scary.

My sister Jane has never quite forgiven me for leading our family group on a 'quiet' walk to digest our first Christmas lunch in the Matuse. We came across an elephant herd feeding peacefully on the green shoreline, the mountain range reflecting beautifully on the mirror-like lake behind. Approaching the herd with my newly learned caution, though a little ignorant and casual about the wind direction, there was nothing to be concerned about. Suddenly, to my surprise, the elephants lifted their trunks, clearly having detected our scent, and in the twinkling of an eye came straight for us.

Jane, definitely not endowed with the Fynn sprinting gene, was lagging alarmingly behind as the rest of us scurried back up the game track we had just strolled down.

"C'mon Janey, don't look behind. RUUUUUUUN!" . . . God, I'm going to have to go back and carry her . . . how fast can these animals run, anyway?!

"Throw your hat down . . . blouse . . . anything!" I shouted. I'd heard that this was a good distracting tactic. Janey's face did not reciprocate much appreciation of her older brother/guide's advice.

Thankfully, the elephants had had a good lunch too—and soon gave up.

Chapter 2

Dung Beetles Mating

The Rhodesian National Parks and Wildlife department was internationally recognised for its professionalism and innovative thinking. Licensed safari operators were something of the future, but the high standards expected were clear. Green and dripping as a newborn impala, I soon found a couple of minor details I had overlooked in purchasing my camp.

For starters—it did not belong to me.

'Parks' had specifically asked former owner, Mike, to leave and find himself a camp outside the park. "Standard policy" I was told.

How he had managed to get in there in the first place, I never discovered.

Nor did the four Land-Rovers and boat belong to me. They were hocked to a hire purchase company who had smartly located the new custodian and were anxious to establish repayment strategies. I wasn't even sure what that meant. At least nobody was interested in the raggedy tents—other than the termites.

Nor had I fully considered the logistics of having two camps so far apart—the one in the northern reaches of the country, and the other, unseen, located below the giant red Chilojo cliffs in Gona-Re-Zhou National Park, about as far south and remote as you could get.

'They' must have had a good reason for its positioning, I reassured myself.

A solution emerged—Rob Hughes and his quietly spoken wife, Grettl, were working for our opposition on neighbouring Spurwing Island. They were also experiencing the difficulties of a shrinking tourist market due to the recent guerrilla incursions Rhodesia was facing. Expressing an interest in running the Gona-Re-Zhou operation, Rob H, an excellent bushman, volunteered his and Grettl's services. He also kindly offered to give me some insight into this new career I had chosen.

I started by asking him how to stalk an elephant without ending up in my normal headlong rush for a tree. He smiled patiently and talked me through the tactics.

"Not too tricky—move slowly and quietly, using the cover. Watch the breeze like a black mamba. And always keep downwind."

"How good is his eyesight?" I asked.

"The old bulls can't see much beyond the end of their trunks and have a laid back attitude for the most part."

"I've witnessed the other part." I grimaced.

"That's right, and although the younger ones are full of nonsense, they're not seriously aggressive."

"Bit like the lads on a night out?"

"Exactly, but the cows, watch out! Always with young—they're different animals—smart, temperamental, highly defensive. They'll 'take you out' at a drop of a hat. Give them a wide berth."

I got him to show me the difference between cows and bulls, as it wasn't that obvious—like a lot of stuff out here.

With Rob H guiding, we travelled down to Gona-Re-Zhou, with Land-Rovers full of equipment, to open the southern operation. From the moment we arrived we were charged by every elephant in the Park. Must be all cows?

By night, however, the gentlemanly bulls appeared, walking between our guy ropes looking for oranges, but otherwise quietly minding their own business; lion sniffed through tent flaps checking the occupants, not quite so minding *their* own business; hyenas and honey badgers scuttled about, eating everything they could find, including cooking pots, cold boxes, and my boots.

Adventurously remote was the wording in the old brochure. Too true.

I checked with my new friends and managers after a couple of days.

"You gonna be okay here, guys?"

"We'll be fine, we love this" Rob H replied.

I headed back to the Matuse, conscious of the size of bite I'd taken buying this business. *Gona* was seriously wild, and a hang of a long way from anywhere.

Well, better get on and find some clients now—shouldn't be too difficult—should it?

I set up a humble marketing and administrative office above the Union Avenue Post Office in Salisbury (Harare). On my drive down Africa I'd met a New Zealander, Lizzie Hope, who was travelling with an overland group, Siafu. She seemed to live on peanuts and fresh air and did a fine job running around in her Morris Minor—standard NZ transport I gathered—organising and sourcing our supplies and clients. Not so easy for a girl a long way from home, and with a bush war flaring on our borders, but she did okay.

We used HF (high frequency) radios between the camps and Salisbury, a twice-daily thirty-minute slot allocated on our licence. HF radios operate over long distances—radio hams use them around the world—but they are prone to signal distortion caused by vagaries in the weather and the time of day. Our morning signal was generally good, but we had one problem—the lady missionary using the half hour before us. She invariably talked into our time:

"Goo' mornin' Mavis . . . shaaaame, dear, that flu sounds aaawefull. Try inhalin' some o' that sage bush boiled up. Sure works good on me."

Lizzie makes a quick note.

"Mmm, orl right . . . I'll try some o' dat . . ."

Crackle, crackle . . .

"You do that, Mavis. You just wouldn't believe the enormous eenzy-weenzy on my wall last night," our mission lady could continue. "It could have eaten poor Lucy . . . honest, it could 'ave . . . naooo, I don' mind about it eatin' mosquitoes, I don' wannit there . . . well, we're gonna try, but I'm not sure Dan's gotten that exhaust fixed yet . . ."

We would desperately try to break through.

"*Uhh, Hello, Mission Station, this is Kazungula, you are in our time . . . hello, hello . . .*"

"Mavis, helloooo Mavis, can ya hear me orl right, dear? The rudeness of these other people! As I was saying . . ."

The more we tried to interrupt, the more she droned on.

The radio signal in the afternoons was always poor and crackly, so we couldn't get much through—even the mission ladies didn't bother to try.

Sometimes, I would take the radio with me if we were out on safari, rigging a makeshift aerial on a tree, an elaborate affair, with directional and angular positioning of the wires being a tricky business. It wasn't always effective.

Not infrequently our problematic communications found Lizzie's clients already en route, and I would only find out about it as they arrived in Kariba town.

Now that was stress.

After a time, I began to consider clients as invaders into our private tranquil world, and envied the research *wallahs* who lived what I imagined idyllic lives studying creepers and crawlers, droppings and bug language.

"Sorry, you can't come today, the dung beetles are mating!" I'd loved to have been able to say. What bliss, and, best of all, somebody else would have to worry about paying the bills.

Daily battle with High Frequency radio – surely it is easier to study dung beetles!

Chapter 3

Winds of War

The *Winds of Change*, as Britain's Prime Minister, Harold Macmillan, called them, were blowing across Africa.

Colonial Governments had taken on the enormous task of developing the vast resources of the emerging continent, albeit to their advantage, and coercing the local population into believing that this was the best thing for them—which it probably was, if the long term effects had been allowed to materialise. Somewhat lacking in sensitivity to local cultures and history, the focus was on education into western systems and the introduction of new skills. This colossal undertaking needed massive resources, while World Wars and insufficiencies back home plagued their good intentions.

In the mishmash of political unrest that swept through the continent in the '50s and '60s, following the growing dissatisfaction of impatient new national parties, it was discouraging to witness the violent upheavals followed by avaricious greed and mismanagement. Over the years Rhodesians had built a successful country, and they refused, under orders from their colonial masters, Great Britain, to submit to the chaos expected from a premature handover. Nor did they wish to emulate their powerful South African neighbour's system of segregation—known as apartheid.

A Unilateral Declaration of Independence from the British Crown, or UDI, was declared by Rhodesia's Prime Minister, Ian Smith in 1965. The country had been a self-governing colony since 1922.

African Nationalist views were regarded as subversive communist ideology. Exiled black politicians, led by Joshua Nkomo and Robert Mugabe of the two major tribes, the Ndebele and Shona, were ever more determined to put an end to white dominated rule. Backed by international sanctions and resorting to military incursions, the nationalists endeavoured to topple the Rhodesian government. A war for 'freedom' was launched.

A running battle in April 1965, near the northern farming town of Sinoia (Chinoyi) launched the *Second Chimurenga*, the *First Chimurenga* being the name given by the Shona to the uprising against the white settlers back in 1896. This first war was inspired by priestess Mbuya Nehanda, who was hanged, along with her accomplices, in 1898 by the colonial authorities. Her last prophetic words on the scaffold were, "My bones shall rise again!"

Which indeed they did.

The first white farming family to be murdered, the Viljoens, was in May 1966. Rhodesian forces reacted quickly. Their commanders had served with the British in the Malayan emergency of the 1950s, and were highly trained and motivated—arguably the best guerrilla fighters in the world. The 'freedom fighters' were no match for them.

War is seldom a solution, both sides of our conflict bearing that irresponsibility and witnessing today our heavy payment for not having pursued a political solution. Initiatives by Britain at the time hugely underestimated the resolve of both white Rhodesians and black Nationalists to preserve the *status quo* and regain 'their rights' respectively.

After a lull of several years, the freedom fighters regrouped having retrained under Chinese and Russian instruction. The year 1972 heralded significant and determined terror attacks in the north and north-eastern farming districts, close to the nationalist bases across the border. Supported by newly independent Mozambique, and led by Commander Solomon Mujuru (later to become Commander of the Zimbabwe Defence Force, recently violently murdered, and whose wife, Joyce, her *Chimurenga* name 'Teurai Ropa', or 'Spill Blood', Zimbabwe's Vice President under Mugabe), these audacious raids marked the beginning of a bitter eight-year guerrilla bush war.

All slightly unexpected setbacks to Rob's safari plans. And incidentally the British Government's, who predicted Rhodesia would fall in 6 months.

Undaunted, tents were patched, staff enthused and the one and only 50hp Mercury outboard powering our 6m open boat, ploughed, tossed and bounced across the tortuously rough 25km of lake separating us from Kariba town—originally built by the Italians to house their workforce in the building of the dam wall, and now our sole source of supplies and off-the-street tourists, the latter a diminishing resource as the bush war impacted.

Apart from delicious diligent Lizzie working her butt off in Salisbury, my only marketing strategy was to ply the pubs and hotels in Kariba town to lure unsuspecting travellers who might be tempted by the tantalising tales of life on the other side of the Lake.

"Hi, I'm Rob, based in the Matuse. You heard about it?"

"Yeah, sort of . . . ."

"Can I interest you in the real Africa, then?"

That line generally worked.

"You got elephants?"

"Yup."

"Lions?"

"Yup."

"Is it safe?"

"No, but we've survived so far!"

"Hmm . . . how about a look-see tomorrow?"

"No worries."

Early next morning there was a frantic rush to buy supplies, refuel, and reappear, professionally kitted out, in time to meet the client, who one hoped hadn't thought better of the previous evening's 'gin-and-tonic' decision.

The most I could muster were eight guest tents—the rest, in poor repair, were relegated to staff and storerooms. Using local *mopane* poles, we erected some rustic structures—a slightly askew new office, workshop and kitchen store had me and my three staff in awe of our combined architectural talent and building skills.

Kazungula – on the trail with visitors on the roof

Ozzy as look-out scout on spare tyre

Visitors off the roof for fording rivers

Mopane is a prolific lowveld hardwood, heavy as iron when dry, making a superb firewood and forever campfire memory. It is not usually used as a building material, being impossibly hard on tools and difficult to find a straight piece.

The dining room came next—a steeply-pitched thatched roof was put up, with no thought given to 'bracing' in its design—my civil engineering skills left behind in university. When the weight of the grass was added to the roof the whole structure started to do the splits. So we wired the two sides together, tensioned by inserting a buffalo rib and winding it, as one does a toy aeroplane propeller. This structure remained standing for the life of the camp and was always a talking point.

"Now, that buffalo rib," I would say to inquisitive clients, "is a good indicator of the tensions in the structure, and should you notice it unwinding, that would be a good time to run!"

"You gotta be joking?" retorted Hank, a real engineer from upstate New York who had been looking forward to a safari run by professionals.

"You'll get used to it!" I smiled, leaving him to contemplate the marvels of bush engineering, and how he had been conned into this experience.

Nevertheless, it made a lovely breezy sitting-out spot. Orphaned darters and herons we had rescued from drowning nests would perch on a huge log that lay across the open front. During siesta time we would relax there, swimming in the shallow waters beyond, excitedly joined by the birds—crocs weren't considered such a problem then as they are today due to their population explosion.

My philosophy towards camp construction could be summed up in two words—'ethnic' and 'available'—any material within ten kilometres of the camp was good. Beyond that, serious budgeting was required.

Clients were encouraged to take a participatory explorer role and to think of themselves as partners in the development. Occasionally, their zest for the safari to encompass wider borders than our immediate area would inspire them to pay for extra fuel, when we would venture as far as the Ume river, collecting reeds, weird shaped poles and stones. In return I made sure we found something special to do or see on the way. My thinking was if you had come from an office in New York, this was as interesting an African experience as you could get.

Fortunately, our clients thought so, too.

I relied greatly on the staff that I had inherited. Ozzy was the major domo. He had worked as a batman in the BSA Police and had several duties in camp. For each of which, he would don a different uniform, changing roles with military precision.

In traditional police batman's uniform—pressed khaki with polished leather belt and shoulder strap—and a gleaming smile topped by a black Fez, Oz's sunny 'wake up call' came with a neatly-laid silver tea tray to your tent.

"Good morning, good morning, evelybody, the sun is awake, our bush is calling!"

"Omigosh . . . sunup already . . . uuh, thank you, Ozzy." A dazed client would mutter.

"You are welcome. Only the hot water, she was taking long to boil this morning. Our Bwana is ready for your game drive, please." Directions were faithfully passed to get folk moving.

The Land-Rover would be waiting, ready to leave. In those days, Parks considered it too dangerous driving around in open jeeps, so our vehicles were equipped with full-length roof racks where clients could sit or recline on mattresses. Oz, now attired in his 'game scout' uniform and wearing a black beret, was perched on the spare wheel up top. It was the same batman's kit in which he had served tea earlier, without the shiny leather.

His eagle eye missed nothing—a constant stream of directions being transmitted to me, the driver below, by signals from his booted foot dangling across the windscreen before my eyes.

Back to camp, and another lightning change—Oz the waiter appeared, in long whites complete with red cummerbund and fez, serving up a much-appreciated full American breakfast to our dazzled clients.

Guests would often comment on how alike all the staff looked . . .

Oz was, indeed, the wizard of all.

My other right hand was our chef, Buhnu, a huge Matabele and retired chief in his own right, who slaved over the wood fires producing unbelievable repasts from our primitive facilities and his own prepared menus. He was kindly tolerant of my haute cuisine ignorance and abysmal lack of purchasing power as I frequently returned from shopping with stuff missing from his list.

"Sorry, Bu, no spinach, tomatoes, nor spaghetti. And asparagus too dear." Somehow, though, there always enough money for beer.

"Aaah, no problem Bwana, we make a plan."

His pained patient response always warmed my heart.

"In time for dinner?"

"Yebo. Mebbe a bit late."

"No worries, Bu."

I would leave all in his capable hands while I dashed off to spruce up and entertain the clients for sun-downers.

He was the *M'dala,* the old man, of the camp, who always had time to listen and to talk while trying another dish, or polishing the silver which he loved. A deep belly laugh was always close at hand, as was his jovial mood—nothing would have been the same without him.

And then, there was Tyson, our general worker and only Tonga, the tribe that have lived in the Zambezi valley from time immemorial. Strong as a buffalo, he tirelessly made up the tents, assisted Buhnu in the kitchen, cut firewood, swept the camp till it looked like a parade square, washed the Land-Rovers, prepared the boat, hand washed our laundry in the lake, and stoked up an old charcoal flat-iron to get those creases in. He never stopped.

None of us did.

We were a fine, cheery team.

But those winds of change were drawing nearer.

Chapter 4

Mamas and Papas

'Robinson Huckleberry Crusoe' Fynn was in his element—on his very own private desert island camp with a whole new world to discover. The only other sign of human life was Jeff and Veronica Stutchbury on Spurwing Island, a kilometre offshore. Jeff was an older Huckleberry and had being doing his Crusoe stuff for many years, totally undisturbed in the Matuse up till this point, other than by a developing bush war and the deteriorating economics in Rhodesia.

Jeff Stutchbury was the John Wayne of the safari industry. Tall, tanned and talented, he smoked a bamboo pipe under a wide brimmed hat woven from palm fronds that shaded his sharp blue eyes, a huge knife strapped to his calf. He was every bit the 'bushman' he purported to be. Veronica, his equally tall and beautiful willowy blond wife, efficiently organised their recently upgraded camp. They had brought new investors into their declining business, taking them into the 'upmarket' safari category, which really wasn't Jeff's bag.

They were formidable neighbours, and coming from their long background in the industry, I was understandably regarded as a 'Johnny-come-lately'. Frowning under his enormous eye brows, his first words to me when we met were:

"Thought they'd thrown you chaps out of there?!"

Quite possibly they had influenced Parks to close down the former operation. So, I was a little wary. He considered the Matuse his exclusive domain and would motor past us in his unique thatched safari craft, always finding a bird or something spectacular to view, anywhere but in the direction of our camp.

"What's that over there, Jeff?" I'd hear them asking, pointing at our tents under the trees, their voices being heard clearly across the still early morning waters.

"Oooh, dont worry about that," Jeff's voice would boom, "one of the new little camps sprouting up like mushrooms all over the place."

"Sounds interesting—research, or what?"

"Ooh, I don't know, you know what they're like—always sniffing out something to upset. Now, there's something interesting—observe that Malachite kingfisher about to drop into the water and catch himself breakfast from the old tree across there." They would all follow Jeff's finger, pointing directly away from the intrusive Old Kaz camp.

Impossible as it was to commune with each other at the time, we were to be led strangely together by the mysterious, oddly-humoured hand of fate and become good friends in the future.

Kariba town was enmeshed in typical small-town resort attitudes, exacerbated by shrinking business in our escalating war. I was greeted stiffly there too.

None of this bothered me. Steaming full ahead, building my kingdom in the wild, I was fairly oblivious of who thought what around me.

Safaris were highly charged, each one a promotion for a potential return-client. I walked carrying a knobkerrie, a great heavy truncheon made from the hard *mopane* roots, as firearms were not allowed in the Park except for their own staff, or honorary wardens like Jeff.

We explored the unknown, my foot safari bravado now tempered by earlier dramas. A request by my clients to 'walk', and jovially agreed to around the nightly campfire, would render me sleepless for that night fretting about the potential calamities that could befall my valued clientele on the morrow.

At first light, stalking as on a combat patrol with every sense alert, I would lead out cautiously. As soon as we spotted anything remotely dangerous, I'd have them flat on their bellies, warning them that the slightest noise they made might be their last. Squirming our way into suitable cover, we would observe the monsters of the wild from a 'safe' distance. Everybody thought it terribly exciting.

The Land-Rover drives were a little more relaxing—except for the clients perched on the roof. They were frequently called upon to jump down and push through soft sand, drag trees off the road, or dig our way out of some chasm that we had fallen into, quite apart from their desperate efforts to cling onto their precarious perch while it swayed over the uneven roads and brushed past over-hanging branches.

Meanwhile, down in the cab, between concentrating on the tricky driving and trying to follow Ozzy's boot indications, I would be swatting up my reference books to answer the questions which I should have known, but didn't, from my trusting clients out of sight above. I would also be organising stuff back at camp on the VHF radio . . . talk about multi-tasking. So much to learn, all in fun, with more than enough stress to keep the senses sharpened.

Oz and I knew that out on the bush drives we were on our own—the only back up being Tyson with no licence in the wood-collecting Land Rover. Depending on what we came across, we were often late back in camp—staff took this in their stride. There was not much they could do about it anyway.

An Italian family had booked the whole camp, arriving like 'rent-a-crowd'. They talked excitedly from the moment they set foot, the level of noise never abating, even on game drives. The children ran unhindered in all directions, exploring and playing happily.

Out on a game drive, I stopped in a clearing where we had surprised a lioness and her cubs resting under a bush. The party on the roof was, as usual, engaged in animated discussion and hadn't seen them. Oz tried valiantly to communicate their presence to the family. Finally, the penny dropped. The sight of the lions acted like fuel to a rocket crash and the noise level increased by decibels, despite our attempts to quieten their fears.

Finally, the lioness could stand it no longer. Her flicking tail straightened, her growls increased, the yellow eyes boring into the offending intruders, and suddenly she charged.

Instantaneously, we had something akin to a soccer stand collapse. Young Italians were sliding off the roof on the opposite side to the lioness, yanking doors and windows open in an effort to climb inside.

Papas cursed and Mamas screamed. *"Santo Cielo! Eccheccazzo!"*

No one was paying the slightest attention to Oz and I's attempts to calm the situation. The growling lioness crouched, only metres away, tail twitching, baring her teeth murderously, looking ready to jump onto the roof any moment.

I engaged reverse gear and slowly pulled back, the family hanging off every side like Christmas decorations. At a safe distance we stopped for a serious talk. The listening silence was electric, their attention riveted to every word I said.

"Calma ragazzi! Attenzione!" growled the Papas. Mammas slapped young sons into order. Not another peep came from up top other than stern reprimands, until we got back to camp, when a celebration fit for the winning Cup Final team broke into full swing.

At the other end of the scale, a young and intense couple from New York arrived with their teenage daughter on the trip of a lifetime. They wanted to experience everything we had to offer, happy to be out all day pursuing it. Their 13-year-old on the other hand was wretchedly bored. She carried a comic book around with her all day and never took her nose out of it.

"What would you like to do today, darling?" mum would ask.

"Whatever . . ."

We made plans.

One morning, from the Land-Rover, we picked up rhino spoor. Climbing out to track its path, the daughter elected to stay in the vehicle and read her comic. We found the rhino half an hour out. As dad fumbled in his camera bag for another film, he dropped a crackly plastic packet. The rhino immediately whipped around, cocking his head at the noise. As Dad bent down to retrieve the plastic, there was a loud snort and the rhino came crash-charging in our direction.

One learned to identify climbable trees when approaching rhino, pointing them out to clients and clearly warning them of the strong possibility that they may be required to climb them. We were all up them in a jiff—amazing what adrenalin enables one to do with no previous experience. The rhino trashed the offending package and then stomped and snorted under our trees for a good while longer. Finally, happy the intruders had been seen-off, he left in a bewildered huff.

Savouring the adventure, fortunately unscathed, we stealthily made our way back to the Land-Rover, deciding we'd had our dose for the day.

"Wher' ave you bin?!" the daughter greeted parents petulantly.

They animatedly related their escapade.

"It's so hot 'n 'ere. I wanna go back. Now!" was her only response.

Looking even more bored than usual, she opened another packet of chewing gum and the next comic.

I felt sad for them and trust she's now over it all and has made up with her parents.

Our small boat was the only transport that we had to get to mainland Kariba. It was also used extensively to experience the unique game viewing from the water, and to fish from while watching herds grazing on the lakeshore. Next to walking, boating was our most popular activity, albeit confined to our one and only 50hp open craft.

It, too, had its moments . . .

Cruising peacefully across a bay one magical afternoon, a pod of hippo grunted their inimitable guffaws at us, and submerged. We focussed our cameras on a fish eagle which was posed majestically on a typical Kariba petrified tree ahead, mirrored in its reflection in the water as we drifted slowly towards it. Suddenly the boat lurched violently sideways with a loud splintering sound.

My immediate thought was that we had ridden over one of the many treacherous underwater stumps. I turned to assess the damage.

"Hhh . . . hi . . . hi . . . hippooo!" an ashen-faced man in the back seat finally managed. The two neat holes at hippo tusk spacing began to spout water and a mangled gunnel showed where the large jaws had crunched. It had come up suddenly, like the Loch Ness monster, mouth agape, wide enough it seemed to the man sitting in the back to have swallowed the whole boat. It took one huge bite and then slid back into the depths, not to be seen again. Fortunately we had all been gazing at the fish eagle, cameras and binoculars in hand, no arms on the gunnel.

Thereafter, I always warned clients to remove valuable wristwatches when we cruised through hippo waters, relating the story. No more elbows rested on the gunnels.

Every outing was a thrilling venture, all trusting implicitly in the guide's long established reconnaissance, research and backyard experience. The enormity of that responsibility was beginning to sink in, while the pristine primeval world we worked in fired up our minds and spirits. I was supersaturated with inspiration.

The end of a day would find us around the campfire, drinks in hand, yarning about our exploits, a canopy of stars above, a gentle wash of the waves lapping the shore nearby. The majestic eerie sounds of the wild were ever-present in the distant dark, all promising another heart-thumping tomorrow.

Business was haphazard, which had its advantages. Having no clients meant time for much needed maintenance on dilapidated equipment, and experimenting with new ideas.

One innovation was a flush toilet.

This luxury was unheard of in the bush camp world of the day, which, till then, had been proud of its wide variety of 'long-drop' designs and picturesque potties under beds. I reckoned flush toilets would cause a stampede from the affluent American market.

But my extravagance extended to only one flush toilet for the whole camp, albeit with the 'latest' 1960's Rhodesian plumbing. The septic tank was a 44gallon (210lt) drum buried underground, the flushing process gurgling, for all to hear, in the still air of an early morning. Magical music to my ears, though possibly a little intimidating to the privacy of newly arrived guests.

The loo was surrounded by a *mopane boma*, as Parks' regulations strictly forbade the use of concrete or any vestige of a permanent structure. It looked much the same as the *bomas* that were used to accommodate newly-arrived rhino in translocation projects—only smaller, but very sturdy. Feeling very secure, the interesting part of sitting on the seat was looking out through the gaps between the logs at all the goings-on around. Nobody could see in, though, unless they strained to peek between the poles. Which of course nobody did, all persons passing distinctly and obviously studying something, anything, in the opposite direction to the loo.

Our two showers, shared by the entire camp, had the famous old 'Rhodesian boiler' to heat the water. This consisted of another 44 gallon oil drum mounted on its side, covered by mud for insulation, under which a fire was built. The only snag was when Tyson made the fire too big and it boiled over through the breather, with scalding water shooting up like an Old Faithful geyser and raining down on the unfortunate occupant of the shower. This was not life threatening, as the water had cooled somewhat by the time it descended. Nevertheless, a little unnerving.

A hinged hanging branch was placed onto a forked stick across the path to warn guests that the shower or toilet was occupied. This signal would often be forgotten by new arrivals and loud, or sometimes discreet, exclamations were a refreshing part of camp humour.

Guests would have hot water delivered to their tent in rose-painted enamel pitchers, morning and evening. A smartly polished aluminium washbasin was suspended in an artistic branch with a small oval mirror above it hanging on a chain. Stone-like tree frogs would sometimes perch on the branch above the basin, no doubt with an eye to laying their eggs in this protected watery haven.

The occupant of the tent adjacent to the dining room arrived at the camp to find what he took to be a thoughtfully-placed ornamental frog on top of his mirror. It never moved for days. While he was shaving one morning, peering into the mirror, the frog decided to jump. Gathering for breakfast, we heard a cry signalling some terrible accident or murderous reptile on the rampage. Our unfortunate guest staggered from his tent, covered in shaving foam, razor arm waving in the air, with a tree frog tenaciously clinging to his nose.

My scarcity of boats, with new craft unthinkably beyond my budget, caused me to work on ethnic designs to expand my fleet. Neighbour Jeff had developed catamarans built from canoe hulls and completed with thatched roofs that made them look like aquatic native huts.

They were touristy and fun.

So I built a raft, not quite so sleek, but on similar lines, by tying drums together. It was powered by a little Seagull engine and we used it for fishing and collecting firewood. The driver had to be sure to check the drum lashings before venturing out, as they were frequently put to the test when the wind freshened and wave action worked them loose. For the cox'n who had not diligently checked his lashings, this meant abandoning his post while he went overboard in croc infested waters to tighten the ropes—not great for client confidence.

I would see the unhappy fishing party returning all buttoned up in their life jackets, a sodden, shivering driver at the helm.

Tourism was taking a serious downturn by the end of my first year's operations thanks to the emerging guerrilla war. Many learning-curves had been rounded off, but the business was bankrupt. The difficult marine passage across to our camp and close to total isolation and the community early warning system were the key to keeping the court's sheriff at bay.

If an unfortunate court official happened to find us, he would spend an uncomfortable day in the hot and unattended camp, with particularly unhelpful and 'inarticulate' staff, who hardly understood English, and who had *no idea when* Mr Fynni would return from safari. Our bureaucrat would finally grunt and give up, leaving a note saying he'd be back.

I'd get the message by radio from camp staff that he'd left, and we would return home from a great day's tracking rhino or studying the bee eater colonies. We'd have a good laugh, and wait for him to hire a boat for another Fynn-trapping trip, when the bush telegraph would once again spring into action.

Eventually he found better things to do.

"This is a temporary camp site, Rob," National Parks staff would regularly remind me, enquiring as to when and where we were moving to.

"I know, I know. I'm looking around. Thank you for your patience." My vague responses were understood by the field staff who were sent to chide me, their kind tolerance delaying my disappearing act still further.

'Old Kaz' camp

Our tent on left, dining tent on right

- with rhino ribs to tension wires & sandbags to keep out lake

I had, however, spotted an ideal position on Fothergill Island, not far round the corner from the Old Kaz camp, but was informed that it could not be made available as it was also part of the Park. Suggestions were that I should look in the TTLs, the Tribal Trust Lands on either side of the Park. These had been set aside explicitly to accommodate traditional tribal operations, and were left to be run in a manner that suited their lifestyles and authorities. Leases to run tourism operations in these areas were negotiable through the local chiefs, who hoped thereby to boost their economies.

The only problem was that there just happened to be a murderous bush war raging and these areas were known hideouts for the 'terrs'(terrorists), as we called the guerrillas.

My mother, family and friends would berate my irresponsibility, reminding me of my perfectly good civil engineering qualification.

"Surely, Rob, it's time to do something sensible?"

"Give me time, guys, I'm getting there."

They would sadly shake their heads at this obstinate black sheep.

I only wished I felt more confident.

Then came the break.

Brian Merriman, a good-humoured well-connected South African, and very much a city boy, had set up an exclusive tour company in New York to enable the rich and famous from the USA to visit their counterparts in Africa, from Cape to Cairo.

He had heard about our camp from a good friend, Freddie Johnson, who ran the fishing lodge at Milibizi on the west end of the lake. Brian was interested in its 'quality with a difference' that he had heard about. The night he visited us we sat around the campfire with the full moon's reflection dancing on the water. Oz served chilled wine and a gentle breeze cooled us off the lake.

Then a fearsome battle shattered the peace. Clashes of tusks and hideous roars erupted from behind the camp.

"Good heavens, man, sounds like the Zulu are attacking!" Brian exclaimed.

"Hippo. C'mon, let's take a look" I jumped up and beckoned him to follow.

"Now don't do anything silly, Robin" Brian chided.

Two male hippos were fighting over territory in our harbour. Bull hippos are the most savage fighters in the wild, inflicting deep wounds with their slashing razor-sharp tusks, on occasion leading to the death of both antagonists.

Sipping our wine on deckchairs from the camouflaging shade of a small tree, we watched the drama, clearly visible in the moonlight, not unlike spectators in a gladiatorial arena. If there was a story to take back home to the American clients, it was this.

The next few days in our Matuse were no less spectacular. Large herds of game roamed the picturesque shoreline, hazy blue mountains shimmered beyond the extraordinary shapes of our stark weathered and near petrified trees, and the myriad birds decorated every scene. And we always caught fresh fish for dinner.

Brian was sold, insisting on my appearance in the USA to help market the next season. Leaving with a cheery "See you there!".

He had no idea what he was asking me.

I begged, borrowed and scraped to buy a ticket and head for the big one. My younger brother, Mike, had decided he'd had enough of university and arrived at camp with his 18 year-old girlfriend, Fruity, who went on to become his wife. The two would run my operation while I was away.

My special VUSA (Visit USA) $300 ticket enabled me to fly anywhere, anytime, within the States for six weeks, only on specified airlines and always on 'standby'.

The plan was to cover 26 major cities.

Brian flew ahead, staying at posh hotels and organising champagne breakfasts, luncheons and evening cocktail parties. Rob, having been up all night on standby at various airports, arguing his way on to appropriate flights, would stagger into the first venue kitted in crisp safari shirt and shorts, to deliver yet another upbeat speech with slides depicting the highlight of their tour, Old Kaz.

"Ladies and gentleman, I present Kazungula Safaris tented camp. Hold on to your pants and your shirt, 'cos you can't have mine!" was my opening gambit, after I'd been asked to donate my shirt on the first occasion for a charity raffle.

Revived by a flute or two of champagne hurriedly snatched before heading out to the next appointment, I would waltz through the remainder of the action-packed day, only to repeat it in a different city and different airports through the next 24 hours.

"Did you score, Rob?" was Brian's invariable query as soon as he got the chance, having regaled me with how beautiful American flight attendants were. I would have given anything for my own bed, let alone anybody else's.

Never have so few covered so much with so little. After this grandiose six-week promotion, I boarded the plane for home, totally exhausted, but with a pocket full of bookings.

Chapter 5

Little Red Car

My eyes rolled as I looked at our boat.

"Where did you leave the keys, Rob?" Mike asked.

I tried not to notice the rifled ignition lock, loose and hanging 'hot' wires, chipped propeller and broken windscreen. Considering he wasn't a Navy man, the hurried handover, lack of spares and safety precautions I had left him with, and that he and Fruity had zero back-up nor experience to do what I had asked, they had done a great job. Nothing less expected.

Lord and Lady Collins of the publishing firm had visited Old Kaz during my absence. As they were sitting down to dinner one night when a thunderstorm developed over the lake and a fierce squall hit camp. Dinner had been served in one of the accommodation tents specially positioned adjacent to our open-sided dining room, where storm winds would funnel straight through one side and out the other.

Guests had to hang on to the poles and anything else they could lay their hands on to prevent the dining tent and its contents from being blown away. Oz fought his way to and from the kitchen under an uncontrollable umbrella, valiantly balancing his laden tray. After an adventurous dinner, the rain subsided.

"Not a bit, my dears—delightful meal," was Lord Collins response to Mike and Fruity's effusive apologies.

And with that, the Lord and Lady retired to their tent.

Except there wasn't one!

It had disappeared into the trees with the squall, their beds and belongings soaked through.

Mike and Fruity offered them their own dry bed and tent, and went to sleep in the storeroom.

The next day, camp trees were festooned with clothing and bedding hanging out to dry—their tent retrieved, repaired and restored.

They noted in our visitor's book:

'Charmingly interesting experience. Well done!'

And then I met Sandy.

I was on a supply and social run to Salisbury, a necessary break for a young bachelor. However interesting it may be, the culture and communication skills of birds, animals and trees needed supplementing now and again.

John Slade was one of our typical innovative sanction-busting businessmen.

"Not going anywhere else—why should I?" would be his response to how business was.

Always making a plan, he would try to sell me boats. When I was in town I made a habit of attending his traditional 'sundowner' in his yard, to greet the end of the week.

"Come for a braai this evening," his girlfriend Clare insisted. "I've got a surprise for you."

I didn't need much arm-twisting.

Relishing the metamorphosis from bushman to party dude, I was indeed surprised. There, at the venue, was this exquisite green-eyed, ravishingly dark haired, gracefully poised, charmingly witty, beautifully proportioned, staggeringly breath-taking model offering me a drink.

She would have stopped a bull elephant in its tracks.

And she did just that to me.

I could hardly wait to invite her to come and touch my wild bush life.

"Boy, I'm not sure I'll manage that," she replied, behind a coy smile, "but I sure do need a change."

She was recently divorced, living alone with her two small children, modelling and running a baby shop.

Boy, did I have 'change' to offer.

Finally, she accepted.

I carefully orchestrated it so as to arrive in Kariba late afternoon. We hopped into the smartly cleaned boat and headed into a golden sunset—the dramatic crimson lake followed by a silver moon shimmering in our wake.

My mind whirred with this sophisticated beauty sitting beside me. Would she take to this wild and isolated life? What about the children? For goodness sake, Rob, how are you going to hold her here?

There was not a glimmer of light on the dark horizon—only Kariba town twinkling in the distance behind us.

After an hour's speeding across this fairytale landscape, navigating by the stars which I knew so well, we picked up the glow of a huge bonfire beacon, made by my staff, which lit our way through a channel in the petrified trees. We arrived to a warm welcome from my exuberant team, all eager to meet the Boss's new girl.

"Wow!" was all Sands could manage.

The magic of Matuse captured her and it wasn't long before she bravely opted to abandon her city life, her modelling, her baby shop and her beautiful house to join me in the wilds.

I could hardly believe it.

The children, Rory and Joanne, were to stay with their Dad during the school term, and with us in the holidays. I really liked them, and understood their difficulties of being thrust into such a strange environment.

Rory, particularly, was struggling with his parent's divorce. His adventurous nature frequently landed him in trouble during his short first stay. He had fallen up to his head in the ghastly grime of our greasy kitchen drain which was, luckily, spotted by Bhunu. Sands washed him down in the lake—and he didn't die of dysentery or septecemia. In his honour, a delinquent young bull elephant that charged and broke everything in sight, was named after him. In contrast, Jo was a little angel, pattering around with Sands, helping with the chores.

Canoeing on the Zambezi, orphaned birds & luxurious flushing toilet

Rob Fynn

Gallant Sands volunteered to drive up from Harare in her little red car, carrying a fridge for the camp. This she managed to squeeze into the space left by the removed passenger seat. Besides all this, she could sew, cook and type!

Life could not have looked fairer.

Nor did she voice her opinions too quickly about the state of our camp. There was no "Haven't you guys had any training in housekeeping?" Her woman's touch quietly transformed the place—in no time her intriguing combination of delightful domesticity and punchy professionalism was the buzz on the lake.

Bright, cheery bedspreads and tablecloths appeared, brass taps shone, equipment was bought for the kitchen I'd never seen or heard of, and she valiantly cooked her creative menus alongside Bhunu, ingeniously converting them for the wood fire and tiny Aga stove whose oven could only handle a single loaf of bread, while half a dozen were needed each day. So it never stopped cooking.

The tap of a typewriter could be heard clattering away in the office, where this elegant lady, dressed in a bikini and sarong, and perched on a wooden box for a seat, motivated everyone more than a visit from the Queen. And I felt prouder than had I been knighted.

Every client was treated as a personal guest and made to feel top of the range, in contrast to my old casual 'Hope everything's okay?' approach. Little flowers from the trees appeared on their pillows each evening with interesting pebble arrangements at their bedside, and decorations of leaves and seeds graced our dining table—things that Rob and Oz had not dreamed about. The visitor's book was no longer full of 'suggestions.' Nor could the staff believe their tips.

And all for the astounding value of an all-inclusive safari at US$ 25 per day.

"Interestingly, the bull calves take longer to mature. We've heard that somewhere else, haven't we?" I was joshing to a group of American 'Friends of Chicago Zoo'.

"Gee, I didn't know bulls had calves!" Sands chipped in, enthusiastically joining in a dinner discussion whilst I was pontificating about how the elephant gestation period varied depending on the sex of the calf—explaining how cow calves took 20 months, while bull calves took 22 months. Which was

36

what we believed in those days. She knew little about the bush world, but liked to participate and at least sound as though she did—copying me, I fear. Her naively ignorant pronouncements always added a touch of humour, especially as it attracted my embarrassment.

Hardened anglers would come to catch our much sought after and famous fighting Tiger Fish. Affectionately, Sands called one elderly bunch of regulars her 'dagga boys', named after old buffalo bulls who spend much of their day lying in the mud—the only difference being that the fishermen lay all day in a boat covered in beer and fish scales. Rising an hour before sunrise and invariably waking the entire camp with their banter, nose blowing and first wind of the day, their preparations before heading out for the whole day were demanding.

The night before, they would hang on Sand's every word about where and when to fish—she loved fishing and would be out on the water herself every chance she had.

"Do you think this moon will favour Impala lures for the Tiger tomorrow, Sands?" They would eagerly inquire.

"Maybe, and try the Repala with a dash of red cotton on the hook," she would suggest, with another of her coy smiles.

Her intricate theories about moon phases, lures and baits would gather the enraptured fishermen around her like children listening to a bedtime story. Well, she was, after all, a super good-looking mum.

Later, when I asked for her recollections, she wrote,

'I was up early to prepare the packed breakfasts and lunches for our special old fishermen. I'd then organise breakfast for those in camp, rush around checking the tents, and especially the toilets to make sure they were shining and beautiful. I'd plan lunch before we headed out to collect firewood, which I would do when Rob was out, as we had no other driver. It was always so beautiful driving through those riverbeds and seeing stuff like the carmine bee-eaters in their incredible colours, or any animal round every corner, even the possibility of a lion kill—sometimes just a tortoise making its way across the road.

**Flying in, canoe game viewing &
background bookkeeping & bird watching**

'Then, home in time for our ten o'clock radio call to Salisbury, organise final details for lunch and open the bar. Our lives revolved around the clients. We were on duty day and night, and it was a pleasure. I was happy to be there for them and see they were enjoying themselves.

'We usually had a swim after lunch (in her flash bikini) with our lovely little friends, the darters and herons, while the camp was resting

'Being there for the *dagga boys* when they came back with their catch in the evening, I'd try desperately to get their fish into the freezers for them to take home, hoping to convince them how good it was to smoke the excess that we couldn't fit in!'

'Boy, they sure were lucky with their fishing trips. (Thanks to her advice!)

'Dinner was our big meal, followed by all the lovely stories around the camp fire. It was very special working with Bhunu and Ozzy and Tyson. They were such amazing guys and were so intricately involved in our lives. We would retire quite late after seeing all the guests to bed. I would stay awake for hours listening to lions, the wind ruffling our tent, buffalo grazing outside, also elephant and hippos ripping up the grass and trees, and our camp cat pretending to be a leopard—all pretty scary.'

The cat, known as Mini Lion, was a black terror that we'd collected in Kariba following one of those *What am I going to do with all these kittens?* queries astutely directed at the weaker sex. A great character, she would love to stalk people at night and jump out at them from behind a bush as they went past carrying their wobbly paraffin lamp that barely lit the path (no such luxury as flashlights). She would scratch the outside of the tent at night, convincing Sands and others of an imminent attack by a leopard. Many a shriek in the night, near heart attacks and confirmed black mamba bites were thanks to Mini Lion.

Chapter 6

Nyami Nyami

A sixth generation African, third generation Rhodesian, and first generation Zimbabwean, *force majeur,* my family are intricately threaded into the history of our little country. Outside politics, we have led a life of freedom and adventure that few experience. Interwoven in the extraordinary African tapestry, however, is the perpetual pain of people stoically bearing up under the extreme conditions this continent is accustomed to from time immemorial?

Sadly, worse with each decade for Zimbabweans.

It was November 2006 when I started to write this from my home in Glenlorne, a leafy hilly suburb of Harare, surrounded by beautiful *msasa* woodland (*Brachystegia spiciformis, Miombo woodland*). Here, I can shut out the horrors of Mugabe's distressing rule that has strangled our beloved country. The façade of our graceful city belies the realities of desperate starving rural communities and overcrowded townships, waterless, workless and powerless, where only disease and poverty are prolific. Unless you are a member of the party hierarchy.

I attended the funeral of an old family friend, Pat Johnson, Freddie's son (of Mlibizi, who introduced Brian Merriman). An excellent farmer, he was once credited as the biggest 'burly' tobacco grower in the world.

Two years ago, he was forced by government sponsored 'War Veterans' to leave his farm at a few hours notice, a farm the family had spent three generations building from virgin bush. The stress of Pat's traumatic loss of his life's endeavour and heritage were undoubtedly a contributory factor to his premature death. A story all too often heard in our former stalwart farming community.

Following Mugabe's defeat in the 2000 referendum, where he'd sought the country's backing to change the constitution, and the stark realisation that he was losing his power grip, 95% of the country's 4,500 commercial farmers, recognised amongst the finest agriculturalists worldwide, were evicted under the charade of reclaiming the land for its rightful owners. They had dared to oppose the President's Marxist policies.

I looked around the church at the sunburnt, weather beaten, life creased faces, the remnant of the farming community still in the country trying to make a new plan, their life's work and joy having been stolen, yet so un-embittered. I wanted to get up and shake hands with every one of them.

They belonged to a generation that had fought, developed and persevered through some of the harshest conditions in the continent's history to establish a farming industry that was called the 'bread basket' of the continent.

It had been initiated 120 years ago in the primitive relentless severity of this country by their grandfathers. And had now been robbed by the paranoid politics of the Honourable Executive President, Robert Mugabe, effectively destroying the vibrant economy of our country in one swoop.

He inherited what he himself termed the 'Jewel Of Africa', at Zimbabwe's Independence in 1980 from the Rhodesians. The Zimbabwe dollar was then valued at 10 to a £, even following a 12 year war. It started at 2 to a £ when first established in the 1950's. Inflation under his rule rose to such that the number of zeros on the Z$ could no longer be managed by computers—in 2008, the Z$ required 48 zeros in order to match the US$, was finally abandoned and the US$ adapted as our official currency, moved by the incoming MDC Minister of Finance,Tendai Biti. The Reserve Bank Governor Gono's printing press simply could not churn out the changing Z$ notes fast enough.

I say 'inherited' this wonderful gem of a country. Some may say he 'won' it. A 12-year war of 'liberation' was fought, in which, as so often with wars, there were no winners. Both sides passionately believed in their cause. The Rhodesians finally dropped the fight in 1980, after long drawn out negotiations with the warring Nationalist parties, supervised by Britain, for the sake of a future for all. In the ensuing election, fierce and ruthless intimidation bought Mugabe the presidency.

To be fair, and to everybody's surprise, his initial few years were a model of reconciliation, prospering Zimbabwe with massive world support.

'If yesterday I fought you as an enemy, today you have become my friend' he said at his inaugural speech, adding that he would 'draw a line through the past'. To all appearances, we had a great statesman.

Sadly this magnanimous attitude was eroded by his neurotic and insatiable hunger for power, wealth and a fostering of tribalism, the sorry curse of so many of Africa's leaders. The statesmanship was all a very clever play act, since when he has forcibly extended his term of office, stealing election after election, believing the people love him.

More than one third of the indigenous black population are refugees around the world, less than 10% of the tribe of whites that used to call Zimbabwe their home are still here.

Sands and I had come to know many of these grand farming characters who had borne the brunt of the war. In our beautiful peaceful camp, their love of the lake, the 'bush', fishing and enabling then to 'do their thing' was top of our agenda to provide. They would arrive frazzled, exhausted and tensed from the traumatic lives they led, yet in typical farming style with their boats and equipment highly organised.

They were fun, drunk lots of beer, and clearly enjoyed breaking from the hard work and tensions of running their farms in the war torn zones. If a boat broke down, was holed on a stump, the camp generator packed up, or supplies did not arrive as scheduled, they shrugged their shoulders, helped fix the problem, and enjoyed another day.

The Lake and its lovely surrounds was their next best to heaven. Our camp the pearly gates.

We thought so too.

Kariba filling in 1959 & Fothergill rescuing drowning animals

Nyaminyami overlooking the wall

'Drink your tea before it gets hot' was the saying in Kariba by those who built it. In temperatures exceeding 50°C, the battle to construct the dam for hydro power and its creation of the biggest lake in the world in 1955, the first on the great Zambezi river, was legendary.

The site, originally surveyed by Rhodes' British South Africa Company a century earlier as a possible river crossing for his Cape to Cairo railway, was situated in the primitive, inhospitable and searing Zambezi Valley, hitherto visited only by tough hunters and die hard conservationists.

The home of the local Tonga people's river god, Nyami Nyami, a great serpent with a fish's head, was reputed to be in the colossal rock that channelled the river into Kariba gorge. The name for the site was *Kariwa*, meaning a trap. The fable went that Nyami Nyami would eat the occupants of any canoe sucked into these swirling waters. Likely as not, the big notorious crocodiles downstream would live up to the challenge.

The engineering and construction task of 120m high, 600m long wall across the mighty Zambezi river bed was formidable, even more so considering the technology of the 50's. Impresit, an Italian firm, won the international tender, much to the pique of the big British companies in this British colony. It demanded completion within 5 years, failing which hefty penalties were to be raised. Eyebrows raised and spectators jostled to observe disaster.

The initial challenge was to establish an access road and construct the massive foundations for the wall, all within the six-month dry season. And substantial enough to withstand the annual floods expected in the rains.

At the end of the first year, the Zambezi river came boiling down in flood of a magnitude only expected statistically every 2000 years, the waters rising 50m in the gorge over night, washing most of the structures and machinery that had been established in the crucial starting phase. The work force of 8000 men, many of them listening to the Tonga legend, wagged their fingers and shook their heads.

The next year, with construction much further ahead, the floods from both the Zambezi and Umnyati rivers met in the confluence just above the Kariba Gorge, and rose the waters 60m overnight.

Apart from the immense loss of structures and equipment, the entire black work force downed tools and threatened to leave.

'Was the white man so stupid he could not hear Nyami Nyami speaking? We are all going to die if we stay here.'

A massive exorcism exercise was raised by the Catholic Church, and only after much persuasion and pay increases were the labour force persuaded to go back to work. To their great credit, the project was valiantly completed on time. 86 men were buried alive in the dam wall's concrete through accidents in the harrowing work, commemorated in a church specially built to resemble the round coffer dams that had deflected the Zambezi from the huge dam wall's foundations.

The Lake filled in 3 yrs, hydrologists having forecasted 5, from continuing heavy rains pouring into the catchment area of the Zambezi, stretching 1000km into western Zambia, Angola and the Congo. It filled a valley 250 km long, and 50km at its widest.

The ecological implications of submerging the irreplaceable wild Zambezi Valley, ancestral home of the Tonga tribe and many thousands of species of rare and valuable fauna and flora were largely glossed over at the time. It's questionable whether it would have been built in today's 'green' and eco sensitive world. The country's ample coal and gas reserves could provide for its power requirements rather than submerging this irretrievable wilderness resource.

All that is left of it today is the 200km portion below the dam wall, known on the Zambian side as the Lower Zambezi National Park, and on the Zimbabwean side as Mana Pools National Park and its surrounding wildlife estate, declared a World Heritage site in 1984.

Nevertheless, the creation of this inland sea with its beautiful shoreline and large tracts of National Parks on the Zimbabwean side is a boon to wildlife and tourism today.

Another of the negative consequences of prioritising power production, with sustained high lake levels, or low in times of drought, is the drowning or starving respectively of immense areas of the nutritious *panicum repens* grass that seeded itself on the lake shore.

Our 'home' Park, the Matusadona, supports 50km of shoreline sloping gently into the lake, covered with the amazing *panicum.* This 'torpedo' grass, so called as it sends runners under the soil from which it pushes up succulent shoots, is greatly enjoyed by grazers. Directly attributable to the *panicum,* 'Matuse' supports five times the game density that any Park inland could be expected to.

The story of the grass is intriguing. As the Lake filled and flooded the gigantic valley, the nutritional content of the water was very high. Fish grew so fast their bodies were disproportionately large for their head size and aquatic plant life exploded. Floating down the Zambezi River, a weed, *salvinia auriculata,* hadn't to date attracted any particular attention. It originated from South America and the story goes that it had been introduced into the Zambezi from a careless tipping of an aquarium. The strong current in the river carried it down to the Indian Ocean, where it dispersed.

The conditions for the *salvinia's* growth in the Lake, however, were ideal. Huge stable islands of the floating weed formed, some so dense that trees were propagating on them, and boats could not penetrate them. Commonly known as 'Kariba weed', it blocked out surface water to such an extent the recreational facilities of this inland sea were endangered.

The authorities declared the weed a pest. They tried every trick they could to disperse it, spraying with herbicide, harvesting it for fertiliser, encouraging hippo to eat it, even importing a bug from its home in South America to eat it. Nothing worked. The islands of weed grew and grew.

Fortunately, as the lake developed to its fuller extent, wave action in the great expanses of water began to break these islands up and they washed ashore in heaps.

In amongst the *salvinia* was the *panicum,* bonding the floating islands even tighter. In a single season, the shallow sloping shorelines were covered with the self-planted grass and neatly applied compost of the rotting weed. It could survive up to 9 months of submersion when the lake rose in the rains. As the lake receded in the dry months and grazing became scarce inland, the *panicum* flushed anew on the water's edge. It became the saviour of the grazers in the 'Matuse', which had been trapped on this high ground by the rising waters, where they would normally have occupied only during the rains.

Now this short term natural grazing had been decimated by the grazer's forced permanent occupation.

Downstream of the dam the consistently high river levels resulting from the continuously heavy power demand cause substantial erosion on the riverbanks. The absence of regular annual floods and consequent rich deposits on the flood plains is bringing changes in the natural riverine vegetation that will have an irreversible impact on that valley. The famous Winter Thorn, *faidherbia albida*, providing nutritious pods to a large game population in the dry months, and the Vegetable Ivory fan palm, *hyphaene petersiana,* the tallest and most beautiful in the valley, with another highly nutritious fruit, are threatened with extinction when the present mature trees die off, the lack of flood plain conditions and pressure of grazing inhibiting regeneration from immature plants.

As so often, the mighty plans of men cause waves untold in nature's world.

Chapter 7

Piece de Resistance

I received an enquiry from a Belgium couple asking if we could arrange a three-week safari around Rhodesia. Having never done anything of the kind before, I immediately replied that of course we could.

Was there anything we couldn't?!

Maasie agreed to swap us her ancient Mazda which was a little bigger and more comfortable than Sands' little red car. A route was planned that would take us to all the most exciting places I remembered from family holidays. Sands behind the wheel, our guests comfortably ensconced on the big back seat, I would surreptitiously swat up the guide book on the area we were passing through, then turn to give them a knowledgeable spiel, like I'd been doing it for years. I dared not look at Sandy's face whose grin would have collapsed our professional-tour-guide couple farce on the turn.

We started at our family cottage in the Nyanga mountains on the Mozambique border, the highest of which tops 2500m. My uncle, Dr Robert Fynn, had enterprisingly invested the few pounds he won in a school prize as an 18yr old in the 1920's into this lovely property. Tucked into the side of a hill of pine, it aired a charm like none I've known, albeit a little rustic. A waterfall on the trout stream below lulled us to sleep at night after lazily yarning around a roaring log fire. Fishing amongst magnificent views into Mozambique and hearty walks up the surrounding craggy peaks filled one's day.

Our Belgians were making a movie that was to be presented at the Cannes Film Festival. We stopped on the way up to catch African village scenes, bicycles loaded with wood to tyre popping levels, women carrying great clay water jars on their head, no hands, and donkey carts driven haphazardly by children moving crops from the fields.

Our arrival at the talked up cottage in the evening was greeted by a cold drizzly mist. Great if we were there to snuggle up round the fire and read. Not quite so for film making.

'Probably clear up by tomorrow' I assured them.

It didn't, for two days.

We thrashed the waters for trout, walked and climbed hills, identified every bird that chirped, visited the lovely mountain farms and hotels, told stories round the great fires. But you can only take so much of smoky indoor scenes and ethereal misty swirls.

We had to find sunny Africa.

The old fashioned phone with a handle in the local grocery store wound to raise the exchange. My old friend, Tim Elton, on his farm in the fertile Cashel valley, had given me my first job on leaving school. He and the unique setting of *Thabanchu* would be a winner, whatever the weather.

'Tim. I'm in trouble here, bud!'

'What's up, Rob?'

I explained.

'The sun is shining here, fella. C'mon down. We'll expect you for lunch.'

'You're an angel, Tim. See you soon.'

Tim's dad, Hallam, had flown his Gypsy Major bi-plane out from England in the 1920's and carved this farm out of thick jungle, setting up a 'Pelton' wheel, driven from high pressure water delivered from a 30cm pipe hooked into the mountain streams. It powered the valley with electricity by night, and a grinding mill for maize by day. Maasie (my mum) had come out by ship with Beryl, his wife, and the two boys, to be their governess.

Tim's stories of this adventurous life, his spirited humour, and his wife Sue's fantastic home cooking from fare grown on the farm entertained us royally. Grand picnics under colossal trees by the river winding its way through the lush valley, walks up the Black Mountain behind the homestead where panoramic views opened across the border onto Mozambique, and tours around the enterprising farm filled three glorious days.

'You make good coffee in Rhodesia' said our Belgian connoisseur in a much better mood as we travelled on through the heart of the country's coffee region in the Chimanimani mountains bordering Mocambique.

'We make good everything in Rhodesia!' I couldn't help but respond. Our Tourist Board slogan of the time was 'Rhodesia is Super'.

We made our way down to the lowveld, the southern arid regions that held the big irrigated sugar cane plantations. Their vivid green splashed an unusual contrast across the surrounding dry bush with its hardy wild life and cattle ranches. Crossing another extraordinary contrast, the gleaming silver painted Birchenough suspension bridge, I recalled hearing of Hallam's victory salute flying under the bridge on arriving from his cross Africa trip.

Three of these spectacular bridges span the great rivers of Rhodesia, the other two being on the Zambezi. Their shiny painted steel, enormous greased cables and great arches were dreamed up by George Andrew Hobson of Sir Douglas Fox and Partners and Isambard Brunel, the 19th century British engineer who's famous Clifton suspension bridge spanned my view at Bristol University. Designed and manufactured in England, these structures were transported by sea and rail, spar by spar, to be assembled on site in the midst of Africa.

Having to leave out Gona Re Zhou as it was closed for the off-season, the *piece de resistance* of the tour was our 'Old Kaz' in the Matuse. Additional to the photogenic safari activities, the *coup de grace* was to be in a tree platform I'd built as a 'hide' from which to observe the surrounding wilderness, game and birds, allowing guests to feel unafraid of the wild yet immersed in it.

I'd chosen for them to spend a couple of nights in this wildly African honeymoon suite.

An elaborate strategy was planned to set up their ultimate 'Out of Africa' experience. Wanting it to be something of a surprise, I was to drive out with them at first light in the landrover for a 24 hour safari away, explaining only that overnight bags were to come later with Sands.

The plan was to stop in a leafy riverbed seemingly in the middle of nowhere, walk the last few kilometres to our tree house for a sumptuous bush breakfast on chequered tablecloths, complete with chilled orange juice, sizzling bacon and eggs, and their favourite, hot black Chimanimani coffee. Their 'bedroom', not forgetting flowers and pebbles, and camera platform would be neatly prepared up the ladder in the tree for them to spend the rest of the day and that night there, alone in the African wild. Scary, but safe, and very exotic.

Sands, in good girlfriend's role, was to head out with the staff, bedding and basic furniture, food and beverage department, with all the extended paraphernalia, or *katundu*, needed to make this an extra special experience. All on the raft, powered by our ancient 4 hp Seagull engine.

As we happily safari'd along, after hectic planning behind the scenes since the early hours, I was a little concerned. Would Sands get there on time? She had a lot to organise and pack. The lake could blow up. As could the ageing Seagull. Not least, she'd never been to this tree platform before. Nor had any of the staff with her.

I took a detour to give her a bit of leeway, taking time to study every bird, tree, animal and insect we could find on the way. On the final walk in, I had worked on building up some suspense of what lay ahead. They had never braved the African bush on foot before, and the slightly anxious lady walked close behind me, putting her foot into my each step as I withdrew mine. When I stopped, she would walk into me, always apologising. We rounded the final bend in the riverbed to arrive at the resplendent breakfast venue.

Nothing. Absolutely nothing beside, in or under the famous tree.

Plan 32B!

Leaving my disappointed guests with a hasty explanation on the empty platform, I went off looking for Sands.

'Don't worry, it makes a good story for the film' he generously assured me as I parted. She was not so convinced.

'Old Kaz' over-water lodge

Bhunu & the girls

Inyanga

'Do you have lions here, Robeen? . . . And what do we do if the elephant comes? . . . Can the eagles attack? . . . Are the snakes coming up into the tree? . . . What if I need a pee-pee?'

I reassured her as best I could and went off to walk the bays and promontories, sweeping the horizon for the raft. Finally, I saw the unmistakable shape of our craft being towed slowly across the lake.

'Yooohoooo . . . . Helloooooooooo!'

I lit a signal fire on the beach. Further wild waving of hat from me balancing precariously on a large petrified tree on the water's edge at last elicited a response and a slow turning of the small convoy in my direction.

Sands, big smile on her face, looking relaxed in the towing boat, surrounded by bronzed young fishermen drinking beer, staff and *kutundu* piled on the raft behind, explained how she had not been able to start the Seagull.

Full marks for initiative. Albeit a suntanned beauty in bikini and sarong waving from the camp's shoreline may have had something to do with the friendly response of these generous boaters.

Back to the tree house, we carried what we could manage, staff like a train of Livingstone's porters with amazing loads balanced on their heads.

To find a pride of lion settled comfortably at the foot of the ladder. Mr was happily filming, Mrs sitting so close he could hardly have worked his camera. Her ecstatic waving and grinning face on seeing us was a fitting welcome.

The tour was a success, although am sorry to have lost contact with the Schellens, thanks to the crazy circumstances we were trying to cope with in Zimbabwe, and never heard how the film fared at Cannes. I look forward to.

Brian Merriman's tours were a regular monthly feature. His advance guest list would include preferences in food and drink, their suitcases when they arrived wrapped in yellow ribbons for quick identification at airport baggage systems. Although the rest of their tour was the height of luxury, they loved the simple comfort and unusual character of the camp.

'Just relax and be yourselves.' Brian would say. 'Your camp and Matusadona do the rest.'

By now, the Rhodesian farming community had discovered our refuge resort too. Living in exposed and dangerous isolation, constantly on the alert for deadly attacks, our camp was one of the few places where they could totally relax in safety. They were also those few prepared to brave the hostile roads, where travel was only permitted in armed convoys, against ambush.

The camp was established and becoming known. Staff and equipment expanding, we were over the hump. Sands was handling the one-loaf Aga with skill, and I was on first name terms with virtually every tree in the Matuse.

'Sorry babes, we've got a booking for No 9 . . . sorry gal . . . at least the moon's good?'

'Don't try and sloosh me up' Sand's green eyes flashed. 'You're lucky that Rory and Joanne aren't here. I won't have them sleeping out under the trees.'

Our eight guest tents already full, and not wanting to turn anyone away, Sands and I would give up our own when an extra one booked. I hadn't minded the holes in the relic of my old 'digs' tent, additional ventilation for those steamy nights. Without a word, she had painstakingly repaired it using Maasie's old hand operated Singer. Her work place stretched across pebbles and sand in the best bit of shade she could find.

As tent number nine booked in, Sand's eyes would roll, and our home's roof would be smartly moved across to the guest wing, leaving us to spend a few nights under the stars. Those guests didn't know how privileged they were. I thought it was quite romantic with Sandy cuddling especially close and whispering.

'What was that? . . . I think it's a lion . . . Isn't that hippo getting a bit close?'

Felt good being the protector.

She had her reservations about how much fun it was.

In my element, I'd grown up on a farm, loved camping, specially under the stars, and was the typical 'make-a-plan' product of that innovative upbringing. Our off-the-beaten-track haven was close to my Utopia, and was becoming so for Sands too.

Chapter 8

Dzimba Dze Mabwe

My family had arrived with the early Rhodesian pioneers. This doughty group were mostly of British descent with a scattering of 'Boers', each sticking to their own culture groups in the areas they settled. The horrors of the Boer war were not far behind and tensions between those two peoples were still marked. Far less was the tension between white (British or Boer) and black.

The 'Brit' attitude to the black community, subtly hidden under tropical topees and sweeping moustaches, held that the advancement and development of local peoples was essential for a happy future. This swung the vote away from Rhodesia becoming a 'province' of the apartheid Republic of South Africa in the 1922 referendum and established it as an independent Commonwealth state under the British Crown with its own responsible government.

Developers were not all angels, nor Hollywood style colonials, nor all tyrants. Fine men and women devoted their lives to building up the 'colonies'. Inevitably, misunderstandings, insensitivities and crass small-minded decisions by inappropriate officials fed class and racial prejudice. But above all, there was development with good heart.

A post WWII policy, seeking to attract more developers, brought a flux of new immigrants, some of whom were elevated to higher social levels and living standards than they had enjoyed 'back home'. These wives, who saw little outside their new homes of the racial interaction in the work place, their only contact with the indigenous population their servants, developed a nervous disposition towards black advancement.

This short-sighted attitude coupled with a growing caution following the successive calamities of the new independencies to our north greatly influenced the voting in of the Rhodesian Front party, who slowed the flow of progressive thought and politics to a dint of the opposition.

Whites whose forbears had fought and been honed through the Zulu and Matabele wars had met and knew the deep dignity of these black nations. They also recognised there was a lot to learn before the African peoples could successfully operate in the new avaricious foreign perspectives of the developed west, let alone the east. They definitely could see them as governing partners in time to come with appropriate training and education.

The industrious economy of our relatively small landlocked country was something of a wonder on the continent, its impact on the world far beyond the expectations of its size and situation. Our sports men and women featured regularly on the international arena. Our farmers, National Parks and general good governance and development were respected worldwide.

It would seem one of the roots of this difference to other former colonial countries stemmed from the Rhodesian pioneer's determination to make this new land their home. Not just another job in the colonies before retirement back in their homeland whence they'd come. The likes of my grandfather and the brave men and women who trekked up in the 1880's and many who came after were there to stay and make this land their future. And it was tough going, honing perseverance and tenacity.

The pioneers found relatively few indigenous Africans populating the country, large tracts of land unoccupied. In the face of modern politics, history shows Man has always been an immigrant, often a belligerent. There is really no such thing as an indigenous population anywhere in the world. Wave after wave of conquering migrants, whether Roman, Nordic, German, Mongols, Slavs or Arabs have swept through Europe from time immemorial. Now we hear that Man originated in Africa. It is the nature of initiative. No different in Rhodesia. Nor surprise that the descendants of earlier migrants did not appreciate the new arrivals.

Sadly, much of what has gone array in Africa emanates from fear. Fear of encourage emerging blacks, and fear of reining in arrogant whites. And then follows shameless greed and raging incompetence, of the new and the old governors. The refusal to allow sufficient time and training under colonial systems has undermined the new governors ability to compete with First World cultures and their long developed cunning. The naivety of thinking the old ways, however powerful and fitting in rural Africa, could challenge the ruthless efficiency of the new industrial world was misplaced.

For all that, back there, a grand optimism in building the new country raced along development at a breathtaking pace, every race, creed and class working shoulder to shoulder to achieve their new vision in this land of opportunity.

And then came politics.

The early country was divided into two main ethnic groups following the last migrations. The Shona, a large and diverse majority trading in the North and East, and the Ndebele, a smaller war-like tribe in the South and West.

The Ndebele were an off shoot of the feared Zulu in the South, who conquered and colonised the surrounding tribes in a brutal highly organized military fashion. They were led by Chief Mzilikazi who had quarrelled with his brother Dingaan of the Zulu and were trekking north to look for land to settle in. Finding Gu—Bulawayo (the place of slaughter), in the south of the Zimbabwean plateau, a most pleasing region, they regarded the Shona living there as their new subjects, raiding and plundering at will.

Mzilikazi's son, Chief Lobengula, was responsible for negotiating the treaty with Cecil Rhodes' BSA Company to monopolise the prospecting rights for the land that came to be called Rhodesia, in Rhodes' honour. The Shona in today's Mugabe ZANU-PF regime have never forgiven them for this and their former subjugation.

The Shona have a more speculative origin. Their historians, and those of the Portuguese, the prime source of early written records arising from their dealings as traders in 15th—19th century Africa, were prone to exaggeration in recording what they perceived the hearer would like to hear. D.N.Beach in his 'The Shona and

Zimbabwe' is recognised for researching this history in meticulous detail and recording the truth as best it may be known.

It would appear the first Bantu migration to have moved on to the Zimbabwean plateau pre 900 AD were from both the Congo basin in the north, and the rich agricultural plains south of the Limpopo, the north east regions of RSA today. These early Iron Age people were responding to the pressures caused by their increasing wealth in evolving from hunter/gatherers to a productive agricultural culture. They needed more land to accommodate their increasingly intensive life styles.

They displaced the Batwa people, the hunter/gatherer predecessors of today's Bushmen, who were chased off the plateau and finally settled in the desert regions of the Kalahari in the southwest of RSA.

These early Iron Age agriculturists from the south, closely related to the Tsanga and the Venda tribes of RSA, were overrun and integrated by the Shona speakers who migrated from the fertile cattle rearing plains either side of the Drakensburg range still further to the south, again needing more land in their increasingly wealthy cattle culture.

The Kutama migration, as these people were called, formed the Gumanye, Leopards Kopje, Harare and Musungezi Shona cultures that dominated the comfortable climate highland plateau of Zimbabwe between 900 and 1300.

Successful cattle herders, the state of Zimbabwe grew and flourished under their rule, fed by the gold and ivory trade with early middle East cartels, and later the Portuguese. Mining was done with hoes, picks and shovels, passing the earth, rock, ore and water out in baskets and bowls, opening the deep slopes and shafts. Once a vein went too far below the water level, a new mine had to be found and opened, with a bit of luck before it collapsed. The milling also took a great deal of labour.

Elephant hunting was carried out with animals being trapped in pits, speared from trees or hamstrung by brave hunters who approached them on foot. Both of these trades were risky and strenuous, directed by the ruling class in their desire for fine cloth, beads and pottery bought in by the cartels. Although the Shona weavers produced cloth, it was no competition to the Indian weaves, which came to be the trademark of the wealthy Shona rulers.

The variable African climate was subject to drought and flood disasters, known to the Shona as *shangwa,* which also encouraged the community to diversify and develop this export/import commerce. Their hardy cattle remained their prime currency, tradable during *shangwas* for crops stored by neighbouring tribes, and was that demanded for a bride, as it is today

This economy developed to the extent that a surplus of wealth accumulated, which was invested into stone buildings, improved through generations to culminate in such as the famous 'Great Zimbabwe' structure, after which the country is named.

This fascinating structure has puzzled archaeologists since its 'discovery' by Europeans in 1868. It consists in essence of the fort like Acropolis on a hill dominating the surrounding valley, with a secret enclosure, or temple, and its famous conical towers, some 30ft in height and 60ft in circumference. The circular walls of the temple alone are estimated to hold 100,000 tons of stone, all hewed square and fitted exactly, as is the entire structure. No signs of any quarry or stone working have been found in the vicinity. Huge carvings of eagle like birds, similar to those found in Egyptian tombs, dominated the great walls.

The theories of who built it and why are as varied as the controversies and prejudices are fierce. The romantics, of whom my Dad was one, gave it to the Phoenicians, the great sailors, traders, miners, and craftsmen of Biblical times, and providers of gold and precious materials to King Solomon for his temple and his fabulous tryst with the Queen of Sheba.

The meticulous science of archaeology has, however, now clearly established it was built by the Zimbawean dynasty of the Shona speaking people. Around 1100, the wealthy Gumanye people started to build thick dagga walls to screen the ruler's lavish life style from the gaze of the ordinary people. These developed into the use of local granite, an igneous rock that forms the great stone Kopjes and balancing rocks the area is famous for. This tends to break off in even sheets and was used to form walls. This practice was developed by their skilled artisans and greatly improved with generations, well established by 1300. Albeit possibly influenced by the early traders, they were impressive builders.

The Zimbabwean ruling class adapted elaborate life styles, in considerable luxury, with a taste for an astonishing variety of imported goods, reported in detail by the Portuguese trading Captains. By 1450, however, the state outgrew itself. Some 10,000 were living in the valley surrounding the acropolis, a sizeable city in those days. The crowded village land would have been trampled bare, enveloped in a great noise arising from such a horde and a smog-like smoke from the cooking fires, with swarms of flies from the primitive toilet arrangements. The contrast between the ruled and the rulers in their palace on the hill would have been striking.

The crops, grazing and firewood collecting lands would have become too far a field to handle in a day's work. Apparently no organisation was effected to address the wider distribution of the people and their activities, nor in sympathy of their harsh and unhygienic living conditions. Complete collapse of that society and dynasty ensued.

It would appear that they were not overly religious, using the priests revered by the 'povo' for their own ends, and the great monoliths, conical towers and birds were not so much objects of worship or symbolism, but of wealth and status. The respect and reverence of these rulers was maintained by their ardour and funds to command and supply large forces of armed men to dominate the plateau and its trading routes to the coast.

All an interesting comment and background to the excessive conduct of the ruling party, their descendants, today. There are possibilities that the structures were built on previous ruins that may go back to the Persian development on the continent, linked in with the extraordinary 'Nyanga' people and their incredibly extensive terrace work (3000 sq kms) and Zimbabwe type walls, the origins of which are a total mystery to this day.

The words '*Dzimba dza mabwe*', house of stone, or *Zimbabwe,* became used for all stone Shona capitals. That this great trade and skill disintegrated was indeed a sad regression for the Shona.

Great Zimbabwe

The Pioneer Column

Another migration of Shona speakers from the south, known as the *Guruswa*, or people of the long grass, replaced the collapsed Zimbabwean dynasty with the Mutapa, then Torwa and Karanga, and lastly the Changamire Rosvi states in early 1600's, each superseding the former in turn. The latter survived through to 1830's, although civil wars and skirmishing amongst their leaders led to 60 odd independent dynasties emerging amongst the Zimbabweans.

Their failure to unite, aided by the Portuguese to give advantage in their trading, collapsed the state's ability to defend and organise themselves. It was into this general confusion that the Ndebele arrived and conquered under Mzilikazi, followed soon after by Rhodes' pioneers in 1880's.

Chapter 9

Neen's Birthday Lion

Back to the Matuse and 1975.

Sands is pregnant.

Marriage, naively, totally selfishly, had not even remotely entered my agenda. Children? Babies? Who's managing the family planning around here, anyway? Certainly wasn't me. And now?

And all we have for a home is a tent!

This turn of events was not the romantic interlude it should have been.

I loved Sands. She was good fun, quick to laugh at herself, and me, and had made a huge commitment to us and our camp. But this new happening was coming in far too fast for me.

C'mon Rob?!

I was bewildered and uncertain.

Were we really right for each other? We don't talk about stuff enough! What stuff? Like a young bull sniffing the air, I was absurdly immature in relationship.

I groan in embarrassment thinking about it today.

Back there, my mind whirred in contemplating a lifetime's commitment. We had such different backgrounds. And outlooks. I had ridiculous expectations that few could meet. I hadn't even thought about marrying now. Gracious me (rather, not so gracious)—we had safaris to run . . .

But surely, Rob, this isn't too much to ask. After all she's put in and given up for you? And children were certainly part of my long-term plan.

I juggled preposterously.

In pathetic panic.

And the penny was slowly rolling towards the edge.

Sands was recovering from a divorce with a man 30 years her senior, his fourth failed wife. Marrying at the age of 18, I wonder now how much she had been replacing the father she had never had.

And now this jerk who couldn't even get it up to marry her!

Sands retreated and left camp to live back in Salisbury. I vacillated. Like a love-sick trumpeter hornbill who couldn't find the tree his naked wife was holed up in.

Devastated, I found her and I said I would. We married in a registry office.

Not exactly the shining knight on silver horse galloping to the rescue.

Our little Karina, or Neen as we called her, was born on the 1st September 1975, in the Lady Chancellor maternity home in Salisbury. I was in attendance, still suffering from shock. After a harrowing, miraculous night seeing my first-born arrive into the world, I received more heady news.

An unforgettable night had been had back in camp.

The young trainee couple, Calvin and Sue, holding the fort in my many absences as the new family man, had spent a particularly dark night. A storm crashed waves on the shore. Moaning trees bent in the wind. It had started as an 'early to bed and snuggle up' evening.

Well into the night, a crying and wailing was heard in the direction of the staff tents. Guests thought there was revelry in the air. Some may have stirred uneasily.

Calvin and Sue were in an exhausted sleep, as all staff were every night. Including Oz and Buhnu who slept by the kitchen.

In the staff tented compound, a lion had clawed its way into where our head bedroom hand, Joseph, was equally deeply asleep.

He awoke to a lion dragging him by the head out of his camp bed. His brave wife took up the challenge, seizing a large cooking pot with which she tried to bash the brains out of the king of the jungle, screaming for reinforcements.

Horrified at hearing lion amongst Joseph and his wife's screams for help, the entire remaining staff of about a dozen bodies crowded into one tent, wailing loudly too, but no ways were they going out there, certain a whole pride were waiting to devour them. Finally, Tyson could stand it no longer. He broke from the tent in a frenzied race through the dark wind-lashed bush for the camp, seventy metres away.

"SHUMBAAAAAAAAA . . . . .!" (LIOOOOOOON!)

Calvin, Oz and Buhnu were quickly wide-awake. Tyson garbled the story. Assessing the situation, the senior staff drove round in the land rover, unarmed as we all still were. Approaching through the trees under urgent directions from Tyson, the lion was picked up in the headlights standing outside Joseph's tent. The remainder of the staff fled round to the back of the 'landy', hurling themselves through the rear door.

Buhnu edged his way to behind Joseph's tent, screened from the lion in the dark. Oz stood by armed with a knob-carry. Everybody watched, holding their breath.

Calvin was poised with his foot on the accelerator, ready to charge if the lion moved. Painfully slowly, Buhnu crept into Joseph's tent, picked up the scalped man in one arm and mauled wife in the other and crawled back to the vehicle carrying them both, all eyes on them and the panting lion standing only metres away.

All fifteen bodies onboard, Calvin reversed out and drove the short trip to the camp. Short in a landrover. Tyson thought otherwise thinking about his earlier terrifying run through the night.

A casualty station was set up in the kitchen, its mopane boma the only solid structure in the camp offering a modicum of security. Oz and Calvin woke all the guests and escorted them to the haven, whereupon a dentist and his wife, returning guests, volunteered to stitch up the sorry two, ably assisted by Sue.

Cups of tea were on the go and stories were flowing. Calvin had tried to get out in the boat to Spurwing to use their radio phone, and returned. Too rough. The long vigil and emergency operating theatre was underway. Nobody ventured outside.

In the early hours, Buhnu, crouching over the fire boiling the umpteenth kettle for tea and coffee, suddenly noticed a movement at the kitchen doorway. Which was simply an opening in the wall of poles. There was the lion, standing surveying the scene, unnoticed by the activity centred on the stitching operation.

Without saying a word, Bhunu pulled a burning log from the fire and hurled it at the lion. A roar, cloud of dust, and the fallen king leaped back and disappeared into the dark. Shock and exclamations. Feverish efforts barricaded the doorway with kitchen cupboards and tables.

In an uneasy calm, the vigil resumed in the emergency room at a renewed level of readiness.

First light found an exhausted but united band of camp guests and staff with two well-stitched and recovering victims.

Our only communication with the outside world sprang to life. The Lake Navigation radio.

'Good Morning Lake, this is Kariba'.

Calvin passed an S.O.S.

An Air Force helicopter based at the airport responded and was whirling over the lake in minutes. Our two stalwarts were picked up and ferried to hospital in Harare, with the RRAF's compliments.

Ensuring my new family and just arrived mauled staff were as fine as they could be, I made haste to the Lake. Finding a fatigued but exhilarated camp, not a single guest had chosen to leave. Such were Rhodesians on holiday. The lion had ransacked four tents. Beds were broken, coir mats torn, mattresses eaten, and Mini Lion covered in saliva, shaken, but intact.

A National Parks team came to investigate. A young research ranger, Russel Taylor, with assistant, bounced out of their landrover, taking charge of the situation. They shot an impala as bait to lure the lion back with the plan to shoot it, and warned all to remain in camp. They nipped over to update the 'Parks' camp site next door, Changachirere, of the action in progress, instructing the occupants to also stay put, and holler if they saw a lion.

As they drove back in the evening light on to the spit of land that adjoined our camp to the main land, there was the lion on the bait.

They jumped from the vehicle and opened up on the hapless beast, momentarily forgetting that our camp lay directly behind in their line of fire. Back in camp, settling down for the evening following the long day, it was like they had been ambushed. Everybody hit the deck as bullets zapped through tents and pinged off metal poles.

All in a day's safari at Old Kaz!

Mission accomplished. Two proud 'Parks' men stood with a dead lion at their feet. On dissection, it turned out to be an emaciated lioness with severe kidney disorders. Bits of tent, mats, mattresses, and boots from the previous evening's spree were found in the stomach. At least no human limbs had been added.

I was on 'call up', our regular military commitment, shortly after this. All the staff insisted on being transported to a small island offshore to sleep every night, leaving Sands, Oz and Buhnu to man the camp through the dark hours. On my return and calling a halt to this inefficient practice, they took to sleeping on the roof of the workshop, only finally persuaded to sleep back in their well-patched tents when the rains broke, months later.

Within weeks of Neen's birth, my new family were heading for camp, all credit to Sands. I had recently bought a small aluminium boat made from pieces of aeroplane by an Air Rhodesia engineer, powered by a little inboard petrol engine from an old DKW car.

I was longing to try it out. In typically task-focused fashion, Safari Fynn loaded his three week old baby and long-suffering wife with all the paraphernalia into this ridiculous boat, not much bigger than a bathtub, to cross the great lake. An old Kariba character, Guy de Barry, who drank his fair share of whisky and bayed to the full moon, saw this and came whooshing over in one of his big power boats, calling me all kinds of uncomplimentary names, and insisted on transporting Sands and Karina across.

I wasn't convinced of her safer passage and thought he had a bit of a crush on Sands, but his gallantry left me with a somewhat ignominious crossing and missing my new family arriving home.

A baby in camp had its complications. Sands, who was the everything in our management team, besides the Boss, coped incredibly. Neen would be papoosed on her back like an African child while the manageress busied around camp.

Swimming with Neen

Tyson & Neen

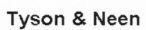

Planning with Bhunu before police reserve call-up

The Taylors with John & Briar

Briar's story is taken up in Chapter 32

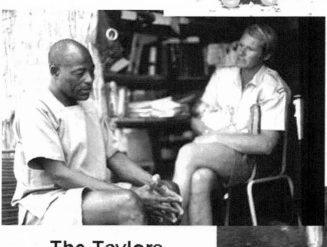

'Do be careful, Rob' Sands would worriedly comment as I took our baby swimming in the lake off the beach in front of camp.

'No worries, you just relax in your slax back there!'

Harry casual! But I kept my eyes open. I'd heard the statistic that estimated a croc to every 10m of shoreline. Macho youth—thanks God we all survived.

Stretched as she was between her work and our guests, Sands always had time to attend to her baby. She had a willing helper and minder, old Buhnu, who soon took the apple of everybody's eye under his wing. Neen would spend hours tucked under his enormous arms against his sweaty armpit, like he was carrying a loaf of bread cuddled against his huge hairy chest. She would be sucking one of his delicious home made buns while he worked away, singing African lullabies.

The terrain in camp was covered in washed pebbles typical over much of the Zambezi valley, from the river having varied its course down the ages. They were comfortable to walk on, but not so easy for the crawler. Neen developed what we called the 'Matusadona rock hop'—bum in the air, moving on all fours, no knees touching, much like a spider on four legs. She learned to walk sooner than usual, being an easier way to get around.

Her increased mobility was another problem.

'Kari? Where is Kari?' Buhnu was asking, calling her.

He had suddenly noticed there was no Karina. Everybody thought everybody else had her. A frantic search ensued, spreading wider, until there was a low whistle from one of the guys behind the bushes backing the tents. Bustling over, we saw Karina in the midst of a small herd of big 'daga' boys, six old bull buffalo. One of the most unpredictable and dangerous animals in the wild.

She was insisting they take an interest in the soggy bun she was carrying, pushing it under their noses while they grazed. They would snort, and move away a few steps. We looked on in awe and wonder, floored as to how to retrieve her without causing a casualty. Her old friend Buhnu came up with a plan. He crept in closer, keeping a wary eye on the buffalo, holding up another bun and calling her quietly.

'Kari, Come Kari. Bhunu's bun, Kari.'

She spotted him, and not having much success with the current bun, she waddled across to get a re-supply. The dagga boys carried on grazing, unperturbed.

'Bhunu, you old scoundrel, Don't think you're getting a raise for that!' I laughed in nervous relief, scooping her up and slapping him on the back. We all had a great chuckle.

Sands, the most conscientious mum you could meet, wondered how this could be happening to her.

Chapter 10

Zulu Fynn

My heritage prepared me for some of this.

The Fynns were originally natives of Donegal, Ireland. Henry Francis Fynn I, born 1775, arrived in Cape Town in 1805. His family lived in London while he owned and sailed with his clipper, trading to the Dutch East Indies and China via the Cape Colony.

His last voyage found him returning two years after his outward-bound Cape stopover. Putting into Table Bay, not knowing that Cape Town had been retaken by the Dutch now at war with England, his vessel together with a fortune in Spanish Gold Dollars and trading cargo was confiscated, and he incarcerated.

On cessation of the Anglo Dutch war and being released with the return of some of his cargo, he decided to stay, fetching his family from London. Acquiring ownership of much of Adderly Street, Cape Town's Oxford St, and running a tavern of the seas, he clearly enjoyed his life. Many complaints of rowdiness and disorderly conduct from his house are recorded in the old town history. He later lost his fortune through gambling and joined his sons, Francis, William and Frank in their ventures upcountry on the east coast.

His eldest son, Henry Francis Fynn II (b.1803), was studying to be a doctor. Following his father's footsteps in maritime trading and exploring, and clearly bored with his studies, he took a job as 'super cargo' on a vessel plying the Portuguese East African route to Delagoa Bay, now Maputo in Mozambique. The super cargo was

71

responsible for selling the goods of a merchantman at the ports he chose to head into, and purchasing the return load. A big job.

A great entrepreneur, and effectively the founder of what is the Port of Durban today and the South African province of Natal, HFF kept a detailed diary. It holds an important place in South African historical literature today.

He was an expert native linguist, as all the brothers were, and a close observer, affording him unrivalled opportunities for acquiring authentic local knowledge, unobtainable by other Europeans in the country. And he was the first white man to meet with the powerful and ruthless Zulu king, chief Shaka.

Zulu folk-lore held the strange white-skinned creatures not human.

'Being a production of the sea, which they traversed in large shells, coming near the shores in stormy weather, their food was the tusks of elephant, which they would take from the beach if laid there for them. Some were put to death by being thrust onto a sharply pointed stake and left for the wild scavengers to eat for being such unnatural and troublesome beings.' (ref HFF's Diary)

Shaka himself regarded the white man as something of a marvel, seeing him as the chief of diviners from whom the Zulu all derived their powers.

'Wearing his garment, though so small as to be held in the grasp of his hand, when slipped over his head it covered his whole body. His hat, which he removed at pleasure, was conceived to be part of his head. His shoes made it appear that he was devoid of toes, and his footprints, showing no traces of them, confirmed this idea. His heel was so long as to penetrate the ground, and he was mounted on an animal of great speed, carrying a pole in his hands which spat fire and thunder, killing all wild animals he looked at.' (HFF's Diary)

In 1824, at 21 years of age, HFF was tasked by the Cape Colony to form an expeditionary force for the purpose of meeting with Shaka and negotiating trading rights into the interior, which hitherto had been dominated by the Portuguese and the Swahili, or Islamised Africans. He was to initiate the arrangements following on his previous experiences in trading at Delagoa Bay.

Their landing in what is the Port of Durban today is recorded in the Diary.

'We set up camp with tents (sails) from the ship . . . . around midnight we were awoken by a thunder storm, and a flood that rushed through our camp . . . . we salvaged what we could and built up the fire. From all sides came the howling of wolves (hyenas) which had to be driven off by burning logs.'

And this following on the four week sail from Cape Town through the treacherous waters of the Wild Coast, a shallow rocky shore with poor charts, some putting the coast line 200km out.

Little was known of the tribes, or the interior. HFF, rejecting the offer of an armed escort, travelled with six porters, an interpreter and a guide to make contact with the king chief. The remainder of the party established a base at their landing. He discovered a land stretching hundreds of miles along the coast and into the interior for as far as he could ascertain, entirely subjugated to the cruel and despotic Zulu.

Victim tribes were impoverished, having lost their homes, livestock and crops. Many were dying of hunger. The warring Zulu nation supported a vast conscript army with a discipline unheard of amongst 'savages', who struck without fear wherever they pleased. No warrior could marry until he'd served his time in battle.

HFF's first contact with them was meeting a returning raiding party. An Impi of thousands of warriors running along the shore towards him 'blackened' the beach for as far as his eye could see. His accompanying party disappeared into the undergrowth leaving him on his own to face this massive army. Dressed in skins and head feathers, they carried short stabbing spears, a Zulu invention equal to the short sword of the Roman legions, and *assegais* (the long shafted throwing and ceremonial spear), each regiment in skirts and leggings matching with their Nguni hide shields, all in absolute military order.

A meeting of civilizations. Equally astonished to find Fynn, they listened respectfully at his attempts to communicate, understanding the name of their chief, Shaka, which he called out repeatedly. They deliberated amongst themselves, then left leaving him no sign of their intentions.

He was awed by their supreme arrogance.

Fortunate to escape with his life in this encounter, on the advice of his interpreter they made camp to await contact from the great king. Over the following three long weeks, messengers came to inform him that Shaka was preparing to see him.

Finally, he was commanded to attend the royal kraal, some 300km distant. This took a further fourteen days to cover. Under tight-lipped military escort and following devious decoy routes.

On arriving at Shaka's monumental establishment, a boma extending around 5km in circumference, he waited another three days for an audience. During his patient wait one of Shaka's many wives, stricken with fever, staggered out from her village to die, as was the custom in such cases. HFF carried medicine and having some knowledge of tropical diseases, administered to the unfortunate lady who duly recovered.

When finally summoned, there were more than 80,000 men in war attire assembled to receive him. Shaka was enchanted to have the fabled white man arrive on his shores, but rebuked HFF for attending to one of his 'dogs', ordering him not to indulge in such time wasting again. Had he not come from the great king umGeorge to see the great king umShaka, not to be diverted by such trivialities?

'I was asked to gallop my horse round the circle in the midst of a tremendous shout "*Ujojo wokhalo*!" (The long-tailed finch that comes over the ridge) A tribute to his quickness and daring. The whole force remained stationary as it had been since the commencement of the reception whilst we were led to the Chief's hut where 200 elders were gathered.

'A long speech was made by our escort chief, elevating Shaka's greatness and achievements, as was the custom of all addressing the king, in the course of which we were frequently called upon to answer "*Yebo*", that is to affirm as being true all he was saying, though we were perfectly ignorant of what was being said. Elephant tusks were brought forward and laid before us.

'Shaka stood and raised the stick in his hand and after striking it right and left the whole mass of warriors broke from their position and formed up into regiments. Portions of each of these rushed to scout the river and the surrounding hills while the remainder formed themselves in a circle and commenced dancing with Shaka in their midst. It was a most exciting scene, surprising to us, who could not have imagined that a nation of natives could be so disciplined and kept in such order.

**Henry
Francis
Fynn**

1803-1870

**Contemporary
drawing of
Shaka, King of
the Zulus**

'Regiments of girls headed by officers of their own sex then entered the centre of the arena in their tens of thousands, each holding a staff in her hand. They joined in the dance that continued for about two hours. Shaka then came towards us, evidently to seek our applause. He desired to know if ever we had seen such order in any other state, assuring us that he was the greatest king in existence, that his people were as numerous as the stars, and that his cattle were innumerable.

'We were then treated to a grand cattle show, each regiment driving towards us thousands of cattle, each the colour of the regiment's shields. This show continued till sunset. During the proceedings we noticed a number of men, it seemed at random, pointed out by the slightest movement of Shaka's hand or head, who were beaten with clubs and executed on the spot by the breaking of their neck by those around them. We understood this was a common occurrence and anyone who offended him in the smallest way, possibly just the expression he wore, would lose his life.

'There were stories of massacres of thousands, such as whole regiments being marched over cliffs to prove their bravery; of other regiments which cared for his *seraglios* (Harems) who together with the women were massacred, up to three thousand people at a time, due to a rumour that one of the soldiers had amorous relations with one of his ladies. Certainly, if you were opposed to him, or simply not subjugated, as were surrounding outlying tribes, no mercy would be shown.

'On his mother Nandi's death, he allowed and encouraged an ungovernable and uncontrollable display of grief amongst his own people, where individuals competed against each other to show the greatest lament, resulting in the death of 7,000. He then sent his army out with the mission to annihilate the entire population as far as the Cape Colony for their not having joined in the mourning. He was personally responsible for the deaths of probably close to one million people in his life.' (HFF's Diary)

Shaka was greatly taken by the sensible and good-humoured HFF. Soon after their meeting, the Zulu king was stabbed by an *assegai* in the chest during a celebration at night, miraculously missing his heart and lungs. Fynn further won his confidence by dressing the wounds and bringing him back to good health. A thousand died in retribution amongst followers under suspicion or neglect.

A lone white man in this midst, thousands of warriors eager to despatch him if he failed to please on the slightest sign from their king, Shaka was clearly impressed with Fynn's skills and courageous, yet sensitive, attitude. They established a friendship that was to protect Fynn and his people for the rest of Shaka's life. The king chief never tired of talking to him and asking questions about the world across the waters. And King UmGeorge.

He constantly challenged Fynn's loyalty. On one occasion they were walking past a pool in a river when one of his accompanying chiefs commented on the voracity of the crocodiles that lived there. Shaka asked Fynn if he was brave enough to swim across, offering him five cattle if he made it. Knowing the point of the test, his reputation as the King's confident at stake, he straight away removed his clothes and plunged into the pool.

On making it across, Shaka asked him if he really thought he would receive the cattle promised, to which he replied 'No', and all the party present laughed. Fynn's commitment and courage to walk and talk on his own with this resourceful tyrant was commendable. And well recognised by Shaka himself.

Modestly hoping for qualities that may be inherited from my forbears, and aware of my own casual approach to dress—mostly made by Sands on her bush sewing machine and never allowed to be discarded—I was amused to read the following description of my ancestor from the hand of HFF's friend and partner, Nathaniel Isaacs.

'If ever South Africa could boast of a Robinson Crusoe of her own, as affable, shrewd, politically sagacious, courageous and large hearted as Defoe's hero, here is one. I met HFF just returned from spending eight months collecting ivory, associating solely with the natives with whom he sojourned. The many vicissitudes he had endured and obstacles with which he had contended, not only in often being without food and ignorant where to seek it, but in daily danger of being destroyed by wild animals, or massacred by savages, were enthralling to hear of. He had from necessity assumed the costume of the natives while with them, having worn out his own.

'It is almost impossible to convey a correct idea of the singular appearance of this gentleman when he first presented himself. Mr Fynn is in stature somewhat tall, with a prepossessing countenance. His face was disfigured with hair, not having an opportunity to shave himself for some considerable time. His head was partly covered with a crownless straw hat. A tattered blanket, fastened round his neck by means of strips of hide, served to cover his body, while his hands performed the office of keeping it round his 'nether man'. His shoes he had discarded for some months, whilst every other habitment had imperceptibly worn away, so that there was nothing of a piece about him.

'He was highly beloved by the natives, who looked up to him with more than ordinary veneration, for he had often been instrumental in saving their lives, and in months of his own pain and sickness had administered to their relief, even pleading on their behalf before the murderous tendencies of the Zulu king.'

Shaka was eventually assassinated by his brother, Dingaan, in1828 (seven years after that other great military leader, Napolean Boneparte). The new hostile chief also found favour with Fynn, although HFF soon discovered Dingaan's crafty treachery. On one occasion he had to swim out to sea to escape an *impi* sent to kill him and his party, while some of his children and wives (some of them local women given him by chiefs) were slaughtered. The new chief all the while maintaining an appearance of friendship with him.

'For all Shaka's bloodthirstiness, he was an imposing, dignified, intelligent and highly organised warrior, holding the respect, and even liking of his people. The guile and cunning of Dingaan were not the way of Shaka, and had he lived, perhaps the history of South Africa might have been written differently' writes the man who perhaps knew Shaka better than any and was so closely linked with the colonial politics of the day.

HFF went on to serve as the British Resident Magistrate for Natal, and died in Durban, aged 68 years, where he is commemorated in the West Street Pioneer Cemetry. The inscription reads;

'. . . . and for 37 years was most actively engaged as a Government Officer in the Colony of the Cape of Good Hope & Natal, much to the satisfaction of both governments.'

Chapter 11

Kunjiri

We bought a larger boat to transport supplies from Kariba. We called her *Boss Jim* after Jim Samuels who had built and owned it for many years and who had loaned her to Rupert Fothergill's famous 'Operation Noah', the rescue operation for thousands of animals and reptiles when the Lake was forming. An open 22-foot steel hull, powered by twin Volvo Penta inboard/outboards, she was an unheard of sophistication in Kazungula's flotilla.

Always loaded to the gunnels on our supply runs, she drove like a battleship, doggedly holding her course while waves crashed over the bows and into the boat. In rough conditions a man would constantly be on the hand bilge pump and another bailing with a bucket. Often it was only the power of the thrusting engines that kept the bows up, with crew shin deep in water. I was the driver on these trips, not trusting anybody else, and when we reached the camp I would take her straight onto the beach, Normandy-landing style. There she'd gently subside onto the bottom when we would bail out the water and unload.

I would pick the evenings for the return supply run when I could as they usually offered beautiful balmy crossings. After one of these long days, shopping completed, with only the family on board, the haze on the lake from the bush fires inland having dropped visibility to a few kilometres and the landfall not spot-on, we arrived camp side amongst the off-shore islands. I felt and heard a big hit on the propeller as we hit a submerged stump and knew we'd smashed the one and only out-drive still operating out of our two engines.

'Ouch, that was a baddie!'

'Oohh nooh . . .' Sands's eyes rolled.

Karina was now asleep in her travelling cot amongst the drums and crates of supplies and we were looking forward to an early bed. With our limited radio handsets in camp, the guides and guests had priority with them, so there was nothing for it now but to sit it out and wait for our camp rescue team who were under instructions to come looking if we weren't back by nightfall. With lots of beer and cokes on board, a paraffin lamp on the bows to act as a beacon, I thought this wasn't too bad—a good bit of 'one-on-one' time with my wife—Sands, wasn't quite so enamoured. The thought of spending the night out on the water with her eight month old baby was not on the top of her page.

Our sun-setting wait was further dramatized by the extraordinary spectacle of a herd of buffalo on a nearby island discovering lion trying to creep past them. Lion would often swim from island to island, checking for stray waterbuck or any other tasty morsel marooned there. These 'dagga boys' were having nothing of it, and chased the lion from one side of the little island to the other. We watched four cubs running for their lives with the thundering herd right on their tails. One was caught with a tossing snout between its back legs, somersaulting 3m high in the air, landing on its feet ahead of the raging buffalo and scampering off to safety into the water. The pride hid for their life amongst the reeds until it got dark when they hurriedly swam off

Our rescue team found us later that night, by which time Sands had resigned to savouring our rare interlude on our own under the stars, and we were all asleep, quite disgruntled at being found.

I had fabricated a game-viewing craft based on Jeff Stutchbury's design—two canoes linked by a platform to form a catamaran. Painted in camouflage, with the clients sitting in bucket seats in the canoe hulls, she was a beauty. I steered from a central seat on the platform between the hulls, my feet on a rudder bar, hands free to man binoculars and 'hold forth'. She was named *Kunjiri*, Tonga for warthog, whose tusks the two canoe bows resembled.

Neen would come with me on boat safaris as soon as her Mum allowed, and would enjoy a break from the onerous task of child-minding in camp. She learned to sit quietly, holding her fingers to her lips if anyone else made a sound. I found that game expressed little concern of the baby noises she sometimes made in her excitement. She would snuggle up between my legs on the seat, pointing, oohing and aahing, copying all of us and holding my huge binoculars to her little eyes. As good entertainment was had inside the boat as out.

One of the problems with *Kunjiri* was that she sat too low in the water and easily swamped by any serious wave action. One windy morning, before I improved the design with higher sides, I pulled out for another mystery tour, never quite knowing what to expect round the next corner. Our harbour channel was marked through the trees with tins hanging from them, all saved from the kitchen. 'Bhunu's tins' Neen would point out as we passed them, waving cheerfully to Sands watching anxiously from the camp as we hit the swell.

Our guests on this occasion were somewhat portly, and heavily slung with cameras and binoculars, and we were sitting particularly low in the water. I took the waves slowly, bows on, for a little distance out to sea, then turned broadside to them, increased power, and raced along between the troughs and the crests for the shelter of the next bay. It looked scary but was a technique I'd perfected previously and worked well.

Not this day, however.

A large roller caught us, breaking into the windward canoe, which half filled with water. And suddenly—as things tend to happen in boats on rough water—we were awash, the entire craft now wallowing at seat level in the lumpy lake, being kept afloat on the mandatory buoyancy tanks.

'Keep in your seats, folks, try to balance the boat. It's okay, this is a retrievable situation.' I was reassuring myself as much as them. Things were looking decidedly unstable. It was imperative not to move around too much, or the whole kaboosh would turn turtle at the slightest imbalance of weight distribution. And we had weight—uncertain swimmers festooned with equipment. And my little two-year-old, untested in these conditions, in crocodile infested waters.

Twilight trip into The Sticks in 'Boss Jim'

Game viewing from 'Kanjiri'

I was confident *Kunjiri* would keep floating, although submerged to deck level, but the guests were probably not so sanguine.

I turned the options over in my mind.

After some deliberation, I tied the wallowing craft to a tree, explained that the radio was waterlogged and the only option I could see.

'I'm going to swim ashore and get back to camp for help. Stay calm and hang in here now, I'll be back soon—okay, guys? Okay Neen?'

I needed to act quickly before hysteria set in or the craft settled further. The shore was some 400m away, but too dangerous with the swell running to beach the boat. I reckoned it was probably too rough for crocs to be around.

Neen understood. "Daddy going for swim. Back soon!" she told them all, and proceeded to regale them with all the other disasters she regularly coped with as a baby.

Intrigued by her faith in her Dad and her presence of mind, our guests floated, distracted by Neen's stories, awash in the sea for about an hour. Sands, who normally disliked choppy water, could not believe what I had done with our child, let alone our guests, and insisted on accompanying me in the rescue boat.

"Thank God, you're back, Rob! Guess your remote control on the crocs works pretty good—we haven't seen one!" the guests joked good-humouredly when we got there, in pure relief I am sure, for us all.

Amazingly, nobody sued. I think they left camp in a state of bemused shock—like they were in a make believe world where the whole thing hadn't really happened.

Although appearing a little chancy in my behaviour, by God's grace we never lost a guest, nor any of my children. They were the most special gems of my life, all of whom I shared my excitement of the journey with as intimately as I could. It's good to see today how they know that and appreciate their unusual upbringing.

What may seem irresponsible risks was just how it was—our everyday life. We did not consider it daunting—in fact, I have to confess enjoying the challenge and exhilaration of it all. It was tough on Sands, though, who had come from an urban background. Nor, sadly, did I give her anything like enough credit at the time for her handling it as well as she did.

I fear I was one of those painful guys who simply would not take 'no' for an answer, demanding impossible standards of myself and of everyone around me. Earning the nickname *Chanyongana* from the workers, translated 'the one who was always running, always chasing, never resting', intense, supremely confident, pushing the envelope as far as it would go, with way too much energy and no idea of how to relax. An exhausting fellow!

Chapter 12

Fynn Tribe

HFF's brother, William McDowell Fynn, was my great-great grandfather. He assisted Henry in early expeditions, following in his father's footsteps and establishing mercantile operations between the Cape and Natal Colonies, and as far afield as America. He later settled in Natal, joining his passion in working with the local people.

He took a different course from his brother. His sympathies lay with the Fingo and Gaeleka tribes who had been demoralised and ravished by Shaka's Zulu. He devoted his life to championing and pleading their cause, serving as a magistrate and the British Diplomatic Agent for these people. The crafty Zulu chief, Dingaan, accepted him in that position and as a trader in ivory, the main source of income from his land at that time.

William was something of an artist, and showed Dingaan drawings he had made of a Zulu warrior and of a young Zulu girl, which he was sending to England to give people there an idea of how they looked. Dingaan was highly pleased but remarked they were not showy enough to be warriors and that he should represent them as the most common of his people. Then to draw another to give an idea of the splendour of the Zulu higher class.

In spite of this façade of friendship, Dingaan plotted to execute all three Fynn brothers. They only escaped through reacting quickly when they sensed what was afoot, although losing some of their family and followers and all their personal possessions in the attacks. William returned to the Cape Colony after his devastating losses to serve under the Cape Government.

The brothers all had an intimate knowledge of local customs and languages and William was later called upon to serve as the British Representative deep in the interior of Kaffraria, now the Transkei and Eastern Cape. He went, happy to serve King and Country, to Butterworth, a mission station.

His isolation was such that he felt abandoned by the administration, and finally retired onto the farm he had been given by the tribes he served, not a little embittered by the lack of response to his cries on behalf of the tribes under his Diplomatic Agency.

One account highlights the relationship between the Fynns and the tribes they were representing. In the course of tribal skirmishes, some overzealous and unruly element of Chief Kreli's people, the Gaeleka, ransacked the Butterworth Mission, and Fynn's camp, for the second time.

In long and laborious letters between the Chief and the British High Commissioner, who goes to some lengths to ensure the offer is being made without coercion, the chief proclaims his regret for the incident and his willingness to compensate both parties—£600 to the Mission and £150 to Fynn—considerable sums at that time.

Both William and his sons were great horseman, often seen riding their spanking horses, with ramrod stiff backs, down the streets of Queenstown, near where they retired. The Chief's family sent William's wife, Margaret, a piano, with this inscription, naming the chief's children:

Moni, Langa, Serumi, Tyali, Nggile, and Lindincowa in acknowledgement of your confidence in the tribe, your courage and encouragement afforded them during the war with Kreli, when no other European woman would stay in the country.

The Fynn women were a doughty bunch. Margaret and her family had been rescued by British troops from the Butterworth incident and taken to King Williams Town, where the family lived thereafter. Her last days were spent with her son, West, my great grandfather, on their farm at Redlands, Stutterheim, in the eastern Cape. She died at 97 years of age.

A story is related by Major D. B. Hook, who was in charge of the British force at Butterworth. In the rescue mission, as the family were mounting a packed wagon loaded with their household effects outside the residency, a young Gaeleka warrior taunted in his own language, which she knew well:

"So you are going back to the sea, where you white people come from. If you come back here I'll take you as my wife."

'In an instant, a Dragoon military sabre, which had been given to Mr Fynn by a Gaeleka after a fight, and was lying on the wagon box, found its way into Mrs Fynn's hand. She pursued at the heels of that audacious Gaeleka with such nimble footsteps that he had to fly as he had never flown before, with the gleaming blade almost touching his kaross. Not until he reached an elevation where he was able to turn around and exclaim in native fashion did he recover from his astonishment.'

The record went on to note that the Fynns have all been good sprinters.

That sabre is still in the possession of the family, hanging in my cousin Claire Agertoft's home today.

West White, my great grandfather, was William McDowell's third son (one of four) and two daughters. He was born in 1845, continuing in his father's footsteps, farming and serving the liaison between the local tribes and the government. The Fynns' knowledge of language and customs and their reputation on all sides made them valuable negotiators in the frequent conflicts in the frontier country. It also put them in an invidious and often dangerous position.

WWF became a close and trusted friend of Chief Kreli of the Gaeleka, 'a fine character, highly esteemed by both the tribes-people and Europeans alike'. Kreli had been badly let down by the British in spite of fervent appeals by William and West on his behalf over a dispute with the neighbouring Fingo tribe. The latter had been raiding his people, and Kreli had asked the British to intervene, which they never did.

Kreli had warned that if these raids were to continue, his Gaeleka would take retribution themselves. In the face of British lethargy,

Kreli' exasperation finally led him to attack the Fingo, whom the British defended on the strength of a protection agreement between them, with the inevitable result. WWF had worked hard to placate the looming battle, but Kreli insisted on escorting him and his family out of harm's way before the attack was launched.

Recorded by Percy, my grandfather, WW's firstborn, 5 years old at the time, writes how 500 fully armed Gaeleka warriors of Chief Kreli's bodyguard escorted them to the Kei River:

'We awoke before dawn to the eerie sound of the women, in large groups on the hilltops, calling the tribe to war. When the bodyguard arrived to collect us, they were very excited, which upset our huge Boar hound. They lost their patience with him and put an assegai through the dog. We forded the Kei River and as the wagons emerged on the west bank the Fingo intercepted the returning Gaeleka, meeting in the middle of the stream in deadly combat. The family had to protect themselves from flying bullets, using mattresses and chests, until out of range.'

Kreli was disgraced by the Colonial government following this war, and went into hiding from where he could not, and would not, be found to negotiate terms. Finally, WW was asked to make communication with him, being offered an escort of mounted and armed police. West would have none of that, and entered the tribal land, still swarming with rebels, alone and unarmed. He knew the country from end to end, and almost every person in it.

News reached Chief Kreli that WW was looking for him. After some days West received a hint to move to a lonely spot surrounded by kloofs (wooded gullies) and thick bush. As night fell he was shown into a lone hut and warned not to light a fire on pain of death. There he sat waiting, until, towards midnight, someone silently slipped into the hut and called him by name. Fynn recognised Kreli's voice and delivered the peace offering from the Governor.

On his return next morning he noticed the sentinels standing guard at every strategic position.

The Chief never came forward, but a makeshift truce ensued after WW's report. Kreli never forgot West's efforts to restore peace and order in his country, and on his deathbed he removed his bracelet which he'd worn since his inauguration, and asked his sons to present it to WW, the highest mark of respect he could bestow, together with a signed tribute from the Council of Chiefs, from which an extract reads:

> '. . . the older members amongst us retain pleasant memories of your services throughout that period of widespread commotion and war . . . following which the years have obliterated all traces of enmity and bitterness; we are convinced that in the difficult and delicate position you were placed as Resident Agent, a position fraught with great responsibilities and danger, you succeeded in holding the scales of justice with firmness and consideration, and discharged those high political duties devolving upon you with a single eye to the best interests of the Colonial Government, and ourselves and surrounding natives, traders, farmers and missionaries.'

This public-spirited civil servant had an equally amazing wife, Elizabeth Fanny (nee Dick) my great grandmother. A missionary, the Rev R.S. Leslie, in the Kreli country, writes a letter sympathising with the lack of support WW had received from the Colonial government.

'. . . there is no doubt in my mind that had it not been for you, there would have been an outbreak of war. Some may say to the contrary, but I can produce dozens of witnesses to prove the truth of this. Yet, Mr Fynn, it is all that men get when they serve conscientiously. God will reward though men may not, but permit me to say you have a great reward in the wife and children He has given you—you have, I can assure you, been blessed in no small degree in that respect.'

He followed his family in migrating to Salisbury, Rhodesia in 1915, owning Emerald Hill, now an orphanage, where he sat, a venerable old man on the veranda, sporting a huge white moustache with pipe protruding under a fine topee, parrot on his shoulder.

West White's son, Percy, or PDL, my grandfather, was born in 1872. He was the eldest of nine brothers and four sisters, and led a wild childhood in turbulent times and places. At 15 years, he left Dale College in King Williams Town because his father was no longer able to support him from the drought ridden farm. He trekked to Cape Town on his white horse where he started work as a clerk in the civil service of the Cape Colony. Ten years later, in 1896, he was asked to join Cecil Rhodes's British South Africa Company as assistant to the Secretary in the new Rhodesia Public Service.

Queen Victoria permitted the ambitious Rhodes, Prime Minister of her Cape Colony, to annex this large chunk of Africa for its mineral rights—all 175,000 square miles of it, three times the size of England. It was named Rhodesia in his honour, and came under the management of the BSA Company. Rhodes had made a fortune through the diamonds of Kimberley, and later, gold in Johannesburg. His avaricious plans to see as much as possible of Africa coloured 'British red' included the famous dream of a railway connecting the Cape to Cairo.

PDL's call to join the BSA Company, based in Fort Salisbury (named after the Prime Minister of England), followed Rhodes's pioneer column. This band of 600 adventurers had set off in ox-wagons from Cape Town, via Mafeking, in 1890. Stories of hills of gold, bigger and better than the Rand of Johannesburg, had spread through the colonies and Europe. The fabled mines, rumoured to be the same that enriched the Queen of Sheba and King Solomon, excited fortune seekers from all over the world.

As with the Zulu, the Ndebele kings were staunch admirers of the British monarchy. A painting of Queen Victoria hung on Chief Lobengula's wall. As rulers of the Zimbabwean plateau, they were happy to negotiate trading and concessionary agreements with Rudd, and later Jameson, as Rhodes's emissaries, under the Queen's authority.

The mineral rights of Rhodesia were sold to the BSA Company for £100 per month, 10,000 rifles, and a gunboat (which never arrived) on the Zambezi. The Company was granted a Royal Charter to make treaties, promulgate laws, establish a police force, and award land and mineral claims. Lobengula later asserted he had been tricked into understanding that only ten white men would come, and would abide by his laws and be as his people. Such are the sad controversies which led to the 'Matabele war', and Lobengulas' tragic death by suicide.

Margaret, married
to William Fynn

Great-grandfather
West Fynn

**Grandfather Sir Percival
Donald Leslie Fynn (PDL)
& the type of coach that
brought him from
Bechuanaland**

Nurse Atherston Fynn

PDL's journey to Rhodesia was typical of the day, with the new railway ending in the middle of Bechuanaland (Botswana). From there, the mule drawn coach averaged 20 miles a day—nine days to Bulawayo and a further 11 to Salisbury. Frequently overturning, getting stuck in rivers, axles breaking, mules dying, always under armed escort in the event of attacks by the Ndebele, it was not for the fainthearted.

The large clan of Fynns in Zimbabwe today are founded from the remainder of his siblings joining him, in spite of losing four brothers in WWI. His sister, Mildred Atherstone Fynn, (Aunt Athy) served in France in the Great War as a nurse. She was awarded the Royal Red Cross, and bar, the 'Nurses VC', a decoration seldom bestowed. The citation quotes:

> *She was universally loved by all the soldiers and the*
> *junior nurses working under her for her gentleness,*
> *kindness and patience. To those who were dying, she*
> *never spared herself, and the way she eased their*
> *passing made a great impression on all the patients.*

The British granted self-governing status to Rhodesia in 1923. PDL, now the Company Secretary, became the country's first Minister of Finance. In 1939, knighted for his services, he acted as Prime Minister in the absence of the PM, Godfrey Huggins, who was in Britain for the outbreak of the WWII. At PDL's crowded funeral in Salisbury in 1940, his quiet and considerable impact in government, with courtesy, commitment and loyalty, resounded in the obituaries.

In researching this history, I am left proud and humbled, and quite awestruck by my family legacy. How our much-torn and deprecated Africa has got into such a mess with the giants she was privileged to bear her heritage, from all races, is a shameful comment on those who have let her down.

The colonial powers *did* disturb the flow of 19th century Africa, along with such casualties as the American Indian, the Australian Aborigine and the hordes suppressed in the Eastern empire-building. However, let it be recognised that from the beginning of time colonialism has been part of the history of man, the legacy of development.

When our ancestors arrived in Africa, there was anything but freedom from strife, peace or tranquillity for the tribe's people. Reign after reign of terrifying despotic powers, unparalleled by few, made war and submission their iron code.

The British colonials made many mistakes, used too much starch in their knife-creased shorts, and gin with their tonic. Nevertheless, in the tumble of spectacular negatives and positives of colonial power, there were good-hearted men who gave their lives to bring order and development into turbulent lands.

The nations of the world at the time of Zulu Fynn were in the fierce and relentless race of empire building. Nationalists the world over have thrown out precious babies with the bathwater.

'Stuff happens' is a crude but fundamental truth—same stuff, different country, smears revolution throughout history. And always, honour, amazing courage and the best of humour arises in its midst. Rhodesia, Zimbabwe, no exception.

The resourceful tenacity of the Rhodesians and the fierce determination of Zimbabwean nationalists inevitably lacked a deeper political foresight that after-sight brings. Do politics, or man's reticence to learn from his mistakes, ever change?

Living through this unbridled, fascinating, historic and cultural adjustment spanning colonial Rhodesia to today's Zimbabwe—under our strangely revered and oppressive liberation leader—I have witnessed sheer guts, giving hearts, awful excesses and disastrous destruction in the dismantling of a nation that was aptly called the jewel and breadbasket of Africa.

It has reeled with a plunging economy described by the IMF as the fastest shrinking ever recorded by a country not at war, whose disregard of human rights is notorious. It boasted the lowest place in the UN 'happiness factor' index, and their worst in the 'Best Investment' country list.

The population express hopeless disappointment. They would have died, and many did, for Mugabe and his cause. Today, they feel abandoned and forgotten by their leaders, watching them grab everything for themselves, leaving their people with nothing—far worse off than they ever were before.

We can't underestimate the anger caused by racial injustices, lack of equal opportunity, and wrong and hurtful policies perpetrated under 'colonial' times, nor belittle that every human being should have the choice of where and how he wants to live. But let us not pretend that any of the above has been put right by despotic regimes in the name of Independence.

Our opposition politicians have stood their ground under frightening oppression, regardless of their families, welfare, indeed their very lives, in their selfless drive to carry the nation forward to a peaceful transition.

Bravo.

Pride and prejudice, colour and class, tribes and trouble may always be with us. We can only determine to participate positively, making changes where we can for the better.

It's certainly time.

Chapter 13

Missiles and Spies

War is one of Africa's sad burdens. In 1974, our guerrilla war was escalating.

Air Rhodesia's turboprop Viscounts flying their regular passenger schedules around the country were being shot at with missiles. Special heat deflectors were fitted to the aircraft's exhausts and pilots developed a tactic of landing and taking off in a not dissimilar display to skydiving aircraft. They would make a spiral dive over Lake Kariba from their cruising altitude to land, and then spiral upwards after takeoff, thus presenting a minimal target at lower altitudes.

It certainly added variety to those plucky tourists who dared visit our strife-torn country.

Every man on the tax roll between the ages of 18 and 40 years was called up for three months of the year, later increased to six. Of interest to note—for every white military personnel on the frontline, there were thirty black volunteers.

I was with the Police Marine Wing. The policy was to hire craft from private individuals who captained their boat, patrolling sensitive areas on the lake where guerrilla incursions were expected. We were based 100km west from Kariba in the Sengwa basin on Paradise Island (which it wasn't)—a deserted spot to relax in during the day, with good shade, fishing and space to walk.

By night we were on patrol, each boat responsible for an allocated mile along the Lake frontier with Zambia. Our job was to find and apprehend intruders crossing by boat to join their colleagues inland. Floating around on this great expanse of water, with little night vision equipment or radar, was not highly effective. We may have been a deterrent, and, as always in that kind of situation, we had some amusing times trying our best to do the job under difficult circumstances. Not the least of which was chasing a fast cigar-shaped, shiny black boat, run by a fanatical Swede acting as a ferry for the 'terrs'.

There are many stories, covered by other writers, of the craziness and bravery of that war, but suffice it to say here that it took up an inordinate amount of our time and resources. Most tragic were the lives of so many fine young men on both sides that were lost. In our small country, almost every person was affected through some connection or other.

Rob Hughes, who'd been running our Gona-re-Zhou camp, was one of the first to go. He was a tracker, as most of our expert wildlife men were, and was killed in crossfire in a skirmish in the early part of the war. Thor Thorrson, a great blond Swede with a list of recommendations as long as my arm, signed up to help us through for the remainder of the season, at the end of which we closed down that operation. We would never have found another 'Rob', and the logistics of camps at different ends of the country were a nightmare.

My dear friend, Tim Elton, on his Cashel farm, was killed in an ambush returning from a day's business in Umtali (Mutare). Mistakenly, it turned out, they thought he was somebody else.

Tim Peech, my brother-in-law, Davey's brother, was gruesomely butchered whilst trying to make contact to talk with the guerrillas. The terrible list grew, and there seemed no end to the madness.

Life in rural areas was nothing short of hell. Soldiers from both sides accused poor villagers of aiding and abetting the other, which they had no choice but to do. Horrible treatment was meted out for the slightest indication of collaboration. Lips torn off with pliers, men tortured to death in front of their families and villagers, as a lesson to the others, whole villages burnt alive in their huts. The realities were worse than the awful stories filtering back.

The harshness for our people was insufferable, civil war their daily experience. Families were divided, none could be trusted. How could it end? How could these wounds ever be healed? The questions burned in every heart. Soldiers suffered the terrible loss of humanity as they carried out their gruesome orders.

Our isolation in our camp was a great blessing. We didn't see or have to deal with the horrendous daily conflict. My call-up stints were shorter, in recognition of our remote situation—two weeks at a time compared to six weeks by the 'townies'. Nevertheless, we were all out for 6 months of the year, and being away so much took its toll on everything and everybody. Family life, business and temperament were heavily battered.

Sands was in charge of the camp while I was away. I would come home to many a story. She would 'guide' if there were too many for John Hepple, my assistant, who'd arrived from a career as an air force technician with a heartfelt commitment to conservation. When he left the country, as many were doing with no sign of an end to the hostilities, Sands was the 'everything'. Guests were quite taken by their flamboyant suntanned bikini clad leader and hung on her every word.

Out in Kunjiri, on one game spotting expedition, she spotted what she announced to the startled clients as a saddle bill stork's mating ritual. In hushed stealth, motor off, her breathless but willing crew deftly paddled the craft to get a closer look. Only when Sands, who didn't have binoculars, could see more clearly, was it discovered that, after all, it was one of the staff wives in a brightly coloured scarf bobbing up and down doing her laundry. I never heard what the guests made of this.

A strange occurrence stopped the USA tourists overnight. An ultra efficient, good looking Swedish lady ran the Air Rhodesia office in New York, which fronted for the Rhodesian embassy which under the world's sanctions was forbidden. We all appreciated her assistance and devotion to duty. Nothing was too much trouble for her. On my 'promotion' trips to gain USA clients, she would do her best to comply with my calling from across the States to send more brochures, book flights, check address lists, whatever I asked. Other than accepting invitations for a drink or dinner!

It turned out she was a CIA plant. After they had collected sufficient damning evidence, they closed down the New York offices and fined agents who'd been booking with the airline, bringing Rhodesia's American business to a dead stop overnight. Which meant all our Brian Merriman tours.

The previous year had picked up enough to get me off the Sheriff's list. We had also established a local clientele in spite of living in the midst of a full-scale guerrilla war. Travelling in armed convoys against ambushes, everyone carrying weapons—women drove, men rode 'shotgun', children trained to lie on the floor.

Mortars and rockets were fired across the Zambezi into Kariba and Victoria Falls towns. The luxurious flagship hotel Elephant Hills in the Falls was hit by a SAM 7 heat-seeking missile and burned down. Airline travel was even more risky and much of the tourist industry was closing down.

Our isolation was again our advantage. No self-preserving guerrilla fighter was going to traverse the 40kms of water separating us from Zambia at night, or the uninhabited and patrolled Matusadona National Park behind us. Apart from our full quota of dangerous game, a human footprint stood out like a flashing neon sign. We were one of the few places Rhodesians could come to on holiday, put their rifles against the wall, and relax.

Our picture was coloured a few shades brighter for a while by the arrival of the Hydrofoil. Actually, its return. The Lake Shipping Company had been formed in the early '70s to run a car ferry the length of the Lake, with a neat little tub named the 'Sea Horse'. Its moment of glory was being shot up in an ambush in the Chete Gorge where the lake's width between Rhodesia and Zambia narrowed to some 150m. The border followed the course of the old Zambezi river which used to run through this famous gorge. The ambush was mounted from the high ground on Chete Island on the Zambian side, from where they shot directly down into the open ferry. One man was shot and killed.

In glamorous entrepreneurship to counter the adverse effect on tourism, the company bought a hydrofoil out from Italy to speed tourists up the Lake while their cars followed at a sedate pace on the Sea Horse, all fully armed and protected by the Police Reserve. A hydrofoil rises up from the water enabling much higher speeds than conventional planing hulls. Carrying 30 passengers she would race the length of the lake in 4 hours as opposed to 20 hours on The Horse.

All worked a treat until the skipper of the hydrofoil decided to liven up the trip with a bit of game viewing closer to shore. And hit a tree stump off Bumi Hills Safari lodge on the mouth of the Ume river. A foil was ripped off, the boat holed and sunk. With tourism declining fast in the war scenario, Lake Shipping sadly abandoned their gallant quest.

Enter Ian F. He arrived in Salisbury to set up a Dale Carnegie school, a famous American course of the day promising 'friends and wealth' to all who signed up. He also set up a finance company through which he purchased the rescued hydrofoil, and had it refurbished, no expense spared. The shiny new craft arrived back on Kariba—a massive boost to our struggling tourist haven.

Everybody who visited Kariba lined up for a ride, skimming across the lake like a visiting space ship with flying spray and roaring motors.

I watched all this as I bounced and got soaked on my way across the bumpy lake with the old 50hp, and decided to approach Ian about coming across to our camp on one of his trips. He was enthusiastic, needing some variety in his schedule. With a charismatic manner that made me feel like a long-standing friend, we struck up a deal in which the hydrofoil would visit our camp three days a week, bringing both supplies and guests, and his own day trippers, who would have lunch with us and go on a game drive into the Matuse.

It was about as close to heaven as I could imagine. No more jarring across the windy lake in our overloaded open boat, guests and provisions invariably wet through, not to mention compacting their vertebrae and bouncing their teeth out. Now, we simply stood by in camp as the mighty hydrofoil roared across whatever weather was out there, watched him drop anchor off the tree line, chugged out on our little old motorised raft, and collected the visitors and stores. It could not have been rosier if they'd parachuted in.

The Hydrofoil – captured in a stamp

'Old Kaz' dining room flooding

Our arrangement was that we'd settle our bills monthly, mine for the carriage of guests and provisions, Ian's for our providing lunch and a game drive to his clients. Each a potential return client for our camp. We punctually paid on his invoice, keen to keep the marvellous arrangement squeaky clean.

Nothing, however, came from him. In the interests of the national emergency, and supporting this budding operation that was so good for Kariba's tourism, and not wanting to appear a little money grabbing grub, nothing was said.

Halfway through the month, our cash flow was beginning to bite.

'Uuuh, Ian, I absolutely realise how busy you must be and what a lot of things must be on your mind, but can I give you just a teensy little reminder that we never received your cheque for last month. Hope you don't mind?'

'Oh noooo! Rob, I specifically asked her (no clear explanation of who 'her' was) to give me the cash to bring over . . . . How embarrassing . . . sooo sorry. Not too worry . . . Next trip,' he responded, with a hit of his hand on his forehead, a rolling of the eyes, and a paternal pat on my back.

'No worries, Ian. Thank you,' I murmured gratefully.

The next two trips produced no cash. On the third trip, a further gentle reminder brought on another rolling of the eyes and a dramatic facial expression, with the promise that it would be waiting for me on our end of the month shopping trip to Kariba town the next week. Our arrangement had now been going for two months, and the hydrofoil's newly launched operation on Kariba for a total of three.

Come the next week, we received a message on our trusty lake Navigation radio that the hydrofoil had broken down. I pounded across those waters again in my old faithful to Kariba, a pain deep down in my gut alerting me that all was not well.

'GONE ON POLICE RESERVE' was pinned to the office door. A common occurrence in those days. Except I'd never seen Ian on Police Reserve anything. Heart pounding and that pain considerably stronger, I raced up to the Police camp to enquire. As I'd already feared, he had nothing to do with the Reserve. I tore back down the hill to his office and smart caravan where he stayed with his charming wife and two children. Peering through the windows once

I had levered them open, there wasn't a paper clip left. Everything was cleaned out, all gone, never to be seen or heard of again.

He had operated a cash business for three months, where everybody who walked across the gangplank onto the boat paid for their ticket on the nail. Not a single bill had been paid for the refurbishing, the fuel companies, the engineers, or anybody, including us. We were tiny in comparison with other creditors, but it wasn't so tiny for us, desperately needing that vital income for our little operation. All had given him the same benefit of the doubt as we battled through the tough times.

He was the first big conman I had ever encountered. How charming and plausible he and his wife were. There couldn't have been a nicer or more supportive couple to work with. Wherever you are today, Ian, "Thanks", from all of us!

Somehow, we weathered it, but tents, Land-Rovers, boats and all our equipment needed attention. I felt like I was sailing around the world in great (times six) grandfather's ship, with no backup nor port to put into. Much like he did.

On the flip side, the camaraderie of my fellow operators in business was consistently amazing. While Sandy was on her own in the camp and I was on patrol up lake, Boss Jim was sent to Kariba to pick up supplies. Parked at the unprotected marina in the main tourist harbour of Caribbea Bay, a mega-storm came down the Lake from the west, pushing up 3m waves ahead of its 250km run. These crashed into the Kariba harbours, wreaking havoc. Boss Jim, amongst many, was a casualty, and went to the bottom. I had been in the same storm further up the lake on a police patrol boat, and expected to hear of heavy damage reports.

I got back to camp a week later. Boss Jim had been salvaged, the engines stripped and cleaned, and was back running on schedule. No charges raised. Such was the spirit of those still on the ground.

Another arrival cheered us following the Hydrofoil debacle. A floatplane landed, out of the blue, flown by New Zealander Peter Anderson who had left his island enclave for adventure. A Cessna 185, normally a 6-seater, but with the drag and extra weight of the floats, reduced to four. Andy Van Niekerk, a longstanding Kariba entrepreneur, who later went on to be captain of the great Mississippi type paddle steamer 'Southern Belle', operated the base in Kariba.

He was on the radio to me one day when it suddenly went quiet, followed a minute later by his controlled voice, saying slowly and deliberately;

'Hang on a minute Rob, I've got a snake on my lap.'

A boomslang, very poisonous, but not quick to bite if you don't make any sudden move, had slid from the tree under which his radio sat (the aerial connection being too short to reach inside the office) and onto his chair while he'd been talking to me. The snake quietly continued over him and into the next tree.

It was a joy to have 'cool and conscientious' Andy organising the Kariba side for us, and a fast and reliable service across the Lake again. Much entertainment was provided as Peter pushed the limits of his load, roaring around trying to jump his own wake in order to get airborne on a calm day.

He holed a float on a tree stump on one occasion, coming in too close to shore. Cool as cucumber, he continued with his take off, and landed back in Kariba straight into the tight and restricted waters of Andora Harbour, charging right up onto the public slipway before the aircraft could settle in the water. All with our trusting clients on board. Safaris were not for sissies back then.

The fancy ride, however, sometimes concealed the nature of the destination. An aristocratic British lady arrived on one trip, pearls and all, stepping out onto the floats to come ashore after the plane had beached in front of the camp. Taking one look at the tents nestled in amongst the trees, with buffalo and elephant browsing in the background, our staff eagerly waiting to welcome her and her huge suitcase, she sighed deeply, and asked me politely, but firmly:

"Young man, please put that suitcase back on the plane. Thank you, it looks lovely, but not for me. I will be returning to my hotel. So sorry!"

And that was the beginning and end of her safari.

I admired her courage and her forthrightness in knowing what she could handle and what she couldn't.

Chapter 14

Island in the Sun

For some time, I had wanted to move camp to Fothergill Island, an offshore and most suitable site. The request had consistently been turned down. It seemed ideal. Legally, it removed us from the boundaries of the National Park. Geographically, it was still very much a part of it.

It was connected, at lower water levels, by a narrow grassy causeway to the mainland, across which a constant stream of game moved back and forth, or simply swam at higher water levels. They will have remembered the days when they'd have walked down this ridge, which the island would have been a part of, into the luscious Zambezi valley, now 120m under water. Puzzling over the large and intimidating expanse of water they found, they would mill around the island for a while and then head back to the 'Matuse'. This meant there was always a higher concentration on the island than elsewhere, and consequently a favourite for game viewing.

It was named after Rupert Fothergill, the famous National Parks warden who led Operation Noah. This operation was mounted to rescue the game that had been trapped on the high ground by the rapidly rising lake. Apart from the dramatic rescue effort, where everything from the 'Big Five' to black mambas were candidates, it was reknowned for its international appeal for ladies stockings. These were the kindest, softest material with which to tie kicking, potentially vicious animal legs together. They arrived by the sack-full from all over the world and we would see pictures of burly rescuing rangers with pantyhose tied around their necks as they dived after a fleeing antelope or escaping reptile. Fothergill gathered a brave band of men who were never thanked by the desperate creatures they tried to rescue. Boats were rammed and overturned, and men jumped, climbed trees or swam for their lives, chased by cantankerous rhino, bellowing buffalo and razor-sharp horned kudu bulls.

I'd had my eye on Fothergill from the time I'd been informed we'd have to move the 'Old Kaz' camp. But plutocracy of government policies disallowed the move from year to year. I was determined. To the extent of planting trees in my future lodge site, already surveyed, building gabions to protect the exposed shoreline from the high water wave action, and completing a detailed design of the buildings down to making 'matchstick' models from stems of grass. Before any such permission was granted.

Each year the National Parks staff would came to enquire where I was moving to. On stating again it could only be to Fothergill, there'd be a wag of the head and I'd have my 'lease' extended at 'Old Kaz' for another season while we renegotiated. No doubt that only the exigencies of war permitted their tolerant acceptance of my continued illegal presence.

In 1976 we could procrastinate no longer. Each year since we'd arrived, following the crippling drought in the early '70s, with the lowest lake levels ever, the lake had been rising. The water was now so high we had to sandbag the camp, like a dyke, to prevent waves from washing through it. Guests would be lulled to sleep with foamy water crashing outside their tent, quite drenching the closed front flaps by morning. The cormorants and darters loved it and were often seen perching on the sandbag wall, eating their catch while intently studying the nearby waters for signs of more fish. A good sight while we ate.

Clearly I could not risk being in the same site for the next high water season—the campsite was below the maximum high water mark. Another slight oversight in my early homework and due diligence before purchasing the company.

It was time to bite the bullet and make a move, even if we had to 'declare UDI' on Fothergill Island.

Chapter 15

That Red Bike

'Go home to Brritaen' is a call Whites in Zimbabwe frequently hear from its President. My family has been in Africa for over 200 years. Many others for longer. How would the myriad nationalities that make up the United States of America, England and Europe respond to such a call from their presidents, I wonder?

Thankfully, our upbringing prepared us well to make the best of whatever came our way.

'If you want it, go out and get it, son!'

Africa is filled with characters as big as hippos. Which why we love it so.

'Jepetaaaaaalaaaa!' Mum's call to the cook echoes across the yard. She's just discovered no sugar, nor flour, tea or bread—essentials expected in her pantry. We lived an hour-and-half's drive over a very bumpy road to the nearest shop.

'I've told you till I'm blue in the face that I need to know when it's *duzi* (nearly finished). And anyway, there was certainly *maningi* (plenty) there yesterday, wasn't there?'

Jepatala anxiously scans for the change in hue of her face, having helped himself to what he regarded as his due. After all, she's saying herself there was *maningi*.

It wasn't easy being a young housewife running an isolated farm homestead with staff who probably understood less than a quarter of what you said, and *you* even less of what *they* said.

Mum, nee Vivienne Hayland Wilson, or Maasie as we affectionately called her, left her Sussex home in 1935 at the tender age of 20, where she'd been tending to her ailing father after his injuries in the Royal Flying Corps from the Great War, to be the governess for the Elton family in the remote Cashel valley.

Beryl and Hallam Elton, Tim's parents, had pioneered a very different kind of farm in the secluded fruitful valley, happily close to Portuguese wine just over the Mozambique border, but four hour's drive from the nearest shopping town, Umtali.

The picturesque farm was a favourite haven for our family holidays, where I would spend hours paddling the rivers and exploring the surrounding jungle. It is one of the few areas in the country without risk of bilharzia, the waterborne disease that ravages much of Africa. A paradise to a young boy, swinging on vines like Tarzan from one bank to the other, a drop into a pool on the way across, surrounded by screaming monkeys and exotic birds.

Utilising the abundant running water that sprang from the hills, Hallam's pelton wheel on piped water from Black Mountain, which overshadowed the farm, was highly innovative technology for the farming community of the day. He also built an hotel, the Black Mountain Inn, which became a favourite retreat for WWII Royal Air Force pilots training in the fabulous weather Rhodesia offered—the young assistant manageress, Viv, being one of the attractions.

Miss Hayland Wilson went off to do her bit for Queen and country, joining the SRWAMS, the women's military service in Southern Rhodesia, driving heavy lorries for the army on supply runs around military bases. She fell in love with a pilot, 'Ginger', sadly killed in an air accident after their first year, leaving her devastated and determined to get back into the thick of the war in Europe.

Cape Town beckoned as the hub from which to find a passage back to England. Meeting a senior officer who gauged her short military background as qualification for a deciphering and intelligence job at the Simonstown Naval base, she was asked one morning to pack her things and board a flying boat, heading north. Destination unknown.

Landing in Cairo after a two-day journey, she was enlisted into the army intelligence. Italy was the next step, where she met the dashing Rhodesian Lt Col F.W.Fynn, CO of No 2 Commando—my Dad. Things happen fast in wartime, and their wedding followed shortly, in good Commando style, the bridal carriage (his jeep) pulled by his men up the steps of the Officers' Mess in Bari. One of their wedding presents was my conception.

Dad, Francis West Fynn, known as Ted (from Teddy Bear, so named by his sister Peggy when he was a baby), was the second son of PDL. In the tradition of the African Fynns, PDL's public-spirited outlook insisted on a professional education for all his sons.

Jack, the eldest, farmed in Wedza following his carear as District Commissioner (DC) and barrister. He died from an affliction of diabetes early in his family life, bequeathing the lovely Francis, a 'pottery' Wedgewood, to bring up her family of Anne, Elizabeth and John, whom we all saw lots of and regarded as part of our family.

The third son, William, also started out as a DC and ended up farming in Marondellas (Marondera). DCs were the representatives for, and liaison between, the tribal peoples and government, a job requiring detailed knowledge of local customs, laws and languages. Very much a traditional occupation in the African Fynns.

William's humour as a raconteur is my great memory. He sustained a war injury which left him with a glass eye, which he would remove and place on a fencepost in the 'lands', assuring his workers he would be keeping his stern eye on them while gone. He came back once to find a hat placed over the post.

Robert, the youngest, whose cottage in Inyanga we all enjoyed so much on holidays, became a general practitioner, much loved and respected, with a humorous library of anecdotes well enjoyed and remembered by family and patients alike.

Their combined children made up fourteen cousins coming together for the frequent family gatherings which were another strong tradition.

All the brothers went to Plumtree, a fine, but isolated government secondary school on the border with Botswana. Each was head boy in turn, their names still on the school boards today, Dad holding the record for the 220 and 440yds for many years. Three of them became Rhodes' Scholars.

Dad was an intense and serious young man, clearly intent on living up to PDL's expectations and making his mark on the world. He read law at Rhodes University in Grahamstown, South Africa, followed by a Masters at Oxford, picking up a Blue for the 440yds. On the outbreak of World War II he joined the London Scottish regiment, soon volunteering for the Commandos. These regiments were the origins of the 'Special Forces' of today, so deadly in combat that Hitler passed an order demanding their summary execution on capture.

A keen archer (his inspiration to name me after the legendary Hood of Sherwood), Dad introduced these weapons into his Commando operations, much to the consternation of the enemy.

The citation on his American Bronze Star reads:

"By superb leadership and complete devotion to duty, in the face of every possible difficulty attached to a waterborne operation, with only one-third of his force in tact, against a well entrenched enemy position, near Lake Commachie (Italy), Lt Col Fynn's inspiring influence materially affected the outcome of a hazardous operation behind enemy lines, as did his encouraging of his weary troops in successive assaults on a vital bridge, and an enemy force of almost 1,000 were captured."

He lost two thirds of his men and half of his officers in the operation for which he was also presented with the British MC. I don't think he ever recovered from that hell on earth.

I was born on 14 November, 1945, in the UK, where Mum was being demobbed before her passage back to Rhodesia.

In characteristic way, she single-handedly dealt with being shipwrecked off Cape Town when her passenger liner went aground in a storm, arriving to find nobody to meet her, many of her precious belongings and baby trappings lost at sea. She boarded the train with me in my cot and the help of a fellow passenger for the four-day journey to her new husband and home.

The old Rhodesian society was traditional, conservative and doggedly Victorian. Their houses were in the gracious style of the colonies, with big verandas, or 'stoeps', surrounding large and rather dark inner rooms facing onto good-sized gardens.

Mum, Vivienne, in uniform & with Mike

Dad, Ted, in commando training & as lawyer

Helensvale farmhouse & '52 Chev Coupe Imp

The custom for a visitor was to present his card to the white-liveried manservant who met him at the door with silver tray. This would be presented to the Lady of the house while tea was prepared and brought into the reception lounge if the visitor were to be received, or he may be asked to return after his card was scrutinised, and he had, in turn, been sent one from the host he was visiting.

On a memorable occasion in 'Mother's' (as my granny, Lady Fynn, was called by the family) home, in Montague Avenue, Salisbury, a long-departed friend had just returned from travels abroad, and arrived to pay his respects. Having just got back, he had not printed any cards. He valiantly tried to explain the situation to the stern-faced African butler before him. The faithful servant continued to push his tray forward in the hope of recovering a card. Finally, in a resigned but determined manner, he politely informed the poor visiting friend:

'Velly solly, Sir—no ticket, no tea'. And firmly closed the door.

'How is your father, Robin?' 'Mother' would ask in a severe tone, bypassing Mum.

As though I knew?

'And what on earth have you in your pocket, boy?' as I struggled to contain the brown house snake that normally had the run of my shirt.

'Good Heavens, Vivienne, surely you know the risk?' scolded Mother.

She knew little about snakes and feared I knew less, certain my knowledge of identification insufficient to be introducing one to her living room. I was to learn more of that wisdom.

Our visits to Mother observed the old order of children being seen, but not heard. After the usual perfunctory short questions and answers, we children couldn't get out of the spotlessly-clean, dark tea lounge fast enough. Toys were few, TV non-existent, and radio only for the news and special music programmes, unsuitable for children. Thankfully, there was always a tree to climb in the garden, a dog to train, or a rope hanging from a branch with an old tyre to swing from, preferably upside down.

Home was a simple ramshackle house on the farm, Helensvale, which Dad had bought on returning from the war for 2/6 an acre. He could not face going back into law after the turmoil of fighting and deeply yearned for the peace of working on the land. An unrealistic romantic, and not being a real farmer, he struggled to make ends meet.

I had two sisters, Jane and Vanessa, and a brother Mike, two years apart between each of us—more by good chance than careful planning, I suspect. Mum in the big kitchen and vegetable garden, Dad busy with farm projects in which he would often include me, as though my opinion counted, our upbringing in this delightful backwater pretty much screened us from the fast-changing post-War world.

Daily adventures kept everybody on their toes. My place as a crawler was usually on a blanket under a big tree in the garden, minded by Ever Nice, our nanny. Once she was away attending to her own matters, when Maasie came to see how we were getting on. An Egyptian cobra was rearing in front of me while I tried to catch it—the fascination for reptiles consistently recurring in my life ever since. Jepetala was shrieked for and managed to deal it a fatal blow with his broom, luckily missing me. Ever Nice was smartly moved on, and the subsequent Veronica vetted more carefully for her child-caring skills, all learned in the farm compound.

I got away with more than I should have, remembering only one serious thrashing after pinching Dad's bag of ammunition, intrigued by all the different cartridges and coloured shotgun rounds. I discovered how to detonate the shotgun rounds by wedging them in a tree and hammering a rusty nail on the percussion cap. I survived the ensuing explosion. But my cover was broken, and, ears ringing, powder smoke burns all over my face, I was whisked off to his bedroom and severely spanked with 'the black slipper'. In relief more than punishment, I'm sure.

My sister Jane was the brainiest, the 'teacher's pet' in school, outshining us non-academics, but always a willing assistant in brother's escapades. Vanessa, with her big eyes and long legs which ran like the wind, kept us all guessing what she'd do next, and was very wacky and 'arty'. Both beautiful girls. Young brother Mike just did his own thing, unperturbed by the goings on around him, his delightful laid-back approach standing him in good stead to this day. We were a close family, with a deep regard for each other and our parents.

I led the healthy outdoor upbringing of a farmer's child, running free through the land with my young black friends, sons of workers on the farm. We knitted into an integrated team with a distinct hierarchy inherited from our parents' status, the foreman's and cook's sons next to me.

We caught and kept snakes, for which we trapped mice and frogs, collected birds eggs, reared their young, started veld fires, cooked tea and flying ants, all far from parental supervision. They would each have been led to believe we were somewhere else than where we were. My most treasured possession was an old red bike with no mudguards or brakes that I called my 'Landy', to go anywhere as would Land-Rovers which I loved and longed to drive. The huge envy of my entourage, they would run alongside me on our expeditions. The pecking order dictated whose turn to ride, *he* mercilessly taking us through the roughest country in his attempt to out-do the last, and test us runners' ability to keep up.

Developing and maintaining a farm is hard work at the best of times, requiring dedication and insightful skill. There was little backup in the early days, and although Dad was a brave and imaginative entrepreneur, and loved the soil, he just wasn't a farmer.

Hitting his share of hard times, he bought cattle to fatten up. They discovered a deposit of arsenic at an old goldmine on the farm. And all died.

Rhodesian law was, and is, oriented towards mining. A licensed prospector could, and still can, follow his nose, register, stake and work his claim, wherever he may please. One rainy Christmas eve, a bedraggled, bearded man in a black leather hat and coat, knocked on our farmhouse door. He announced to Dad that he was coming to work his gold claims on the farm. I didn't like the look of him, but Dad kindly asked him in for a Christmas drink, and heard his story out. A bit of a down-and-out, he fortunately faded after a few weeks of digging and panning, clearly not on a rich enough seam to warrant his efforts. Dad checked for arsenic left behind on his site.

He became very sick himself from an allergy to the poisons in cattle dip and crop insecticides, not helped by the aftermath of serious dysentery he suffered in the war. Two Italian ex prisoners of war waiting to be repatriated were employed to assist. One was a superb cabinet-maker, the beautiful mahogany dining room suite he made sits in my sister Jane's home today.

The farm was battling to pay the bills, not least of which was our education, always on his mind. Much of the land was sold up for residential plots to the expanding city of Salisbury. Still passionate about the soil, he started a small brickfield on the farm on the site where the arsenic had been found, no longer suitable for any development. Exhausting the clay deposits there, he donated the land to The Borrowdale Country Club, and bought AMAC, a brickworks out by Mount Hampden, an hour's drive from home.

I loved going out there with him. The soft texture of the rich clay, sheds with bricks stacked to dry and smelling as sweet as a dairy cow's breath in the carefully regulated high humidity, big machinery everywhere, all fascinated me. Dad would point out the changing colours that came out of the firing processes, each kiln burn treated like a painting. He would explain the chemistry while we watched the fiery process of the almost transparent white to red-hot bricks through special inspection hatches.

I never imagined there was so much intrigue to making a brick.

The world depression of the early 1950s, however, brought building and development to a standstill, bankrupting Dad's pride and joy. Reluctantly, he went back to law.

None of this helped make a happy marriage.

I carried the fascination of bricks with me onto Fothergill Island and to my own children, where we baked our own from the termite mounds. These industrious 'white ants', more correctly termites, collect the clay in the soil, bonding it with a saliva, producing a fine material for bricks. Gangs of men from the rural areas who specialised in the art would make them to order.

Their first job was to demolish the termite mound and turn it into a mud bath. Apart from the large amount of energy this required, it also took a vast quantity of water, which was something of a juggle with the camp's demands.

One man would stand up to his waist in a hole in the mud they'd churned up, slopping it into forms on sliding poles before him, which a team of runners would then pick up and deposit on prepared ground, leaving the bricks to dry in the sun.

These would be built into intricate kilns, with their own fireboxes running through the base. These required mountains of firewood, picked up from the old mopane trees lying on the lake shore, relics of the forest before the bush clearing exercise and as hard as coal. The fires would be fed and burn for a month.

The process, making around 30,000 bricks at a time, was repeated every year in the dry season for as long as we needed bricks. Our children were intrigued by it. They would sit for hours watching the clay covered men running up and down with their forms filled with clay, delighted by the man slapping mud from his slimy hole into the trays, each neatly squared off by a stick wiped along the top. As soon as the men knocked off for tea, and their Mum wasn't looking, the children would jump into the slimy clay pit and have a great mud fight.

I can remember Mum always looking and smelling very feminine, in spite of the farming rigours. Full of bounce and fun, the 'doer' in the family and good wife and mother, she was not an intellectual and couldn't spar with Dad's philosophical mind. I could see him often exasperated by her disjointed understanding and irrelevant questions. And she with his head so often too high in the clouds.

Dad was the dreamer, thinker and launcher of plans. We would be spellbound by his stories, theories and viewpoints. A bit of a showman, he loved making us laugh and would entertain us with tricks like jumping on to a drum lying on its side and rolling it by walking around the barrel. He once fell, spraining his wrist badly. Mum wasn't sympathetic.

He loved his woodwork, treating it as both a discipline and a therapy, spending hours on the fine detail, and making the most exquisite joins from old bits of wood to fabricate such items as a simple drawer, just for the fun of it. I loved being with him in his workshop, him helping me with small jobs while he made big things, like pigeon cots, and repairing ageing furniture and farm equipment.

The workshop, an open-sided shed, held a plethora of fine off-cuts of wood piled against the wall, all collected from farm-grown trees, and any piece he liked the look of while wandering. Buckets of rusty nuts and bolts and broken chairs were suspended from the ceiling. Doors, and everything that needed fixing were gathered around his workbench which was stained and engrained with paint and oil, deeply etched from chiselling and sawing, with the vice standing strongly at one end. Always a delicious smell of pipe smoke, wood shavings, and linseed oil, and a tray of tea balanced among the debris. Sometimes we just sat there, and talked and pondered over 'something other than'.

He loved music, classical, jazz, or 'honky-tonk' as he called it, Parisian café New Orleans style. Rachmaninov was his favourite, when a look of intense serenity and peace would fill his face as he settled with his pipe and a gin, the Angostura bitters always burned, the blue flame dancing in the side tipped glass, then gazing out the big window onto the farm that he could never make work.

And trees. He would spend hours pruning and shaping them, in the homestead and surrounding bush, followed by the house cat, Tiddley Push. Anything to do with water fascinated him, from boats, to dams and irrigation projects. I must have inherited some of that that. He made a swimming pool with an intricate waterfall tinkling down rocks running off the filter pump.

We were treated like young adults from an early age. I was allowed to drink beer and wine at the age of fourteen, and smoke after sixteen, as long as I did it at home and with him. I did and would feel quite sick, but continued simply to maintain the privilege and hold my status as the oldest son. Fortunately, I dropped smoking thanks to the tobacco in the Royal Navy issue (RN Blue liners)—dreadful compared with our Rhodesian *gwaai*, surely the best in the world.

Our family Christmas would always have single neighbours and friends invited to the table, where a huge pile of cotton wool sat, decorated to look like a snowy mountain, never mind Africa's mid-summer. Underneath, were hidden little presents tied to pieces of string. Each led to tags with our names on them. The mystery surprise at the end of *our* string caused unbearable suspense as we sat waiting for the signal from Dad to pull. The moment was invariably accelerated by brother Mike and myself surreptitiously manipulating a candle and torching the cotton wool mountain, whereupon presents had to be quickly retrieved.

New Years Eve was Scottish dancing and 'Glühwein', with all the locals we could muster. An inseparable guest on these occasions was a confirmed young bachelor, David Goldsmith, very English, very musical and uproariously funny. In between teaching music, he worked for Caltex public relations, driving a huge red Chevrolet van crammed with a generator and projector equipment. He would disappear for weeks into the rural areas, putting on film shows in the villages. Always ready for a party on his return, usually starting at the Fynns, we would know to expect him when beautiful piano concertos would waft across the valley from his neighbouring cottage in the trees.

Family holidays were often oriented around sailing and camping. Morgan's Bay on the Wild Coast of South Africa was a favourite. Children packed onto the top of *katundu* in the back of our Morris Minor station wagon, carrying as much from the farm as possible to reduce cost of restaurants and pricey tourist shops. We would stop at roadside hotels on the three day journey, averaging 80 kph on the long hot African roads. We little ones would be intrigued with every detail of the journey, asking persistent questions, and finding the very ordinary motels so spicey and exciting.

Two days into one trip, in the middle of the Karoo, with temperatures touching 40 degrees centigrade, the fan-belt broke. We weren't carrying a spare. Dad battled to tie Mum's stockings onto the pulleys. Us kids headed for a nearby cattle trough, filled from a clanking windmill.

"All fixed!" a harassed, but smiling Dad, covered in grease and sweat, came over to tell us, and was pulled in to the reservoir. We limped into the next one-horse Boer farming town to learn the head gasket was blown and a two-day engine overhaul lay ahead. Undaunted, the holiday started and we wandered the village, as much an attraction to the dour community as they were to us. Our frequent inspection visits to the Scottish sounding garage man fixing our car would be met with indifferent enthusiasm.

"If yer ask me one morrre taame when it'll be fixed, young kerrel, aa'll be charging yer Dad double!"

Chapter 16

Cobras and Caravans

The downside of this paradise was being sent to school. I was dispatched as a boarder at the age of six years old to a government school, Highlands—today a fifteen minute run from our old home in Helensvale. Back then, it was an hour's journey bumping and winding along tracks and. as we approached town, we drove on the 'strips', which made up most of the country's main roads.

These consisted of two strips of tarmac about half a metre wide, set apart at the width of the car's wheelbase. If another car approached, each positioned itself with the right hand side wheels on a strip and passed, watching carefully where one's left hand side wheels were running, as great ruts were dug on the road's verges by the hard rubber tyres, not forgetting cavernous drainage ditches for storm water.

In time, precipitous drops would develop the sides of the strips and passing manoeuvres became quite tricky, often turning into a game of 'chicken' when aggressive drivers would sit squarely on both strips, only swerving dangerously at the last possible moment. Traffic was so infrequent that if you passed another car, it was customary to stop and chat. Kettle, tea set and 'tea boy' were specifically carried for the occasion. Dad related when, as a boy, his father owned one of the first Oldsmobiles, on which headlights were lit and run on paraffin.

We were only allowed out from school for one Sunday a month, and home overnight at half term. Away at school, it seemed a lifetime as a little boy, and I would look forward to the outings for days ahead, hardly able to sleep with excited anticipation. In that short break home, I would cling to my family and my band of little friends as though I might never see them again, filled with an awful dread that it would all be over so quickly.

I missed home terribly as a young boarder, feeling almost a stranger when I got back for the far too brief holidays, and quite cheated of the home life and family love I yearned for. The desperation of having to leave home, and that sense of homesickness for the first few days back at school, is a heartache that I have never experienced to such an extent since. Yet there were some who obviously thrived on it.

Arguably, it toughened and prepared one for the rigours of life ahead. Personally, I felt those early boarding days set up complexes and psychological barriers that put me back in relationships and self-confidence that took me years to get over.

My strongest memory is of 'Stingers', a nightmare game that would continue for months. Played only amongst the boarders, who regarded themselves as an elite, the stinger threw a tennis ball as hard as possible to inflict maximum pain on whom he chose. Once 'stung', you had to keep stalking with the ball, looking for a victim. No rest for the stinger was allowed, other than in class, after lights-out, mealtimes and out of school. When free of the ball, you lived like an impala being hunted by a hungry predator, constantly keeping your eyes peeled. To some it was probably a stimulating challenge. Too young to appreciate that, I lived in a perpetual terror of being 'stung'.

De-motivated, I would sit in the back row of class, spending most of my time looking out of the window, relaxing, but worrying about everything—in between swats on the ear by the teacher to checking that the stinger wasn't hiding behind the door.

Fortunately, Dad spotted there was a problem, although he didn't really know what it was, and I couldn't explain it. Still committed to the idea of boarding schools, he moved me to Springvale, a small private school in the farming district of Marandellas. For me it was a happy new start, their wide curriculum including Gilbert and Sullivan opera productions, art school, a carpentry workshop, bird watching club, a whole new different life and assembly of activities—like dung beetle racing.

Dung beetles become active during the rainy season collecting and rolling balls of dung in which to hatch their eggs, and which then act as the larder for their newborn. We'd look for the biggest, capture it in a matchbox, and rush off at break-time to the stables to see whose would make and roll their dung ball fastest.

What a great improvement on 'Stingers'.

Peterhouse was the next-door secondary school, run on the lines of an English public school. We worked hard, played lots of sport, and enjoyed another wide range of education and 'club' options. My favourite was still the carpentry school, the smell of wood and glue reminding me so much of the good times with Dad in his old workshop.

I joined the snake collectors, our specimens housed in a pit or in lines of glass tanks where we watched them doing 'boy' things, like mating and catching mice that we'd trapped. Snakes were frequently spotted in the school grounds, and we, the *Ka'nyokas* or 'snakers', whom all the staff knew, would be summoned, even from the classroom. We would dash out with our nooses, special sticks and bags to catch the offending reptile. I was more of an assistant than a catcher, which entailed performing dubious jobs like holding the dustbin lid up as a shield while the catcher dropped the cobra into the bin.

My fourteenth birthday present was finding a beautiful brown house snake, or so I thought, at home in the swimming pool. On retrieving its cold stiff body, which quickly became more lively as it warmed up in my hand, it bit me. Thinking nothing of it, I put it in a jar and went to find Dad to show him. By the time I found him my finger was throbbing and quite painful. Fortunately, Uncle Dr Robert was visiting, who suggested we nip down the road to our neighbours, the Thompson—real snake collectors—to identify it for certain.

It turned out to be a burrowing adder, a little snake that lived underground and which had one of the most toxic venoms, designed to terminate its prey rapidly in the confined spaces. Most recorded bites ended with amputation, some death. Uncle Robert got to work, my whole arm by this time looking like a football. Thanks to his expertise and timing, I still have all my limbs and only the scar left to show for it. Old 'Mother' was only too right.

We had fun, and learned lots, in and out of the classroom. Sundays were something completely different. Tradition held that we head off where we liked for the whole day in the 2,000 acre school property, carrying whatever we could, including the issue pack lunch.

We walked out with our little bundles, like small herds of David Copperfields, heading who-knew-where, wondering what would befall us. The day was to be spent 'anywhere but back at school', in the virgin bush that was part and parcel of the grounds—birds egg collecting, snake hunting, kopje climbing, sailing and canoeing, or just lounging under a tree and enjoying the peace, and perhaps a smoke, having dashed across the main road in commando style to purchase a packet of the cheapest from the local store.

A member of staff, Phil Ward's wife, owes her life to the scheme. She was walking through the school area to the next door farm, when she fell into a rocky ravine from one of the many balancing rock features the area is famous for, breaking her leg. After being missing for three days, the entire school was sent out to look for her. Sixteen year old Anthony Kaschula and his mate, Sean Smit, who had explored the property every Sunday for four years, found her while searching in one of the remote spots they knew well, which certainly would never have been thought of otherwise.

She was then extracted by a professional medical team and hospitalised, and survived the traumatic experience. Another day lying in those rocks would have been the end for her.

The Mozambique coast and the ancient port of Nova Sofala was a favourite for family holidays. Initially Arab, and later a Portuguese trading post, it was fabled to be the port used by the Mutapan dynasty for their gold and ivory trade. It hadn't developed much since its early beginnings as the Bubi River whose estuary it was based on had changed its course to flow out where the port of Biera is today.

We joined the farming families who would meet there every year for their annual break. The access road was a sandy track winding through the wild hinterland of Portuguese East Africa (Mozambique), our vehicles crossing the rivers on ferries pulled by men heaving on steel cables.

Dad borrowed a caravan for Mum from his long suffering secretary—a major breakthrough for holiday comfort. We had busied ourselves for months on the farm veranda, making our sailboat, 'The Fish', suitable for the sea. At 23ft, bilge keeled and gaff rigged, her hull looked like a big Flying Dutchmen—Dad's passport to heaven.

The girls packed all our catering and camping *katundu* into the caravan for our four weeks away—when there, we could expect to find nothing other than fresh fish. Our grown-up cousin, Wendy, from England, 18 and very 'cool', directed operations. The girls hung on her every word. For all her lovely characteristics, she just didn't know about packing caravans.

'See you on the road,' they cheerfully called, heading out, blissfully unaware to the dangers of caravans loaded heavily in the rear. We boys were still putting finishing touches to 'The Fish' on the homemade trailer and packing our Land-Rover.

The family car had by this time had graduated to a big 1948 Chevrolet—'The Cathedral'. Mum had never towed a caravan and thought it was quite normal for it to be swinging from side to side—isn't that's what caravans *do . . . ?*

Halfway to the border town of Umtali she was heading down into a valley at the bottom of which was a narrow bridge, common on arterial roads back then, allowing only one lane of traffic to cross at a time.

Another car was approaching.

She braked, the caravan getting into a greater sway, sweeping the whole of the road. Mum braked harder, and the caravan jack-knifed, pushing the whole sliding screeching enchilada with its screaming female cargo towards the bridge at the bottom.

The car eventually came to a halt with its front wheels over the edge of the bridge, caravan on its side, totally blocking the road.

Trundling along miles behind, happily enjoying our open jeep 'landy', dreaming of sailing the ocean waves, we were flagged down by a passing car.

'Are you Ted Fynn?'

Dad nodded, a questioning expression on his face.

'There's been an accident with your wife and family up ahead. They're not hurt—caravan's a bit of a mess tho'—some blokes are helping get it back on its wheels.'

Dad's smiley relaxed face whipped back into the all too familiar wrinkled brow. Trundling as fast as we could, we arrived an hour later. Other travellers had stopped to help in the way they all did then. A local farmer had brought his tractor and labour to tow the car off the bridge and move the clutter.

We spent the rest of the day retrieving and repacking our precious goods into the boat and Land-Rover, peeling eggs off the smashed-in caravan roof. Mum said she'd scramble them for dinner. Dad had apologies to make, and some re-planning.

Sans caravan, holiday still on, our somewhat over-laden convoy continued. A message from the Commandant of Sofala somehow reached us that a special tent had been arranged for Mum. Dad's smile was slowly returning.

The last few hundred kilometres were sandy, potholed bush-tracks, rutted by heavy lorries and buses. The best strategy in the face of an approaching 'heavy' was to pull right off the road till it passed, or face being swiped off by it. Conditions were hard on our laden vehicles and it wasn't long before the struggling boat trailer took a sharp diversion into the bush after the over-stressed tow hitch collapsed.

Dad picked up the axe and went looking for a *mopane* tree. We slaved through the sweaty, fly filled day making a new towing boom. Camping that night under the stars, all loving the adventure, Mum a little quiet, Dad opened our Portuguese 'Vinho da casa' demijohn and we celebrated being on holiday.

We arrived in Sofala the next day to a great welcome. The commandant laid on a superb prawn dinner at his mansion with his best ice-cold Dao wine. We made our camp under the coconut palms before a beach stretching as far as the eye could see, fresh prawns and lobster delivered by hawkers each morning. The farming community already camped offered us every assistance to ensure our wellbeing.

Launching our boat in the lagoon next day, we sailed out across the bar at high tide and beached her for the night on the shallow sloping sand, expecting an early morning sail on the morrow. Unfortunately, the wind came up overnight and the boat took a pounding in the surf. By morning, all we could see was the top of the lopsided mast. The camping community gathered again at low tide to retrieve the wreck. After days of attempted repairs we abandoned the effort. Dad reckoned the boat was no longer seaworthy but it had been worth the try. Others with their more practical beach-launching power boats offered us places on their offshore fishing trips.

Walking the coast on some days, we explored the Arab fort that had protected the ancient harbour, dug up barnacled cannonballs and found pieces of ancient pottery. The Portuguese had made the mistake of cutting back the mangrove swamp surrounding the fort. Consequently the sea swirled around its back, where the wave-hardy vegetation had been removed, and claimed the entire establishment. Planning skills in Africa were clearly no higher back then.

After 3 weeks of sun-filled, gloriously different days to the hardships of our parents making their living back home, surrounded by friends in this wild and remote outreach, we headed home, uneventfully, the good things of life deeply restored.

I had always wanted to be a game ranger in National Parks, but Dad didn't think there was a future in that, pushing me towards engineering. It didn't look a good swap to me.

We talked about the Royal Navy, the service he'd always wanted to join, but couldn't—the wartime waiting list just too long for his ardent spirit aching to get 'stuck in'. The complex and thorough selection process finally led me to an interview in Simonstown, the RN base for Southern Africa. A four-day train ride to Capetown took me before a panel of nine senior Naval Officers, grilling us candidates for two whole days, throwing initiative and leadership tests, observing us closely.

It seemed a lot of trouble to go to for just one possible future cadet—I was learning a little about how the RN functioned.

'The Fish' - Sofala

Jane, Mike, Ness & Rob in school days

Back home, while waiting for the selection results, I looked after my friend Tim Elton's farm in Cashel while he was away on honeymoon with his new wife, Sue. Getting to see that it wasn't so simple managing a labour gang or a farm, I returned to a job that Dad had lined me up with as a clerk in the Water Court. From one extreme to the other, it was all part of that great learning curve of life out there in the big world after school.

I earned enough to buy my first 'wheels', an ex-police 650cc BSA Golden Flash motorbike. These came up regularly on the auctions. Dad helped me overhaul her. She was a beauty, and in shorts and open shirts, no thought of helmets, our Helensvale gang revelled in our throaty machines and newly found freedom.

'A telgram, Sah!'

Delivered by a smartly uniformed Askari on a shiny black bicycle with a brown leather briefcase to our family on holiday, deep in the middle of Wankie National Park, it confirmed that a cadet had been chosen from Rhodesia to attend Dartmouth Royal Navy Officer Training College, only one being selected from each Commonwealth country every year.

In 1964, it was Mr Robbie Fynn.

Chapter 17

Two Years before the Mast

'Orl roight then, fall in three abreast . . . down the end of the platform, Sirs! . . . that's it. Close up now. Dressing from the roight!'

Everybody else seemed to know what that meant. All I knew was it had nothing to do with what girls wore.

Arriving in Dartmouth by train from London, direct from Rhodesia, was like landing on Mars. Arranged into a ragged line on the platform by ramrod Chief GIs (Chief Petty Officer Gunnery Instructors, whom you addressed as 'Chief' while they called you 'Sir'), black swagger sticks under their arms, brilliant white caps with shiny black peaks pulled over their eyes, screaming in decibels that must have been rocking houses on the other side of the River Dart, we heard where we were.

'Welcome to the Officah triaining collidge of the Royal Naivy, Gennlemen. You daon't look it, but you maiy well be the craim de laa craime of the future maritime foighting force of 'er Majesty. Koindly maike every effort to look like that now, Sirs! Belly flat, butts in, chests out, chins up! By the leeeft, Quiiiiick March! Lep-ri-lep-ri . . . keep your dressing, Sirs!'

What *is* this 'dressing'?!

Marching down the little Devon road to the river ferry, I try hard to keep in time—wondering some just what I think I'm doing coming all this way for this . . . ?

Crossing the river, I am stunned by its beauty and sea village tranquillity. This regal establishment had trained the empire's senior service officers for centuries. You could feel it embodied in every stone. And now I was one of them. Awesome.

There wasn't much time for conjecture, though. Haircuts, uniform fittings, lectures on naval history and procedures, getting to know your new mates, checking out pubs, and girls. A new world, which couldn't be more different.

'Double cadet!' The new buzzword. 'Double' meant 'run', raising your knees as high as you could. Cadets were not allowed to walk which we were reminded of every time we saw a GI.

We spent six months learning the fundamentals of Royal Navy life, in classrooms by morning, and on the impressive Dartmouth fleet of boats in the afternoon. These training craft were a cross section of the smaller vessels in service in the main fleet, varying from sailing cutters to 50-foot twin engine 'picket' boats, even some racing yachts taken as prizes during WWII from Germany.

On duty picket boat patrol one afternoon, we watched an open sports car run down the ferry ramp and into the sea. Racing across to assist survivors, we found a happy little Frenchman with his pretty *petite* wife waiving jovially in an amphibious 'DUKW'. He motored down the Dart on a riptide, round the corner and out to sea. Fascinated, we followed.

Once he hit open sea and swell, which *we* knew about but *he* didn't, waves were breaking over the bonnet. Windscreen wipers on, now unhappy wife nervously pointed to the land. He tried to turn. As he came broadside, waves broke over the side windows into the car. We manoeuvred upwind of him to act as a breakwater while he turned in the calmer waters, scooting back up river, *petite* wife gesticulating furiously.

'No 5, front rank, you bleedeen' clockwork orange, Sir! Bye the naivy *left*. Not the blitherin' armies, you git! Your mum may think you're lil' King Arthur, or Admiral Nelson, but you might just find his sword up your arse if you don't get your mind on the job! Squaaaaad Halt! Bye the Naivieee's Leeeft . . . Quiiiiick March!'

How had the windows in this great establishment survived the centuries of these falsetto parade ground screams?

Parade training was the backbone of teaching unquestioning discipline. With WWII .303 rifles, in No. 1 uniform, white 'blancoed' belts on navy blue serge, GI's bawling, Royal Marine band playing 'Mary Poppins', chest out, bum in, our hours at rigid attention, not a tremor showing, had to be for some reason?

We watched a line made of seagull guano spat across the parade ground and up the straight blue back and cap of the GI out front. He never flinched. Smirks, hidden we thought, or indeed any parade misdemeanour, were greeted with 'Round the ramps, cadet, Sir!'. Doubling around the rampart, 150m distance, rifle above your head, entire route accompanied by screams to lift your knees and rifle higher, your loud response of, 'Aye, aye, Chief', was sobering stuff after any party the night before.

The next six months was at sea in the Dartmouth training squadron's three anti-submarine 'Leander' frigates. They were normally dispatched on 'showing the flag' missions. Ours was to voyage down the West African Coast, specifically to sell the ships to the new African Navies. 'Home from home' was my first thought . . . little did I know what lay ahead.

If Dartmouth was Mars, joining HMS *Scarborough* was galactic. The Navy's plan was that cadet officers were to live as any sailor would, in what would normally have been the junior seamen's mess, the most aft part of the ship just above the propellers, where comfort was not the primary consideration.

RN ship's companies are split into three watches, shifts of 4 hours on, 8 hours off. On our first night at sea—destination Gibraltar across the Bay of Biscay—our 'oppos' were taking the 'first' watch (2000hrs to 2400hrs). My lot was for the morning watch (midnight to 0400hrs).

Clearly rough out there, the ship rolling through some 60 degrees, 50 white slung hammocks swung cosily in unison, lit up by the red safety lights. Excitedly we tried to get some rest before we were called up on our first watch on an HMS ship at sea.

A sound of rushing water surged back and forth as the ship rolled.

Another one of those new sounds you need to get used to?

But this water was rushing by underneath us, whooshing across the deck below our hammocks each time we rolled. It started to wrench open locker doors. Soon, all our kit was tumbling around as in a huge washing machine. Suicidal to have got out and done anything, we lay in our hammocks, eyes on stalks, trusting that HMS ships didn't go down without letting the junior seamen's after mess deck know.

The problem was only discovered when the change of watch came down. The cadet opening the watertight hatch was greeted with a wall of water, tumbling uniforms and toothbrushes.

'We're sinking . . . ! Chiieeef!' was our encouragement as the cadet yodelled down the gangway, our kit exiting on a tidal wave with him through the open hatch.

It turned out the fresh water tanks beneath our mess deck had been over filled and were overflowing through the breather pipe, a fault on these ships in rough conditions. Pumps and experienced seamen soon restored order, and we were on watch.

Life at sea promised not to be boring.

Cadets were to experience every aspect of the ship—engines, equipment, weapons, early warning radar systems, maintenance, seamanship, navigation, even cooking. This formerly landlocked Rhodesian now inside and part of a fighting warship was enthralled with each and every moment.

Heading towards the Mediterranean one night, I was on lifeguard duty, a stern lookout stationed alone on the quarterdeck to alert the ship in case anyone or anything fell overboard. I watched as huge waves, bigger than the ship, lit up by the stern light, rolled towards us. The afterdeck, sucked down by powerful propellers, was way below sea level. An immense waterfall in reverse towered above me. Occasionally, a wave caught up and crashed over, a wild torrent halfway to my knees, threatening to sweep me overboard but for the safety line. Exhilarating. And so very different from anything I'd ever experienced. Quite a responsibility for this new raw cadet, though.

Arriving in Gibraltar, we scampered off to the dives of dubious repute. Life in Port behind the scenes was not for the fainthearted either. In the interests of common decency, details are omitted.

Proceeding down the coast of West Africa, we visited newly independent Ghana and Nigeria. Government dignitaries representing the potential buyers were invited for sea trials to show off the ship's versatility and firepower. One manoeuvre involved a frigate steaming at full speed past the flagship (carrying 'the brass', including our admiral of the fleet) firing a full salvo from the main 4.5 gun turret and another from the antisubmarine mortars over the superstructure of the flagship.

Our ship was designated for this role. We approached at full speed, around 35 knots, all hands at action stations ready to fire. Sudden frantic signals were flashed from the flagship bridge. We made a spectacular high-speed turn away, dipping the upper deck into the water as the ship heeled crazily, no guns fired.

It turned out that the president Kwame Nkrumah of Ghana aboard the flagship feared for his life as he saw our approaching warship, all guns trained on him.

African cities were a shock to most of the cadets, who'd never experienced the striking contrast of wealth alongside abject poverty, a sad anomaly that the third world is all too well accustomed. Open sewers, fly ridden markets, begging populations, all alongside the attendant sumptuous receptions put on by our hosts, cadets attired in 'Dress' uniform, our best and most formal.

Overwhelmed, one of our shipmates described the scene in a postcard sent home to Mum. Unfortunately, the card was intercepted by the local post office and handed to authorities. We were summoned for a special gathering on the quarterdeck, where the Captain read the offending work.

'Gentlemen' he addressed us 'as much as we admire Cadet McHugh's diligence in keeping Mummy abreast with conditions on the African Front, we are here representing the Queen, and trying to sell some bloody ships! A minor international incident has been caused by this offending mail. Try to be a little more fucking diplomatic. If you can! Thank you. And kindly leave the resident officer's daughters in peace at the ship's cocktail party tonight. Dismiss!'

Days at sea were filled with painting, chipping, cleaning, polishing and lookout duties, where our standard dress was shorts only. Or we were 'on watch' over something or other in the engine rooms, in air conditioned ops room on sonar and radar sets, or with the ship's driving team on the bridge, endlessly learning about procedures, equipment, weapons and machinery.

'Runs ashore' were when we weren't in uniform at some function, where hopefully we'd meet some of the local girls and pursue that entertainment, assiduously keeping out of the way of military shore patrols. There was always an abundance of 'guides' to show us the ropes, or whatever. Really all a young guy could ask.

Returning from the training squadron in September of 1966, we were fully commissioned officers with the heady rank of Midshipman, and posted to ships around the fleet. I was sent to HMS *Lincoln*, an anti-aircraft frigate in Singapore. On finding the ship was in dry dock on a refit when I arrived, I further found other plans were in the Navy's store.

The Indonesian-Malayan conflict was waging at the time. Singapore was being infiltrated by guerrillas, who dashed across the narrow Malacca Straights from the Indonesian Island of Sumatra in 'sampans', big dugout canoes with powerful outboards.

The Navy was pulling out of 'mothballs' the gunboats that had last seen action in WWII. I was assigned to HMS *Ickford* as the third officer.

The compliment of 30 men was trawled from other ships in the Singapore fleet. The newly formed crew on our gunboat, not a little put out to be summarily posted, insisted on retaining the name on their cap tally from their previous ship. A band of pirates if ever there were. Exciting, and slightly intimidating for the newly commissioned officer.

Two weeks of sea trials and we were operational.

Our job was to patrol the Malacca Straights throughout the night on a line five miles long, differently allocated each night. Some 25 other ships did the same. The Singapore side was lit up by the glamorous city while the Indonesian, with its hundreds of little islands, lay in darkness. We steamed slowly, blacked out, manoeuvring between the islands within our patrol line, taking care not to stir up the phosphorescent marine life that would illuminate the ships waterline to waiting sampans.

Any movement from them would show up as a fast moving blip on the radar, when we would steam at full speed in its direction, all hands called to action stations. As soon as in range, everything we had would open up, a considerable fusillade of tracer lighting up the night sky, and sometimes a sampan. If we hit our mark, which was rare, a blinding explosion blew up ahead. Only floating debris would survive from the deadly cargo they carried.

We knew well they would be ruthless killers themselves if they had the advantage. Nevertheless, shooting to kill was not easily adapted to by this newly fledged officer, only lessened by an instance when a sampan had been trapped and ordered alongside one of our patrol ships, the occupants called upon to standby for boarding. They blew themselves up, killing a midshipman and sailor who were about to step aboard. Orders from then on were to command the occupants of any boat caught to swim across, when they would be carefully, albeit roughly, searched, after which their craft would be blown out of the water.

Returning to base one early morning, we spotted a boat adrift. We warily turned towards it, coming across a smart looking speedboat. A pretty blonde head bobbed up into view, and disappeared again. Arms and legs floundered about above the gunnels, after which a scantily clad couple reappeared, clearly embarrassed. They were duly ordered to swim over and were pulled on board. They'd been snorkelling the day before, ran out of fuel, and had spent an interesting night at sea. The poor girl in her bikini was the centre of much matelot attention as we continued our passage, their boat in tow, lucky to be still afloat.

A few nights later, our mustard keen crew were put to their first real test. A radar contact right on the Indonesian border was identified by our radar operator as one of the Russian gunboats used by the Indonesians. It was slowly heading into our patrol waters. This would be a serious engagement. They were modern, fast and armed with missiles.

'600 yards, dead ahead, closing . . . 400 yards dead ahead, and closing . . .' the radar operator called out the range as we proceeded with great anticipation towards him. Our old style open-plan ship had the ops room immediately below the open bridge, and all gun stations and hands on deck could clearly hear the radar reports on the calm and balmy night.

'200 yards, dead ahead, still closing . . .' Totally blacked out, we had no vision into the darkness other than radar. Tension was high.

'Fire starboard rocket.'

The captain ordered an illuminating rocket that would fire a flare some 500m above and ahead to light up the scene. I was starboard lookout on the bridge, next to the rocket launcher. A loud click echoed underneath me. The rocket had misfired. This required changing the firing cartridge. And a short delay.

The captain, a young lieutenant in his first encounter on his first command, called the order to fire again. A Junior Seaman next to me on the starboard bridge Bren gun, in his tense readiness, simply heard the order, 'Fire starboard.'

And opened up.

Every gun on the ship followed. A deafening roar of tracer barrelled into the night sky ahead. An instant later, the rocket went off with a noise like a jet fighter on a low level pass. A small explosion above transformed our night into day. There, some 100 yards distant, was a Malaysian Police boat. These never normally venture more than a kilometre offshore and were not known for their bravery. They, of course, were on our side, but absolutely not expected to be out here.

'Cease fire. Cease fire!' bellowed from the bridge.

In the minute's silent observation that followed, just the crackling of the flare overhead descending on its parachute, the pandemonium on the police boat was clearly visible. Cries echoed across the water, crew abandoning ship, leaping into the black sea.

'Half astern both engines' was quietly ordered from the bridge, and we unobtrusively removed ourselves from the scene, having ascertained they were not sinking.

The Captain gave a subdued and short talk on the tannoy to the ship's company.

'Bad luck chaps. Big bugger up. We're all as keen as matelots on Singapore's high streets to get stuck in, I know. Bloody good show, just a pity it wasn't the enemy. Put the lid on it. Let's get back on patrol.'

Midshipman Fynn

**HMS
Lincoln
off
Singapore**

Nothing more was made of it, nor was anything said ashore. Other than a furious weapon cleaning session with insuppressible grins on the faces of the gunners.

A few days later we read an article in the local newspaper reporting a Malaysian police boat had sunk at its moorings in port following damage suffered in a fierce encounter with an Indonesian gunboat a few nights before, which they had valiantly fought off. No casualties, we were happy to hear. What they were doing there, we never found out

The regular stint of the morning watch, midnight to 0400hrs, had my crew of ten, and me, with Her Majesty's ship to ourselves. My cox'n, the man on the wheel, through whom all messages to the engine room were passed, was an enormous Able Seaman Hardiman. Navy procedure called for the wheelhouse to repeat every order back to the bridge, and then steer accordingly, relaying the relevant orders to the engine rooms.

'Wheelhouse, Bridge . . . port fifteen, revolutions one two zero,' I would call down, smugly superior, navigating 'my'ship.

'Port fifteen, revolutions one two zero, Sir,' would repeat AB Hardiman

'Roger that, wheelhouse' and minutes later, 'Wheelhouse, bring her to midships.'

'Midships she is, Sir'

'Good . . . starboard ten . . . midships . . . port twenty, revolutions eight zero.' And on, and on, and on would be calling the crisp Dartmouth trained orders down the voice pipe as we zigzagged our way thru the myriad islands, having a whale of a time.

Only, the repeats were getting slower and slower, to the point of insubordination and embarrassment. Finally, there was no response.

'Wheelhouse, this is the bridge, any problem?'

Long pause . . .

'Yes, Sir . . . the wheel's come off.'

'Say again, wheelhouse.'

'The wheel, Sir, it's come off.' I walk three paces to look down the hatch into the wheelhouse. The wheel was clearly still intact.

Do I have a mutiny on my hands? My adrenalin races.

'What the hell's going on, Hardiman?' I nervously break tradition down the voice pipe.

'Would you come down into the wheelhouse, Sir,' Able Seaman Hardiman requests. With great caution, wondering why they hadn't issued me with a service revolver, I descend the steel steps.

"Ave a go on the wheel, then, Sir.'

'I beg your pardon.'

'Just 'av a go, Sir'

I do, with great difficulty. It was an old World War II cable system, very heavy to move. He explains that it would make his life a lot more enjoyable if we didn't have so many course alterations, as would the engine room over their revolution changes.

Understanding each other better, I go back onto the bridge, a little chastened, and the patrol resumes, further out to sea, with fewer changes to course and engine settings. Not quite so much fun, but more acceptable to the working parts of the ship and the men. And a slightly matured Officer of the Watch.

The closest I came to disaster, driving home the responsibility I carried, was when we were patrolling one night in the deep channel that the major commercial shipping used to enter Singapore harbour.

One of the tricks used by the sampans was to hide behind these big ships in their radar shadow. We were required to check each side of them as they passed. I spotted two large tankers making their way up the channel from the other end of our patrol line. Having checked the one side out, we needed to get across the path between them to make an inspection of their other side. I set course accordingly.

A ticklish problem at sea at night is distinguishing between a small light close by and a larger one in the distance. A matter of experience—a quality I was low on—I misjudged and reckoned the tanker was a lot further away than it actually was.

'Steady bearing, Sir, red two zero' my bridge lookout called. This means that if nothing changes, we would all arrive at the same point at the same time.

We were on a collision course.

I called down to increase our speed.

'Still on a steady bearing, Sir', the lookout calls a few minutes later, gripping the bridge rail so tight his knuckles were white in the darkness.

I called for more speed.

Shortly after, in the frightening way that things happen all too fast at sea, in spite of being on emergency 'Full Ahead Both Engines', it was clear we were not going to make it.

'Hard a-port!' I called down, another emergency command to turn as hard as the ship would go. For a few sickening moments we were swinging round into the line of the oncoming ship, with a closing speed of some 40 knots (85kph) between us. Our ship was heeling hard in a tight turn at full power when we hit the huge bow wave of the tanker, almost rolling us over onto the opposite side.

All hands asleep below were thrown out of their bunks, including the captain, who crawled up the hatchway in his pyjamas.

'What the f . . . !' The massive bulk of the tanker rumbled down our side, searchlights flashing from high on their decks to see what was going on down there. There wasn't much that needed saying. The white faces on the bridge told him we'd learned our lesson.

'Call me earlier next time, Mid!' He growled as he went below to catch up on the rest of his sleep, having just missed his first Command disappearing with all hands, without a trace.

HMS *Lincoln* was now through her refit and ready to patrol the Borneo straights. A similar job on a bigger scale.

I sadly bade farewell to our gunboat and rejoined my 'proper' ship.

We were taking over from a Royal Australian Navy frigate which was going home after 6 months in these waters. The RN protocol for the arriving ship was to steam past the departing one, all hands on deck in Number Ones, piping a salute. The departing Aussie ship was 'all hands on deck'. But dressed in shorts only, lounging on the guardrails, watching us, and smiling.

At just the right moment, there were three loud reports from their anti-submarine mortars. Was this the beginning of a gun salute? Oh, no, no. Thousands of toilet rolls shot into the sky, raining down on us, tangling into radar aerials, being sucked down air intakes, and draping the entire length of the ship and assembled ship's company. A raucous cheer and message flashed from the Aussie bridge.

'That should help clean up the shit around here!' And they sailed over the horizon.

We were out of commission for two days cleaning up the mess.

Life on board a larger ship was different. Discipline and order escalated as the ship size increased. 'Mess dress', a formal monkey jacket, was required in the wardroom after 1800hrs. Dinner was served by stewards, also in fine uniforms, on our polished Mahogany tables set with the ship's silver (dating back to the first of the ship's name, often as far back as Nelson's Navy), chased with the best of wines, followed by port, more after dinner drinks, and 'mess' games.

Sometimes that was cards, throwing dice, or simply stimulating discussion, but others were more boisterous. One involved a relay where two teams were to race a course by climbing out of the porthole, clawing one's way up the outside of the hull, over the guard rail, up to the bridge and back down into the wardroom.

No sobering up experience beats clinging by one's fingernails and toes of boots to the rivets and joints in a ship's steel plate while the sea whooshes past in the darkness below. Knowing for certain, that if one fell, that would be that. You'd never be found in the dark

All part of naval officer training.

Chapter 18

Yo Ho Ho

In the days of sail ships, the only way to persuade men up the mast to change sails in harsh weather was to give them some 'dutch courage'—a good sized tot of rum. Also issued to spur on matelots going into battle.

The tot was about the only perk a sailor had in signing up on HM's ships back then. The Navy arranged contracts for the vital rum with the Caribbean Islands, lasting one hundred years at a time. I joined when the current 1870 contract was to expire in 1970.

The 'Rum Issue' was still religiously distributed at midday. Every detail of 'how to' was written up in the QR&AI (Queen's Rules and Admiralty Instructions), the Navy's 'bible'. The venerable book covered everything from who was to man what part of the ship at action stations, down to what questions to ask, and answers to expect, in a disciplinary hearing when a man was brought forward for molesting a maiden ('teaching deep breathing exercises' was not an acceptable excuse.)

Rum was stored in the bowels of the ship in large barrels with 'God Save the Queen' inscribed in brass on their side. The officer and midshipman of the watch, together with two Leading Seamen, known as 'tankies', solemnly stood outside the closed and locked hatch for 15 minutes before entering, while extractor fans were pulling out the bacchanal breath. Even then, intoxicating fumes rendered the 'Rum Party' considerably happier after the issuing routine.

This entailed running through a list of the ship's company entitled to receive rum, those under punishment, sick or registered as 'temperance' not entitled. Two pence extra per day would be received by those who admitted to 'temperance', who weren't many. A tot of the dark oily 100+% proof rum was $1/8^{th}$ of a pint (100mls). The calculated total issue would carefully be measured out in copper jugs, also with 'God Save the Queen' emblazoned on their side. One tot for 'spillage' for every 25 tots issued, was added.

After locking the rum store with its threefold padlock system (more than any armoury or weapons magazine had) and turning off the extractor fans, the Rum Party proceeded to the upper deck, 'piping' the appropriate tune on the ship's tannoy, calling 'Rum Issue. Rum Issue!' The entire ship's company 'off watch', 2/3rds of the men, excluding petty officers who were allowed to have their rum issued directly in their 'mess', gathered on the quarterdeck (No rum for commissioned officers.)

Each name was called in alphabetical order from the daily list. Our Seaman would step forward, salute smartly, 'Aye, Aye, Sir!', and down his 'grog', a tot of rum mixed with two tots of water, before the Officer of the watch. He'd place the empty glass back on the issuing table, do an about turn, and stagger off down the deck. On the completion of all tots being issued, the QR&AI instructions clearly stated that 'the remainder was to be ejected overboard into the sea'.

What actually happened was that this remainder, amounting to over a bottle on a frigate such as ours, was tipped into the scuppers (guard rail drain) at a carefully selected point, where it would run overboard at the next break in the scupper, below which a seaman would be ready with a bucket hanging out from a suitable porthole. 'Tanky's perks.

More court-martials took place over the misuse of the rum issue than any other offence in the Royal Navy. Not to mention the virtual incapacity of the entire fleet for several hours after the daily issue.

The Admiralty sighed in relief, in 1970, when the contract was not renewed. Thereafter, each man was given two cans of beer instead.

Ian Smith's government, during my time as a Midshipman in 1965, declared UDI, Rhodesia's Unilateral Declaration of Independence.

The 'Winds of change', as described by Harold Macmillan to the joint South African parliament in Cape Town in 1961, had been blowing down through the African continent. Nationalists were ecstatic. Alarming and destructive consequences sadly seemed to ensue.

The Gold Coast in the west had erupted, horrors of the Mau Mau had decimated Kenya, the Belgian Congo had dissolved into chaos, the Portuguese evacuated from Angola, and later Mozambique. The birth pangs and atrocities accompanying African independence were not pretty reading. Always backed and exploited by the Eastern bloc.

UDI was the Rhodesians' response to the British Government's demand that it submit to the immediate step-down of their government, followed by a general election. The Rhodesians, self-governing since 1924, had set up an evolving constitution, requiring an electorate with certain educational or financial status. Their argument was that this eliminated exploitation by unscrupulous politicians of the mostly uneducated population, and that the largely white electorate of the time would gradually be added to by the black community as education and economic opportunity built them into responsible voters. Too slow for some. Too fast for others.

They deemed the British demand would do nothing short of plunging the country into the anarchy, chaos and rampant corruption that had ensued with every newly independent country to the north, and so refused to cooperate.

Britain was incensed. Their African trade was in jeopardy, a six billion dollar oil investment in Nigeria alone. World sanctions were determined, the demise of the renegade regime forecast in six months. Nationalist parties declared war, backed by China, North Korea and the USSR.

Fifteen long tortuous years later, in 1980, a truce was called and an election held, enshrining a constitution to protect a 1/3rd white minority in parliament for ten years.

Meantime, every British military unit with a Rhodesian serving in it, was ordered to repatriate the rebel member. My Captain called me into his cabin, explained the situation, and sought my response. I was far too busy enjoying life and the Navy to be troubled with politics which I was happy to let take its course and expressed no urge to be flying 'home'. Nor did I think I could seriously make any contribution that would greatly change the situation.

'You won't be throwing bombs down my engine rooms, then?' he humoured.

A stoic defence of my position as a loyal serving member of his ship's company ensued with the Admiralty. 'Sparks' in the radio room kept me privately informed on the daily discussion. It was finally agreed with Whitehall that the orders for me to be flown home should be deferred until the ship returned to England in six month's time.

We were called to join an exercise that took us to Vietnam and on to Hong Kong. It was a poignant time being with the American fleet, watching squadrons leaving on sorties from their aircraft carriers, counting so many less coming back each time.

What extraordinary invincibility has the faith and ego of the military man who risks his life, often in somebody else's war, on the whims of politicians, courageously confident he'll be going home at the end of it. You might not be so sure about your oppo, but 'no worries' about yourself. The odds were you would live to fight another day.

Our stay in Hong Kong was extended thanks to problems in our variable pitch propeller mechanism. A development that wasn't too hard to bear. I vowed never to be a ship's engineer as they struggled to fix our ailing propulsion system while we all had great runs ashore into this exotic city.

I qualified as a ship's diver while in Singapore, the course finale being to jump, fully kitted, off an aircraft carrier's deck, 40m to the water below. The technique was to jump feet first, flippers locked together, holding your air bottles to prevent them from hitting you in the head when entering the sea. And not to look down whatever happens, or face a devastating belly landing. Counting while dropping, I reached a frightening seven before plummeting in, plunging ten metres deep before swimming back up. The inspiration behind this terrifying leap was that there would never be a higher platform you'd be called to jump from.

The purpose of the diving team was to enable a ship's bottom to be searched for limpet mines in emergencies and to deal with regular underwater maintenance. Of the happier outcomes were the exercises mounted in glamorous diving locations abounding in tropical waters.

Crossing the Indian Ocean, we came across a deserted island in the middle of this vast expanse of water. The ship's diving officer immediately requested an exercise. For three amazing days we camped on the beach, swimming with turtles, while the ship sailed away on another exercise. In the exquisite silence of our island, we could hear the ship's engines hours before it reappeared on the horizon to fetch us.

We received a signal to standby for the Beira blockade, set up to prevent sanctions busting ships from docking and supplying Rhodesia. The Captain called me to explain he would not split my loyalties if the ship was diverted, and would arrange for me to stay over with the Minesweeper squadron in Aden.

'Let's lock the Boss in his cabin, and take the ship', a young lieutenant suggested that evening in the wardroom. Hijack the ship and keep the Beira corridor open for the beleaguered Rhodesians. A memorable discussion ensued.

'Absolutely bloody not! What of our sworn allegiance to the Queen? No pipsqueak African tin pot is changing that!' Others argued hotly that that was exactly the Rhodesian stand, bar the politics. I was amazed to find the wardroom split 50/50. Although tongue in cheek, it was a sharp reminder of the divisions the British were battling through over this conflict.

The order never came, and we steamed on through Suez back to Plymouth. The ship having been abroad for seven years, a great reception awaited us, with an attendant flotilla hooting and tooting, as was the tradition for a returning foreign based ship.

Over wardroom cocktails for the families and welcoming dignitaries, I was enticed into some careless conversations with cleverly camouflaged journalists. The next day's headlines featured such articles entitled 'Homesick Sailor Not Allowed Home', 'Rhodesians still serving', and other unhelpful anecdotes for an ailing ex Rhodesian RN sailor trying to go home on leave.

In consequence, my meeting in Whitehall with the Admiral in Charge, Officer Postings Abroad, was glacial. Trailing down the austere corridors of the Admiralty, their historic role in two World

Wars and beyond quite overwhelming, I was ushered into an office with a door as high as the 3m ceiling. The Admiral, busy writing on his enormous oak desk, raised his bushy eyebrows to notice my entrance, gave a deep 'Huuumph', and continued with his business.

After several minutes of silent standing, I was finally waved to a chair.

'Midshipman Fynn?' The great shaggy head raised.

'Aye, Aye, Sir!'

'I've been reading about you in the morning papers', he growled.

'Sorry about that, Sir.'

'Hhuuumph! Not as sorry as we are. Need to be a damn site more discreet, dear boy, hmm? Damned reporters. Turn a duck's fart into an international incident! Bad luck. For all of us . . . So, tell me, Fynn, what do you want to do?"

'I'd like to go home on leave, Sir, and come back and continue my career in the Navy.'

'Hhhuumph . . . don't see why not . . . pick up a few tips on what those Rhodesians are thinking while you're there, Hmm? Not a bad fellow, that Smith. Pity about the mess, Hmm? All right Fynn, carry on.' And he bent back over his desk.

I flew back in an RAF transporter as far as Lusaka, then made my own way.

For all the joy of seeing my home and family, most of my friends still abroad, I had no desire to stay. It all seemed a long way from my world, like landing on another planet. I found I'd lost touch with former colleagues, all completely immersed in this struggle, which I wasn't part of. I loved the few excursions into the bush, but couldn't wait to get back and on with the next Navy adventure, certain this 'storm in a teacup' would soon settle.

How wrong I was.

Back there, the Admiral in Charge, Officer Postings Abroad, was more sympathetic than he showed. After recommending I be allowed home on leave, I was permitted to continue with entering the Royal Navy Engineering College at Manadon.

I had elected for my specialisation the job of maintenance test pilot with the Fleet Air Arm, firstly reading aeronautical engineering, then being trained as a ship-born engineer/pilot, the most exciting career I could possibly imagine. A policy was developing at the time to phase out aircraft carriers and the fixed wing fleet, leaving that to the RAF, whilst the Navy would specialise in 'chopper' squadrons. All okay by me.

Manadon in Plymouth was fun. In between lectures, we tuned and rebuilt our sports cars, raced yachts, flew Tiger Moths, and frequented the delightful pubs and ladies on Dartmoor. We bought an old fashioned fire engine to carry us on pub crawls, 16 on the open back, one driver to remain sober. Insured as a 'sports lorry'. Some of the guys took it to Paris, where they plugged into the metropolitan fire mains and sprayed the streets and all who moved thereon, including the Gendarmes, earning them a night in a Paris jail.

We dined in typical wardroom splendour, the tables laid with the old HMS *Thunderer* ship's silver, again dating back to Nelson's days. A special mess dinner when girls were allowed was laid on monthly, a Royal Marines dance band livening the evening.

My good friend, Richard Goodfellow, who later survived being blown up on HMS *Antelope* serving as the ship's Engineer Officer in the battle for the Falklands, asked my sister Vanessa down from Cambridge. After all the frivolities were over, 'Ness' slept over in our cabins, her having no other place to go. The following morning, we dressed her in naval uniform, hair tucked into cap, and walked her in close formation to the car park to get her out undetected.

On another 'morning after', a local contractor was extremely unimpressed to find his heavy machinery, which was parked neatly each evening on the new development he was working on, had been raced around the yard in a massive 'dodge 'em' cars escapade, left randomly where they stopped after running out of fuel.

I have always admired the British Police Force. Somehow different to any in the rest of the world. We all owned character cars, refined in the college workshops. I was driving with a trainee Navy pilot on our way to a reception, in our uniforms, in his 1948 MG. At the bottom of a long hill we were flagged down. A police officer walked over to inform Hugh that he had been doing 70mph in a 40mph zone.

'Good golly, was I really? Look, Officer, would you mind giving me that in writing, I'm actually trying to sell this car!' Hugh's British Navy accent responded. The policeman rolled his eyes, smiled in bemusement, cautioned and waved us away.

Next time I met them was driving to Gatwick Airport from Plymouth in my newly-done-up Triumph TR2 open sports car to collect Dad who was flying in from Rhodesia for his first visit. Halfway through the trip, the car had complete brake failure. Due to the important occasion, I decided to chance it using gears to slow down, keeping an eye on the traffic a long way ahead.

The exhilaration of my open car roaring along the outside lane of the motorway caused me to forget the problem existed altogether. Until a slow travelling van on the inside lane crawled out into the fast lane to overtake a lorry. My casual touch on the brake pedal, producing no result, soon reminded me as we closed rapidly. I tried to pass by riding one wheel on the middle barrier hump.

All avoidance manoeuvres failed. My front end locked firmly into his rear end and we staggered like mating cars to the verge and stopped. At least ten Jamaicans jumped out, patently ready to renege on the Navy's 100 year rum contract. They ripped the entwined metals apart, suitably glared down and admonished me in ripe Jamaican style, and drove away.

I was left with a punctured radiator, a sorry front end, and still no brakes. A kind AA man stopped, towed me to a garage and got me back to the Gatwick road where I jauntily thumbed a lift, conscious of my Dad's imminent landing.

Nobody stopped.

After many snubs, with the clock ticking, I was desperate. I stood in the middle of the road making myself as obvious as possible, flagging down cars with an agonised expression and wild shouts to try and stop them. Understandably, they swerved and accelerated past.

And then a Police patrol car came round the corner.

'Allo, allo, what might the problem be here, Sir?'

I did my best to explain, looking and feeling increasingly forlorn. They listened patiently, and after some minutes, the officer in charge asked me to get into the car.

Mortar deck

The bridge, HMS Ickford

TR2 sports car in the workshop

Great! Now to the Police station for more questioning and breathalyser tests . . .

'What time did you say your Dad's flight arrives?' He turned to ask again. Checking his clock and switching the siren on, we sped for Gatwick, arriving with five minutes to spare.

'Good luck, lad. Say hi to Dad from us.' And off they sped.

Thank you, officer. Whoever and wherever you are.

Yet, for all this, it was too easy—too good to be true. I yearned deep down for life to be more real, more relevant, less laid on. I wanted to understand something of how the rest of the world lived, and to experience its ordinariness, its depravities and extremes, its beauties, cruelties, opportunities and challenges, outside the stereotyped, comfortable, albeit appealing Navy life.

I spent a Christmas working for an ex-paratrooper who had started a house in the west end of London, taking in and rehabilitating street people. I helped him with soup kitchens under railway bridges and in the Parks, trying to establish relationships with proud, honourable people to whom life had dealt some tough cards.

It was a moving time and added to my train of thought that life had to be more than an exciting job, smart uniform and having a good time, all of which I nevertheless enjoyed to the hilt. Meanwhile, my home country was in turmoil ; Dad had taken the plunge to live the simple life he yearned for, divorcing Mum and immigrating to Portugal. Tough things were happening, and I felt I was out of the stream.

After much soul searching, I resigned, much to the anguish of the Navy who'd done their best to support me in a paternal and endearing manner through all the confusion, and I headed off to discover what it was all about out there. As my Australian son-in-law puts it so aptly today—'If you never, never gao; you'll never, never knaow!'

I decided to finish the engineering degree I'd started at Manadon, but switched to read Civil Engineering which I thought might be more useful in Africa, and was accepted into Bristol University.

Walking away from my security was scary, but in the glorious invincibility of youth, I'd tell myself 'No worries. It'll pan out.'

Little knowing quite how.

Chapter 19

A Tiger in my Moth

In 1967, as a 22-year-old new 'Uni' student, all I knew for sure was that, with my degree, I'd be heading back home to Africa, confident I could contribute to its development, somewhere, somehow, sometime.

The quest to discover more about old Dad's 'something other than' pulled as strong as ever. On my Easter vacation, I decided to try for a job on a fishing trawler. I'd heard the going was about as tough as it gets, and I wanted to see how I'd shape up.

I had no idea how or where to start, nor could I find anyone who did. I headed up the east coast, hitching my way on big trucks so as to talk to the drivers as how to go about it—Destination—Any fishing port where I could find a boat to take me.

I quickly found that working on an English fishing boat required certificates, which I didn't have, and foreign boats weren't keen on Englishmen who had no previous experience and couldn't speak their language, however hard I tried to persuade them otherwise.

Then an Icelandic boat, leaving on the turn of the tide, relayed to a fish merchant I'd befriended that they'd be happy to take me, quite where to, or to do what, was unclear. No second invitation was needed. Throwing my rucksack on board and offering thanks to the captain, we sailed off in a small 50 foot herring boat, heading gloriously north.

Only one man spoke English on board, but all were friendly and encouraging. Soon after we'd lost sight of land we met up with another boat that appeared from nowhere, to whom we passed a number of boxes, contents unknown. Interesting . . . looked like I'd picked a smuggler.

To the delight of the crew, we found a shoal of herring a few nights out, the extent of which luck I would appreciate more later. We hauled on the net through the night and into the next morning, filling the holds. Then sailed north again, now heavily laden. Two more days landed us at the volcanic Westmannaeyjar islands, parts of which were still steaming, so newly pushed up from the ocean bed were they.

The houses and factory wharf on the island were built in the lea of foothills to protect them from lava flows that erupted every now and then from the volcano behind. This was the end of our journey, my wages set against the lift I had been given, with another arranged to mainland Iceland.

I only began to discover the proud nature of these people and the devastation their economy had suffered when some young students aboard the onward ferry asked pointed questions about what I was doing, and how much money I had. On learning of my vagrant agenda, they were angry that I should be travelling in such a meaningless and unconstructive manner in their country.

'Don't you know what's happening here, man?'

'Well, no, actually, I don't. Sorry.'

They explained that Iceland had been robbed of its herring by the Russian factory ships, which arrived with their accompanying fleet of fishing boats and processed huge tonnages of fish on the spot out at sea. The local boats would have to steam back to port to empty their holds before returning, a journey that took several days, during which time the Russians depleted the shoal.

The entire economy of Iceland depended on the herring industry, and now it was seriously troubled. Their currency had devalued four times that year, unemployment running the highest ever.

'What are you doing, man, coming over to take our jobs, with no money, and no plan?' they accused me.

I got the message. Not prudent to go looking for a job in Reykjavik. I headed off on a sightseeing tour instead—with no plan and no money, to discover a country more different than my wildest dreams could have conjured.

'Who is eating at the little table?' I asked the kind folk who were hosting me for the night.

'The Little People,' they replied straightaway, looking at me curiously in wonderment at my ignorance.

I nodded, sipping my beer. Belief in fairies wasn't my strongest, but it led them to leave out food and drink in their gardens, which these folk clearly took as a normal and right thing to do. I felt a bit ashamed about how little I knew of these people and their strange land I was visiting.

Proudly jealous of their heritage, they had a special radio programme warning the public of slang appearing in their language, which purports to be one of the oldest tongues in the world, spoken by their ancestors, the Vikings.

There was only one road connecting the south of the island to the north. It looked more like a farm track than a national road, following a rocky trail around the coast. The Vatna Jokull volcano (down which Jules Verne started his 'Journey to the Centre of the Earth', and recently erupted) dominated every scene. Iceland had declined an American offer to construct a highway connecting their two military bases at Reykjavik in the south and Akureyri in the north. I set off on it in anticipation of the adventure, but with some trepidation, still knowing nothing of the language or quite where I was going, nor having any means to support myself.

'We drop you here?'

Taking lifts on whatever route they happened to be going, I decided to spend the night in a refuge I spotted not far from the road at the top of the pass we were climbing through. These little shacks were constructed and stocked with basic provisions for mountain wanderers, a donation box covering for whatever one used.

'Thank you, this'll be fine.'

My quizzical transporters drove away, no doubt remembering something about 'mad dogs and Englishmen'. Surrounded by a lava moonscape, I made noodle soup on the little gas stove, enjoying the solitude in the soft evening light on the remote rugged landscape.

Next morning, refreshed and eager to get out, I trekked across the rough, rocky ground down to a fishing village I could see as the only patch of green along the coastline, again protected from lava flows by the lee of some foothills.

I walked the docks, watching herring being pulled ashore and packed, going over in my mind the precocious student's stories, conscious that everyone else was aware of a stranger in their midst. A white haired old man approached, and in perfect English, invited me for tea. He talked while I ate hungrily, his delightful little wife busily keeping my plate filled with delicious cookies.

'We've been expecting you,' he assured me. 'You will stay a few days?'

'You have?!' Slightly taken aback, I gratefully and curiously accepted.

He was clearly a leader of the village and gently introduced me to their philosophy of life, based on ascending levels of consciousness in the different realms of the senses. I found it intriguing, learning much about Iceland at the same time. I began to feel like I was some kind of a pilgrim in this land, strangely welcomed by the spirits.

Setting off north a few days later, I got a lift in a WWII vintage MAC truck. Superbly maintained in its antiquity, carrying a 30 ton load of timber, we traversed precipitous drops along the coastal trail, labouring so slowly up hills that I could have walked faster. After hours of engine noise and diesel smell in the steamy old cab, I did just that, thanking the sweating driver for his kindness.

It was the first time I had experienced the northern summer and never setting sun. The huge red ball simply moved along the horizon for a few hours through the middle of the 'night', rising again for its low daytime orbit. It felt quite surreal wandering in this stark country, alone, with no idea where I would be sleeping or eating that night, but greatly at peace in this perpetual sunset.

Approaching a farm, I presented the specially written note from my previous philosopher host. I had no idea what it said. The farmer read it, his eyes opened wider, and he generously offered his hay barn to me for the night, providing me with a meal of sheep's knuckles and yoghurt.

My 300km journey, much of which I had walked, ended in Akureyri's famous hot springs and the best bath ever, surrounded by snow. All this time, I had virtually no money in my pocket. But armed with my note, I was welcomed everywhere as family. The note mysteriously disappeared on my trek home and I never found out what it said.

Back in Reykjavik two weeks later, it was time to get home and I searched for a passage.

'We don't know where we land. First we find fish, then we see where the price best. Maybe Canada, maybe Norway, Denmark or Scotland, or back here! Okay?' The herring boat captain was at pains to explain.

'Okay!' I hopped aboard.

A brand new adventure.

Three days out to sea, coded communications crackling amongst the Icelandic boats, they located the shoals around midnight. I came up on deck, thinking we'd made port, lights all around us. It seemed every herring boat in the North Sea was gathered there.

For all the coded Icelandic communications, the international fleet had found the shoal too, a rusty old Russian factory ship rising to the swell in their midst, literally sucking the sea dry of herring. I began to understand the student's concerns.

The anguish in my fellow fisherman was heartbreaking. The harvest which the generations had conserved and survived on was being stolen before their eyes.

Fortunately for me, it turned out the price in Scotland was good.

Arriving back in Bristol a week later, a sunburnt Rob was feeling very different on the inside. Discovering some of that 'something other than', over which I had turned my world upside down to find, brought a peace and stimulation into the heart wrenching decision of leaving my Navy career.

Bristol's engineering degree expected a summer vac job as a practical experience in the industry. Most of the guys picked a serious career move, working with a company they hoped to join in the future. I took a job in Barcelona, it looking the most fun place to be in what was on offer. One of the qualifications asked for was a working knowledge of Spanish, which I ticked, knowing not a word. Ness, my sister, joined me and we headed across the continent in my camouflage painted mini van.

'Como estas? Hablas Englis?' Ness would test me from 'Learn Spanish' as I took my turn at the wheel.

We booked into the Torro Bravo campsite, right on the beach. I found my job as trainee engineer on the main sewage works of the city. The senior engineer gave me screeds of information while he whisked me round the site, to which I nodded sagely.

'Si, comprendo . . . si, si.' I would lamely add. The young Spanish engineers accompanying us soon cottoned on and valiantly covered for me, filling me in with a quiet translation.

'She worksa where?' My new found friends at work were horrified when they discovered where Ness had found a job as a bargirl. They explained that young English girls regularly disappeared from this place into Eastern harems and the Marrakech white slave trade. They helped find a more suitable bar for her, where we would gather at the end of our day.

We both enjoyed a wonderful month of Spanish hospitality and sun, not advancing my engineering skills greatly, but definitely our cultural understandings.

Back at 'Uni', the 'Air Squadron' expanded student life further for me. It was set up to train reserve pilots for the RAF, in the hope of attracting some for their career. We flew old de Havilland Chipmunks, a two-seat trainer that really looked and felt like an Air Force plane. Filton, our base, sported a huge runway that we could have landed and taken off our little chipmunks five times in the same direction. The Concorde and new Harrier jet were being built and tested there by British Aerospace. We were forbidden from flying over their hangars in case we messed up.

I had a beautiful girlfriend, Anna, who liked to wear my navy submarine jersey as a dress. We lived in a flat overlooking the Clifton suspension bridge and Bristol docks. I flew as often as I liked and tried to fit some engineering in between this delightfully different life from the Navy one.

Waiting for results at the end of the final year, I took another construction job in Spain, now having passed the second page of the language teaching. Well paid and humdrum, we erected grain silos, day after day. I was reading Francis Chichester's autobiography, 'The Lonely Sea and the Sky', half of which dealt with his famous first solo circumnavigation of the world, the other half his epic quest to teach himself to fly, navigate, and take his Gipsy Major, a bigger and earlier version of the Tiger Moth, from England to Australia. He crashed and rebuilt his aeroplane, single handed, on the way.

Trawler bound for Iceland

Tiger Moth joyriding

DH80 Tiger Moth, with Digger at Filton

A seed was sown, with large doses of inspiration. If Chichester could do it 40 years ago, why couldn't I fly back to Rhodesia in a Tiger Moth today?

My every waking hour was consumed with thoughts and plans until, with apologies to the foreman, I couldn't stay another day. The grand idea had not a cent to back it, which didn't lessen my enthusiasm. And never did in the many wildly innovative ideas that would fill my life ahead. I stowed away on the ferry across the channel doing the traditional hiding in a lifeboat to leave harbour and sleeping in baths on the passage.

Arriving back at Bristol, my ambitious plan found a few smiles, knowing nods, and an excellent reason for another party in the mess of the University Air Squadron. Aircraftsman 'Digger' Farley, an RAF mechanic, pledged his support and committed to flying with me.

First thing was to find an aeroplane. I headed for Bicester, an RAF base just outside Oxford, where I had done some gliding courses and remembered the motivated aviation community there. One evening in the flying club bar, a guy who had made some money in a pyramid cosmetics company, Holiday Magic, volunteered to put up the plane and advertise his cosmetics on the fuselage through the venture.

Whoopee!

He knew of an aircraft in the south of France, where the warm dry climate had preserved the fragile wood structure and fabric. The de Havilland Tiger Moth is an open-cockpit tail-wheel biplane produced as a trainer for the RAF in WWII. It cruised at 80mph (130kph), and stalled at 30mph (50kph), which meant you could land it in about 50m, and take off in just a bit more. Pretty useful in a cross Africa trip. They were sold at the end of hostilities, in boxes, brand new, for £50. We bought ours for £1,000. Today it would fetch £100,000.

The Bristol squadron offered to strip the plane down, check it out, and convert it to a British registration, a formality that would make the paperwork easier crossing Africa. Apprentices at BA made an auxiliary fuel tank to fit into the front cockpit. This increased our range from 300 to 400 miles (650km). The local model aero club donated a wind driven generator that could be strapped onto the undercarriage, providing 12v power to run a radio/navigational aid donated by an avionics company—equipment no Tiger Moth normally had. Starting the engine, however, would still be done by swinging the propeller.

I planned a route via the west coast of Africa to Angola and then inland to Rhodesia. I found out later that it would have been wiser to have taken the eastern route which most of the earlier aviators preferred for its kinder weather and more favourable aerodromes. The squadron gave me maps to cover the route. These filled a briefcase that would be the heaviest bag on board. Flight planning was laborious, requiring permission and sourcing fuel from 26 different countries, most of which were at war and suspicious of our motives.

The stretch down the Spanish Sahara coastline was 450 miles (720km) of unbroken sand and sea. The meteorological service assured me that at the time of year we were planning, we should find a 50 knot (100kph) tailwind above 2,000ft (600m). Even if it was half that, we'd make it with our 400 mile range. But 'met' boys have been known to be wrong.

I'd met a Spanish girl in London whose father was the diplomatic attaché. It turned out her uncle was CO of the foreign legion in the Spanish Sahara. He agreed to an exercise with his troops to establish a fuel dump halfway, in case we needed it.

Gambia and Portuguese East Guinea refused us permission to over-fly, suspecting us to be gunrunners. Their coastlines—50 miles (80km) and 200miles (320km) respectively—were flyable by rounding them out to sea, holding the coast within gliding distance in case of engine failure, always a consideration for any single engine flight, especially in our 35-year-old Gipsy Major.

The squadron generously covered our fuel requirements for local flying, but we needed sponsors to cover our cross-Africa flight. A big breakthrough came when the chairman of the Tiger Moth Club agreed to see us at their flying base at Biggin Hill.

We were to meet on a Sunday morning. Ruefully watching the weather worsening as we prepared for the flight—a wet, cold front having blown in from the Irish channel—the met briefing suggested that if we left smartly we could fly through the front into reasonable conditions ahead of it, and on to Biggin Hill.

159

We hurriedly took off to follow a railway line through the immediate poor visibility and low cloud. Digger would keep a sharp lookout from the front cockpit for hazards in our track. (The pilot flew from the rear cockpit in a Tiger Moth.)

Not only did the weather not improve, it got decidedly worse, driving us down until we were flying dangerously low under the cloud base. I hung onto the railway line just visible below. On approaching obstacles, Digger, up front, would indicate by flapping his arms upwards. I would ease up into the low cloud, desperately trying to maintain visual contact with terra firma through the gaps. A train or a bridge would whoosh past underneath. I'd cautiously descend so we could see the line again. Very scary stuff, but we were committed. I knew it was worse behind, and I didn't dare veer off the line to look for somewhere to land.

Half an hour on, nothing had improved and decision time was looming. The train line led us into central London, clearly not helpful. The 'Hogs Back' was approaching, a road that would lead us to Biggin Hill. Not good was that it climbed a hill, likely to be in heavier cloud. Good was that it crossed another railway line on the other side, leading directly to our destination.

No choice, I picked up the Hogs Back and started to climb with it. Very soon we were flying in fog, double-decker bus height, barely able to make out the traffic headlights below. Not a continuing option. I had to climb and get above the cloud.

I'd made a serious blunder.

This now meant flying in instrument conditions, for which neither the aeroplane nor I were qualified. And if we did make it above the cloud, we were likely to find a blanked out carpet underneath us with no way back down.

I tried with every ounce of concentration to keep that aeroplane flying straight in the climb with far too few instruments and absolutely no visual reference to the horizon, or experience to accomplish this. Sweat was pouring off me in the ice-cold open cockpit. And I was losing the battle.

The inevitable happened. Pilots need vigorous consistent training and an appropriate instrument panel to cope with 'white out' conditions, where the lack of reference to which way up they are plays extraordinary tricks on the senses. None of which I had.

I lost it at about 1,000 feet (300m) above the ground, falling into a spin. I believe in angels more strongly to this day and have no doubt one was with us back there. My thoughts particularly went out to Digger in ending his life this way.

Then, we broke cloud, and not onto the hill as I expected. Miraculously we had fallen into a valley. I quickly recovered the aircraft from the spin, and gained flying control again at 100 feet (30m) above a forest.

Giving thanks to a generous God, it was back to the drawing board for what next, and where were we? Crossing a railway line, I flew along it till we passed a station, dropping down close enough to read the name on the sign.

It was the line that went past Biggin Hill. But heading the wrong way, London ahead. Tight about turn, and minutes later we were landing.

Taxiing in the drizzling rain up to the flying club, we climbed out feeling we'd done extraordinarily well under the circumstances, half expecting a little praise for making it. A big man walked up from a surprised crowd gathering at the club doors, all flying abandoned due to weather.

'And where the hell have you come from?' he asked. The Chairman of the Tiger Club. On learning his worst fears, he erupted, regarding me as less than worthy of owning, let alone flying, such a precious plane.

'And if you think I'd risk my hard earned mula, and a bloody good Tiger Moth, on some damn fool idiot who'd risk one in these conditions, you'd better have another!'

Which we did. A few ales went down a treat while grumpy chairman frothed at the other end of the bar. Sadly, that was the end of that. Apart from dealing with a complaint made to the control tower that a Tiger Moth had nearly wiped an old lady's chimney off.

We needed an injection of enthusiasm, let alone cash, at this point, and I knew where to go to get it. Back in Bicester. At least we could expose our project to a more appreciative audience, and earn some income by towing gliders, giving the plane a good testing at the same time. Even offer rides in between glider tows.

The queues lined up, and I flew my pants off. I watched with amusement this plump young boy in the line, holding his dad's hand, school cap pulled down over his eyes, a Brownie box camera hanging on his protruding tum. He could not contain his excitement as he waited his turn, bouncing on his feet.

'Wanna fly yourself, or do some aerobats?' I called my usual query as he stepped up onto the wing, under Digger's careful instruction and watchful eye, the propeller idling.

'Aeros, please!' Brownie slung school boy shouted back.

Thumbs up, chocks away, we rolled out for take off, Dad waving.

I had been practising a difficult manoeuvre called a 'four-point roll'. Imagine an aircraft corkscrewing around the longitudinal outside of a barrel, holding for a moment at mid point on each side, and again at the top. When upside down at the top of the roll, the engine would stop because of the gravity fed fuel system from the tank in the upper wing. Normal and fine. As long as you had enough speed to carry you on through to the other side.

If you didn't, the aircraft would stall, quite violently from upside down, and fall out of the sky like a tumbling leaf, which would turn into a spin, recoverable only after a considerable drop. It was tricky, although quite safe if you started off with a good height and speed. And grand fun.

Climbing to a safe altitude, I dived to pick up speed and enter the four—point roll, avoiding some birds halfway through, which messed up our speed.

As we rotated at the top of the roll with insufficient speed, hanging upside down by our shoulders on the straps, I knew, 'Oh dear! Here we go.' That turbulent stall.

No worries, we had bags of height, I recovered into straight and level flight after dropping 1,000 feet (300m), aware of a strong forward-pressure on the joystick. Was something broken? Concerned, I looked around to see what might be causing the problem. To my horror, there was no little head sticking up in the front cockpit.

My immediate, sickening thought was that he'd dropped out. The harness straps had somehow come loose.

Aghast, I banked sharply to look for a spiralling body below.

'Oooh Nooo! Poor little guy. Bloody fool, Rob. We should have been checking the strapping-in more carefully. Maybe instructing our passengers on parachute drill?! And this whole operation is probably illegal!' A hundred more recriminatory thoughts raged through my mind.

Feeling like I wanted to vomit, I turned for home, not bearing to think what I was going to say to Dad.

As I was levelling out to land, still with this great pressure on the stick, my head full of bees, I suddenly felt the pressure on the stick release. And a little head popped up in the front cockpit.

I could have kissed it.

Rolling to a stop, I switched off, apologised to the waiting queue we'd not be flying again for the day, and listened to an excited little voice that I treasured more than anybody could know. He related how he'd got such a fright up there, hugged onto the stick and had held himself under the instrument panel with all his might, the parachute slipping from under him and jamming further against the stick. Hence all the pressure. Bidding our 'Goodbyes and Good lucks' to him and his Dad, I headed for the pub with Digger, thanking God for another chance and determining we would not take any more rides.

I had to fly back to Bristol a day later, to collect some documentation, setting off a little late in the afternoon. A headwind built up, slowing my speed on the ground to a crawl, and I began to realise I'd not make it to Bristol before dark. Cirencester, another RAF base, was ahead. I'd land there instead.

It was almost dark as I approached. I could no longer see my instruments. Thankfully, the lights of Cirencester runway showed clearly ahead. This was an emergency, no time to fly past the control tower as was normally required in approaching an airfield with no radio (we'd never managed to get ours working). Only hoped there was no other aeroplane on finals. I aimed straight up on the lights and prepared to land.

But the lights were moving. They were not the runway lights, but the city's main street—one of the old roman roads, dead straight, running through the town. Too late to start looking for the runway now. Flying blind, I spotted a large dark space to my left. Whether it was a farm, a forest, a bog or a lake, I had no idea. I had to land.

I turned and slowly descended into the dark patch, not sure what would happen next. To my huge relief, I finally felt the wheels touch, running free. No spray, no mud, no fences, no trees.

Dear Angel!

I rolled to a stop outside a dimly lit pub, to the delight of the patrons. On the edge of an old wartime aerodrome, now used by the local model aero club, and cricket team.

I flew on the next morning, only the worse from an almighty hangover.

Digger got a job offer at Bicester. A good idea considering the uncertainties of sponsorship for our African trip. My cousin, John Fynn (Jack's son) whom I'd been at school with, offered to take his place. 'Fly Africa's pilot may have been a 'ball's up' in a Moth, but was not in 'moth balls'. Yet.

Needing a break from preparations and fundraising, we accepted an invitation from our girlfriends, and to join them for a party in Cambridge. We were to land in an old disused wartime aerodrome they had identified near their home. Illegal, but flying with no radio had its advantages. They were given instructions to hold up a white silk scarf as a windsock.

On a beautiful clear April Sunday morning, we arrived over our destination. I circled, looking for the aerodrome. Spotting the girls valiantly flying their scarf, I made out a stretch of tarmac that would have been part of the original runway. No more than a 100m was still intact, with a double storied house on one side, electricity cables crossing the runway halfway, a pile of beet down one end and a haystack at the other.

Tiger Moths have no brakes, relying upon the tailskid to slow them down on grass or earth. I'd never landed on tarmac before. Every bit of aviator in me was saying this wasn't a good idea.

But there were the girls . . .

'Okay!' . . . the eternal optimist took over . . . 'Let's give it a go.'

I lined up for a slow, flat precautionary approach, a crosswind springing up in the last few hundred feet.

A Tiger Moth is very susceptible to crosswinds with its biplane's high wings and narrow undercarriage. The technique was to tilt the aeroplane into the direction of the crosswind and land on that wheel. If done too heavily, the plane would jerk towards the direction of the wheel landed, when a burst of power was required to correct the direction and straighten up.

There were men working on the haystack, watching us aiming straight for them. Laughing at their frantic exit antics caused my concentration on the last minute crosswind correction to stray, and make a consequently too heavy a landing on one wheel.

We lurched off the centre line, heading for agricultural machinery parked on the verges. I throttled the engine up to straighten the plane, the only steering control on the ground. We were now well over halfway down the runway, with no room to take off again and too fast to stop with the negligible braking effect on tarmac before we hit the beet. I took the only option and turned into the green wheat field running alongside. The wheels caught in wet black soil and we were over onto our nose before I could wink. Our beautiful wooden propeller splintered, stopping the engine.

We hung in our straps in the ghastly silence, looking down at wheat growing between the wings.

'Shit!'

The local 'bobby' patrolling on his bicycle had watched the incident. He pedalled down at a furious rate, blowing his whistle. The girls followed in hot pursuit, enquiring if we were alright. The house owner, woken by a Tiger Moth flying straight at his bedroom window, came out with cups of coffee on a tray for all of us. The 'bobby' kindly agreed not to make a report and enjoy the coffee, as they tend to. The paperwork, fines and 'red tape' involved for a crash on an illegal unregistered strip would have kept us all unhappily occupied for months.

But poor old Moth was not in great shape.

'Aaaggrrh, Oi 'tink yoi're gooin ta bee orighte, me suns!'

The girls happened to know this old WWI engineer who knew wooden propeller biplanes backwards. We retrieved a propeller from a flying club wall, which he tested with his pocket knife for internal damage. The club was happy to swap it for our shattered one, and the story that went with it.

'Noaw, youe'll be aible ta registurr dat prop oonder de 'ol Moth it caime off, see?!' Thus solving the legal problem of its airworthiness.

We straightened struts, repaired broken spars, patched torn fabric, and made a thorough inspection on the engine, our old veteran spraying the crankshaft with a fluid that would show up cracks if there were any. He finally passed the plane as airworthy, but warned us that the crankshaft would have to go back to Roll-Royce for an annealing process before the African trip.

He was also careful to explain that old wooden propellers, if previously over—revved, can suffer internal damage almost impossible to detect that can be a shattering experience on a full-power take off.

We flew out of that field, hearts in mouths, successfully.

Sadly, Rolls-Royce explained they'd have to wait for a 'batch' to build up before they'd do the job. All this was going to cost time and money we didn't have. The trip wasn't going to happen in the timeframe we had planned to take advantage of weather constraints en route.

I discovered that flights in small aeroplanes going south usually took the drier and more stable eastern route through Africa. Almost certain calamity awaited us on the path I'd naively chosen for our venture, where down the lower end of Africa wall to wall jungle lay along the coast, with unstable weather patterns. Aeroplanes and airmen regularly disappeared without trace.

By God's grace we had not, finding the soft green fields of England on our nose instead. Albeit a little too far up. Never-the-less, an escape from inevitable disaster. By His grace, again.

'We could take the landy?' John suggested 'I've been thinking about that trip for a long while.'

We had all the visas. It seemed a grand way to fill the chasm of failure.

Selling the plane to a couple of New Zealand Air Force pilots seconded to the RAF, within weeks we were driving out.

Destination: Our African homeland. Planning: None.

Chapter 20

A Funny One

John's landy was a virtually new Series II, short wheelbase, diesel open jeep. Army green colour was not the best for travelling through Africa's war torn countries, but that wasn't putting us off. We prepared the vehicle with all the stuff you don't need when driving around England. Sand ladders, extra spare wheel, digging tools, high lift jack, lock up cover for the rear section. Every spare space filled with jerry cans of water and fuel.

In February 1970, we left to stopover with Dad who was now living in Portugal. His neighbour, Mr Thomas, heard about our trip, and phoned an old friend.

'Ganthrup, I've got a funny one for you here. Two lads want to drive across the Sahara. I've told them you might have a bit of advice for them. Are you game?' His aristocratic accent could not have been more British.

'Of course, old fellow. Send them over.'

Following appalling instructions, we finally found the enormous iron gates in the village of Caravelos, marked 'Quinta Morval'. a Rolls-Royce and Aston Martin were parked in the garage. The maid let us in to a great hall, at the bottom of which was a curtain with a red chord which she pulled. The curtain parted, and there stood Ganthrup, in front of a fire, impeccably attired.

'So, you'd like to know about the Sahara?'

A Dane, with an excellent command of English, he offered us whisky and we listened for three fascinating hours. He had driven a racing Mercedes to the Ivory Coast and back, and the Rolls in the garage from Norway to the Sahara. His Norwegian wife joined us and poured herself an enormous cocktail. She'd travelled with him, loved it, and embroidered his stories in a delightful and charming manner.

We spent a grand few days with Dad in his Quinta Passerinos do Alto in Ranholas, near Sintra, the last time I'd see him before he died a few years later, prematurely, thanks to his pipe smoking. We worked more on the Land-Rover, sourcing last minute spares, enjoying the gentle winter sun by day and drinking mulled wine round the fire late into the evening, talking about those 'things other than'.

A week later we landed on African soil in Morocco—the first for a while for both of us—en route for home. We made for the British Embassy in Tangiers to enquire whether we could head directly for the Sahara.

'Wouldn't do that, old man.'

'Why ever not?' asked John.

'Too risky, old chap.'

The man from the embassy gave us a great deal of advice and warnings about going directly south into the desert, apt twenty years earlier but quite wrong in the present day we later discovered. Suitably deterred, we headed along the coast and the recommended route down through Algeria.

Helpful and friendly, the Moroccans' chief interest in tourists seemed to be practising their English. Ten-year-old Mahomet led us to a campsite.

'Only to hussle tourists,' he responded with a big toothy smile on our enquiry into his occupation. 'No money. Just to help.'

True to his word, he insisted on cooking supper, which he ate with us.

A major trading item to tourists in Morocco was hashish, or marijuana. Illegal in most Western societies, it's been around a long time in Africa. We walked up the hill in the first village outside Tangiers, through ancient houses painted in a deep, cool arctic blue. There we bought some bread. The bakers, standing not two metres from the ovens, from which the heat neatly escaped through vents in the roof, had developed cooling systems that worked as good as any air conditioning, based purely on convection.

Little children in brown 'hobbit' hooded coats stumbled up the steps with us, offering everything from their sister to bead necklaces. One produced a small packet of greenish seed hashish. Knowing nothing about the intricacies of the market, we succumbed to the feeling of 'try everything once'.

'You will dream you are in heaven with twenty virgins!' was his guarantee.

'We pay eight dollars and a packet of Benson and Hedges. Final!' was our offer.

'Aahh, you are ruining me, Sirs', he needled.

Looking forward to the heavenly experience, happy we'd paid more than the market price, we prepared in a more menial manner for our Southerly sector into the desert.

Crossing borders in Africa can be laborious, the volumes of paperwork preserved from colonial times, with a big dose of corruption added. In Algiers, there was special desert insurance, fuel coupons, prefecture reporting (a system to establish the whereabouts of desert travellers and their possible need to be rescued), British Consul reports and information, a police vehicle inspection, food and fuel purchases. Only towards the end of the day were we finally on our way for the great trek south. We motored out in high spirits, exhilarated by the thought of crossing the huge continent ahead, looking forward to whatever it had in store.

We stocked up in a little town called Blida with what we thought would be our last fresh provisions for a while. The ironmonger welded one of the sand ladders that had got damaged on the journey down and offered us mint tea, chatting amiably about 'Le Grand Sud'. His speciality was scorpions and vipers, which he preserved in jars. He explained how to masticate a limb in the event of being bitten.

We learned we might meet *Leiurus quinquestriatus,* aka death-stalker, a scorpion up to 10 cm (3.9in) long. Its neurotoxic venom is very dangerous, the victim running the risk of anaphylaxis. In any case extremely painful.

**North
Africa**

Discussing Bedouin directions

Next were *Cerastes,* Sand vipers, small snakes less than 50 cm (2in) in length, of relatively stout appearance, with a pair of horns, one over each eye. These fold back, streamlining them for easing passage through burrows, and maybe our sleeping bags. Active at night, they usually lie buried in the sand with only their eyes visible. Bites are painful, but rarely fatal.

We felt better after hearing all that.

Within twenty kilometres of leaving town and Media's lush grape-growing valley, we were in semi-desert. We turned off the road at evening to find a camp and were invited in by an Algerian family to eat rice and brown sugar with them. We tried to get them to eat some of our steak and drink some wine, which they would only taste. It was good to sleep in their house before the fire, it being bitterly cold outside. Extraordinary, considering the fiery furnace literally just down the road.

Reaching El Golea, we camped in warmer climes in what seemed a deserted Oasis. The romantic vista was soon broken by a gang of ten kids appointing themselves as our guides. They bustled about helping us unload and erect the tent, inspecting everything as it came off the 'landy'.

It was the Prophet Muhammad's birthday and we set off on our mandatory tour with the gang. Great festivities were in the streets. Drums, firing of rifles, rows of men stopping frequently to face each other, bowing twice and chanting. Much to the amusement of our kids, one fierce looking fellow turned his rifle over to shoot into the ground, and the bullet dropped out the end of the barrel.

'Now we go eat,' they announced when they got bored with all that. Back in camp a fire was lit from palm fronds, potatoes peeled with fingernails, our food boxes scrutinised for a tasty number while others played our guitar and mouth organ, beating a catchy rhythm on empty jerry cans. Another had his own flute. The celebration increased in tempo until they insisted we all crowd into our tent to eat.

Our start was a little late the next morning after the previous night's 'hoolie,' and then having to drive them all back to their village at the end of it all. Thundering along massive corrugations in a landscape with few landmarks, we arrived at Fort Mirabell, a deserted French foreign legion base. Graffiti from passing travellers through the ages covered the walls. Not convinced we should contribute, we drove on into a completely featureless plain, a thin layer of pebbles covering the sand, as if the tide had just gone out.

The sun set and a sudden darkness enveloped us. We drove off the track, simply indents where wheels had pressed the pebbles down, parked the Land-Rover facing the direction we'd be heading out in the morning, and erected our tent. The site could not have been chosen with less distinction. The silence and staggering emptiness of our surrounds was almost overwhelming.

Waking at first light next morning, after loading the 'landy' and driving straight off across the plain that stretched from horizon to featureless horizon, we hardly had to touch the steering wheel.

'We're making good time, Rob. What about checking out that grave site?' Johnno comments after noticing a monument marked on our RAF map (visible from the air). After several hours of following the main track in the sand, having passed no vehicle or landmark, we felt like a break from this featureless planet.

We trekked 'off piste' to explore. Several more hours, motoring along quite easily in two wheel drive on a compass course, feeling a bit like a ship at sea, some dunes appeared which we had to drive around.

To our concern we noticed that the compass didn't move as we zigzagged thru them. Clearly it was not functioning. Abandoning our search for the monument, but not feeling too worried, we estimated a course to get us back to the main 'piste' and set off to rejoin.

We crossed other tracks engraved into the pebble-covered sand, wondering how long back they might have been made, and what their purpose was. Perhaps from the last war, maybe even the Great War, or maybe someone lost. Those tracks, together with ours, clearly left imprinted in the sand behind us, would remain there for aeons. There was no movement of sand or debris of any kind out here.

Three more hours. No glimpse of anything remotely resembling the main piste. Fighting a twinge of panic, we drove on. Half an hour later we abruptly arrived at the edge of an escarpment which dropped several hundred metres onto another desert plane stretching relentlessly into the shimmering distance.

Had we missed the track? And where were we?

We took a long think. Poring over our map, doing calculations, we retraced our times and speeds of the morning, going over again our dead reckoning. We pondered whether it was possible for there to have been a slight curve to our course, unnoticeable to the eye, as you hear about when people walk in the bush.

An agonising decision had to be made.

Go left and carry on, or right and backtrack.

The cliff edge, with absolutely no landmarks in sight, gave little encouragement. We made calculations about fuel.

Finally we put our money and our lives on going left. Our gut feeling was that the track was still ahead, although the terrible doubt that we might be wrong was undeniable. We made a proviso that if we had not hit the main 'piste' by 300km from where we had started out on the trip that morning, we would turn back and try the other way.

At 290km on the clock, suddenly some tracks marking the outer extremities of the piste. A few more kilometres and we were winding our way down the escarpment, within a whisker of heading back to a grisly fate. It appeared the piste itself had gradually curved away from our original course to make this pass down. We had been travelling more or less parallel to it. The taste of the cost to be lost in the desert was a sobering experience. Our deep sympathies lay with those who had.

Late evening we reached a small oasis called Jafon, just before the hustling, bustling big oasis town of In Salah. Again the wonderful desert hospitality descended. We were invited to join a Taureg family to eat. There were two distinct villages around the oasis pool, one with brown squat houses where the black workforce lived. The larger, painted white, surrounding a burial shrine dating back to the eleventh century, was where the Tuareg landowners lived. We sat and drank tea there in the cool of the evening, moving across to another house later to eat couscous. Two of our hosts brought sand in the laps of their coats, which they poured into a pile in the middle of the room onto which they built a fire with firewood brought from 300km away.

One broke a chicken into mouth-sized bites with his fingers and put a piece at each place. We sat cross-legged on the floor and shared the meal while the old man plied us with pertinent questions he wanted answering about the situation back home. He was particularly interested in the ratios of blacks to whites in Rhodesia and South Africa, and what the work ethic was, expressing his unhappiness with the local workforce from Niger. After a long evening of discourse, we were escorted to sleep on a rug in another room with six others.

They took us on a guided tour of their irrigated gardens in the morning, after which we departed for In Salah, where we were to buy provisions and check in with the prefecture before heading out into the real desert ahead. Traditional Taureg territory, a people impressively adapted to living in this harsh environment.

The People of the Veil, the men, not the women, wearing veils over their faces to protect themselves from evil spirits, descend from the Berber of Lybia. They adapted to camel nomadism and dominated the interior, expertly defending their famous trans-Sahara camel caravan routes.

Formidable fighters, their broadswords were no match for the modern weapons of the French, who subdued and colonised them in the early 20th century, although longstanding feuds with their African neighbours to the south from whom they captured slaves continue to this day. The goal of the Tuareg in modern uprisings is economic and political control of ancestral lands, their never having taken kindly to French colonialism.

Chapter 21

Sahara Sands

Before setting out to cross 'Le Grand Sud', we opted to take a small break from the rigours of travelling at a small restful sounding oasis village shown on our map, Augustinia, some 30km north of the nearby Jafan airfield. Driving straight down the runway, simply a hardened surface strip on the desert, exhilarated to reach 80 kph for the first time since reaching the Sahara, always in 4 wheel drive through soft sand on the vague track across the desert, we arrived at this picturesque little oasis surrounded by date palms—the perfect image.

Planning to have a restful day, reading, writing, washing clothes and generally getting prepared for the big journey ahead, we made a big mistake. A merchant appeared, selling two leather bags which we swapped for two old shirts. For the rest of the day, locals besieged us with everything from chickens to camels. At one point 67 people crowded around us. Towards sunset, we took it in turns to walk up the nearby sand dune and admire the peace and beauty of our surroundings away from the madding crowd below, who lingered well into the night before finally leaving us alone.

The next morning we found two of our jerry cans missing. Some schoolteachers were amongst the first to visit us in daylight. They scoured the village and returned with them.

After a brief shop in In Salah, an hour into the long sandy haul to our next town, Tamanrasset, we found a Citroen Deux Chevaux, the classic Parisian roundabout hopper, driven by a young French couple, hopelessly stuck in the sand. We pulled them out, with ease.

'*Merci beaucoup, merci.*' This was their first encounter with *le sable*. They looked a little worried. Like seasoned desert travellers, we made light of it and assured them they'd be fine.

'*La Deux-chevaux, c'est excellent dans le sable*. No worries, see you later.'

We never did—although we had a high regard for the Deux Chevaux trans Sahara capabilities, but knew they'd be slower and more cautious.

The Sahara, in Arabic, 'The Greatest Desert', is the world's largest. At over 9,000,000 square kilometres (3,500,000 square miles), it covers most of Northern Africa, almost as large as the USA or the continent of Europe. Some of the sand dunes can reach 180 metres (600ft) in height.

Churning along in 4-wheel drive, charged with anticipation, we were beginning to savour the confidence of being in a Land-Rover—the development of this wild continent largely dependent on them and their like. The deep sand was very tough on the vehicle—engine, clutch, gearbox, differentials and half-shafts consistently under heavy strain. There was no cruising, no down hills, just hard pulling all day, always with vehicle laden to capacity, never quite knowing what was ahead or where the next fill up would be. Landy kept going.

The main 'piste' is marked with piles of stone every few kilometres. We drove on the fringes, avoiding the deep ruts caused by the big heavies that ploughed this route. The further into the interior we moved, the less frequent became the marks, until for kilometres we were on compass only (now working again).

The all-metal cab of the landy got very hot with its limited ventilation—engine temperature gauge sitting permanently in the red, cab heater switched to high to draw some heat from the radiator, not adding to our comfort.

That evening we took a celebration joint from our Moroccan hash, causing everything to seem hilariously funny, some reprieve at the end of a long day. A big desert truck passed us as we lazily packed our camp next morning, from which two French Canadian girls unexpectedly jumped down for a chat. They were hitch-hiking to Tamanrasset and accepted our invitation to join us. Perched on the back behind our seats, we set out looking like we were on our way to the beach. Camping that evening they cooked us an excellent meal. 'Loo' arrangements in the huge expanse of nothing but sand and the star-lit night were extended.

We routed through Djanet's amazing rock formations, part of the Ahaggar (or Hoggar, as previously called) ranges—'Cowboy' movie country, with sheer rock pillars rising from the ground hundreds of metres high. Most of the Sahara is not horizon-stretching sand as one imagines, but mountainous, with peaks reaching to 3,400m (11,200ft).

We took a bath in an irrigation canal in the mountain village of Ideles where the Touareg had ingeniously initiated vegetable and rice gardens. The slaves for this project had been brought in from the south hundreds of years earlier and were now totally integrated into the community. We were invited by an older man to join him for tea. He changed considerably in appearance when he removed his veil and put on a white cloak over his blue robe, his bared head under short-cropped hair giving him an added dignity of ancient nobility.

Our usual fan club of kids congregated. They offered to find and kill a chicken for our supper. When we saw them preparing to cut off its head with a rusty knife, we relieved them of that duty. I swiftly put it onto my knee to demonstrate the neat western farm technique where one broke its neck with a smart turn of the wrist, painless and humane—something I'd done hundreds of times on Tim's farm. But the more I snapped and twisted to bring about its demise, the more it clucked contendedly.

Chongololo, so named by us for his ability to appear in the most unlikely places, as is our southern millipede similarly nicknamed, was a bright and amusing youngster. Noting my inept ritualistic approach, he took hold of its head, told me to stand on its feet and hold the body, whereupon a mighty tug of war ensued to decapitate it. In desperation, we finally gave Chongololo back the knife, who slowly put the poor bird out of its misery with some laboured sawing, and then let it go while it spayed everything and everybody with blood, much to the amusement of our young crowd. Two hours of boiling still resembled it to a reinforced washing up cloth.

The mountain pass through to Tamanrasset, frequently finding us in low ratio gears scaling the rocky gradients, weaved its way through spectacular pillars and scenery. Relaxing and servicing the landy in the desert city campsite, a social spot filled with desert travellers and their vehicles in various states of repair, no-one seemed in any great hurry to move on. We decided to experience some real Tuareg stuff and went looking for camels.

'*Allez! Vitement s'il vous plait*! For goodness sakes, Musta, can't we go any faster? Be quicker to walk, man!'

'*Non, non, non!*' was all our excessively cautious guide, Mustafa, would respond.

He insisted on tying our camels and leading us through the vast sandy wastes at a snails pace, when all John and I wanted to do was gallop over the horizon, turbans streaming, Lawrence of Arabia style.

We felt a little out of place in our shorts and open shirts while our guide was covered from head to foot in his blue robe and white veil, although we relished the change from our hot and noisy landy cab.

The camel's pace seemed very leisurely, perched up on the uncomfortable saddle, and John decided to walk for a while. It wasn't long before he found he could not keep up and requested our guide to remount. The stride of a large camel is 3 metres and they move amazingly efficiently through the sand at around 14km/hr (9 mph) without exerting any apparent energy.

Our exasperated badgering finally forced our hapless guide to release us. The camels seemed as delighted as we were with their newly found freedom. Mine picked up its head and charged off with great strides, long neck stretched forward. It was slightly concerning since no advice had been offered as to how we should control them. John's was lagging, the distance between us opening alarmingly, our guide now beside himself with one of his charges way ahead and the other way behind.

Shouting '*Alta, Alta!*' which meant nothing to John other than a hope it might be, 'Go, go!' he was taken by surprise when it promptly took a roll in the sand. John in turn did an impressive parachute military type roll off the saddle. The salutary performance, after

Mustafa's strenuous shouts to get my eager mount to return, resulted in us all being hooked up again onto our guide's tow rope.

We noticed camels walking unattended in the distance. We found out that they came into season in the winter months, when the breeding females and stud males were let out to wander, and find themselves a mate. They would return to their owners after ranging, everybody satisfied. We learned that even while trekking, if a female camel 'in heat' passed a good looking male, the owner was quite entitled to lead his ravening mare(?) up to the excited bull(?) and have them mate. Anytime, any place, no matter what the business was on hand.

The camel arrived in the Sahara around 900 BC from the Middle East, becoming the major transport of the vast sands. The Tuareg ran the Saharan routes, protecting them from raiders, with caravans of up to 12,000 camels taking 3-4 months to cross, carrying salt and manufactured products south to the Ghana and Mali empires, returning with gold, ivory and slaves to the northern Ottoman empire. The European shipping trade that opened with the Portuguese in the 16th Century was the death knell of the harsh and inhospitable Saharan routes.

Midday brought our little caravan to a spindly acacia, Mustafa making a pot of tea with just enough kindling to fill the palm of his hand. This brought the small kettle to boil exactly as the twigs were consumed—neither a calorie of heat nor a gram of precious firewood wasted. The camels munched on the dry looking bushes, happily lapping up the large thorns with their leathery tongues, constantly groaning as though in pain, apparently their equivalent to a cat purring.

Like camel, like guide, we mused.

We arrived at a pretty oasis in the late afternoon, where preparations were being made for a ceremony—some kind of run-up to young men's circumcision. Uncertain of the precedure, we quaffed refreshing mint tea and smoked something that went straight to our heads, and waited to see.

Dancing began. Dust flew, strange music wailed and cries filled the air. A crimson sunset followed, with a crystal night sky shimmering above.

Sahara – camels, water collection & dune walking

Trail through Hoggar Mountains

The women, dressed in black, drummed a slow steady rhythm on steel jerry cans, eerily akin to a heartbeat. They chanted a hoarse grunt in a compelling key that built up in tempo. Others swayed and hummed to the beat.

The men, starting slowly, danced in an inward facing circle, becoming more energetic, jumping and wheeling and ululating. Many collapsed and were carried off, returning as soon as they recovered from a strange ceremony where, surrounded by women in the dark behind the dancers, a knife was drawn across their belly and chest. John and I joined in until we too collapsed in dusty exhaustion. We, however, didn't get the knife ceremony. We slept on the sand as the party ended, waking early in the morning to find others asleep around us.

Encouraged to be heading back by Mustafa, an hour or so into our homeward journey, a beautiful sleek white camel came charging towards us, a fine looking 'Blue' Tuareg carrying a WWII .303 rifle proudly mounted and sitting head and shoulders above our mounts. He was menacingly fierce and exchanged strong words with our guide, gesticulating towards us. We guessed we were in trouble, perhaps about something we did at last night's ceremony. After snarling a deprecating sneer, he charged off in a cloud of dust, our guide shrugged and rode on, leaving us none the wiser. We pictured the terrifying foe such a warrior would make and were thankful he wasn't our enemy, at least in war.

Our now more friendly camel man, bonded in some strange way after this encounter, offered us water from the goatskin hanging by his saddle, which tasted and looked like the goat was still in there. Expressing our thanks, we offered him some of our tinned grapefruit segments, at which he turned his nose up in equal disgust.

That evening, back in camp, a cool breeze whistling through the open canopy of our army green friend stoutly parked beside us, aching limbs and sunburnt arms were good reminders of the swaying saddle and soft padding sounds we had become accustomed to as our shadows passed under us on the two day trail.

It was time to get back on our own trail.

Chapter 22

Flying Landy

'It's a taxi, a London taxi!' John was saying.

Two days into a never ending sea of sand since leaving Tamenrasset, a dot in the shimmering distance did indeed begin to look like a black London cab.

Mirages already? We swigged more water.

'Hello, would you like some tea?' Asked a suntanned English blonde, loosely hung in Arab cotton, brewing tea in a colourful enamel pot, sheltered under the shade of a sarong draped over the two open doors.

'Well, that would be nice, thank you.' Our astonished reply hardly raised her eyebrows.

'Cookies?' Mixed with hashish on a strawberry and flower patterned plate.

Two young men in shorts, one French and one English, emerged from behind the vehicle. They had been repairing a puncture. The seventh that morning, the one hundred and fiftieth that week. We tried not to stare at the amount of baggage they were carrying, their bald tyres, tube covered in patches and worn out hand pump.

Commenting on their foresight to have a big heavy spare gearbox strapped on the roof rack, we gathered they had already replaced the one they had set out with, and this one, jammed in next to boxes of provisions, fuel and water cans, was burned out and awaiting repair.

We nodded sagely and laughed with them, hoping we sounded encouraging, as they told us their destination was Cape Town.

We could not abandon them and spent the rest of the day towing, listening to their London streets automatic gearbox changing up, down, back up, down again as it laboured through the sand. Our fuel gauge was dropping as fast as their box of puncture patches.

'I don't think we're going to make it all the way to Agadez, the next Oasis ahead,' we explained, camping that night. 'Fuel isn't going to last.'

'Cool, Man,' the Englishman replied. 'We'll pick a trucky if we need one, no worries. And thanks for your help so far.'

They had taken three weeks to cover a distance we had done in five days. Quite philosophical, they assured us they had observed enough traffic passing that would assist if they needed. Theirs was a flexi-timetable. We promised to report their problems to the prefecture in Agadez. They promised to look us up in Salisbury on their way through. Parting the next morning, we marvelled at their optimism.

The next stretch was so sandy we had to use our sand ladders—reinforced wire mesh lengths of about two meters. The laborious process required they be laid in the soft sand for each wheel to drive across. Reaching their end, they would be picked up and carried forward for the next two metres.

We imagined the taxi and its inevitable addition to the many abandoned vehicles that were scattered along the route. And wondered at how the three had reckoned they would fare, so ill-equipped for such a trek.

We never saw or heard of them again.

'All done?' I ask. We were sweating over the landy, doing the first oil change of the journey, having camped the night a few miles after crossing the Niger border.

'Yup, ready for the oil.' called John, passing out spanners from under the engine.

'Great. Then we can nip back to that customs post for some water and a wash.'

'Good plan!'

After cleaning up at the fort, we realised we'd lost a spanner and went back to look for it. Not found, we carried on.

Twenty minutes later, another fort appeared surprisingly on the horizon, with some military looking figures whom we asked to confirm our direction.

'Retournez! Retournez!'

It was the same customs post we had just left. We had gone round in a circle. One more sobering experience of how easy it was to get disorientated out here.

Three more days and we began to emerge from the harsh beauty of the desert into the Sahel, a belt of dry tropical savannah with summer rains of average 150mm (6 in) that demarks the southern limit of the Sahara. Precipitation, however, varies strongly from year to year, often coming torrentially after lengthy droughts. We understood this belt of sparse savannah moved south by as much as 50km (30 miles) per year, expanding the Sahara.

There was still no road as such, simply ruts in the soft sand heading roughly in the direction we anticipated. We developed a driving technique to build up speed in the bush verges, where the sand was tighter, maintaining as straight a line as possible through the scrub. On reaching terminal velocity, we'd career back onto the main piste with enough momentum to stay on top of the soft stuff.

Every time a truck came past, or goat, cow or human appeared, we'd have to slow down, then grind our way back onto harder bush sand, charging off again like a float plane trying to lift off the water. It was hard driving, both on the driver and the vehicle.

Our engine temperature still hovering on red the whole time, we'd regularly stop to top up the radiator. We came across a well where hundreds of cattle, goats, donkeys and camels were waiting to be watered. The herdsman had to haul water from 30m down in a huge skin bucket, rope attached to an ox which would slowly walk the distance from the well. The water was then tipped into the surrounding trough for their animals to drink.

It was a long process, with a solemn queue. Our turn looked hours away. We offered to pull up the water with the Land-Rover. After 30 minutes of reversing and forwarding, we had watered all their animals, douched ourselves for commission, and filled our containers.

As we drove, our eyes were peeled for the famous Sahara Cheetah, wild dog, and the illusive addax (Addax nasomaculatus)—a threatened species of large white antelope. Adapted to the desert, they can go for months without drinking, even a whole year, surviving on the moisture gained from browsing and grazing. They are able to track the scent of rainfall, bringing new plant life, over hundreds of kilometres. Closely related to the oryx, it differs from other antelopes by having large square teeth like cattle and lacking facial glands. There are fewer than 500 addax left in the wild.

We didn't see any, most likely as we were so preoccupied with the tricky driving.

'This permit is for a flying machine?' asked the Nigerian immigration official looking at our visa and vehicle documents. So far, we'd got away with it. Had he been watching us through the bush? Well might he have thought our Land-Rover was on its take off run.

'This is a'Tiger Moth' Land-Rover,' we tried to convey, 'now crossing by land.' Our devious explanation was to no avail, nor did we like the idea of bribing. We needed fuel, but there were alternatives.

Some dreadlock 'guides' whispered that there was no need to cross here, and that once headed east for Lake Chad, we could simply cut down one of the many unofficial routes that led into Nigeria for fuel.

A jaunty dash some 100km (60miles) further on into Nigerian territory to fill our tanks at the risk of being arrested, topped up the adrenalin. It was good to speak English again to the man in the street, the first time since leaving England.

Without having to explain our Tiger Moth Land-Rover to anyone else, we continued to Maine, fighting a constant headwind of white dust, the Armattan, a layer of ancient fish bones dried out from the days Lake Chad covered a large section of the Sahara.

'Can we help?' we asked two guys broken down in their jeep station wagon.

'Yeah, man. Know anything about turbos?'

'No, you'll need a *fundi* (expert) for that. Wanna lift back into Maine?'

'Think I'm crazy, man, 'n' find nothin' but a chassis when we get back?'

We drove back into Maine to alert the police of their problem, leaving the phsycho with his vehicle. On our way back, roughly following the track we'd taken the first time round, we spotted our Michelin map, which had blown out of the cab, lying in the bush. We would have sorely missed that. A good turn . . .

A few miles before arriving at the lake shore village and fishing port of Nguigmi, we crossed a large sand dune and came down into the more humid air surrounding Lake Chad—the first smell of moisture since leaving the Mediterranean. Better than fresh flowers.

The lake was continually receding, leaving swampy shores and battalions of mosquitoes. The great expanse of water remaining was no deeper than two metres at any point. The local boats were made of papyrus, which became water logged over a period of time, until they sank. I'd seen a few ships like that. Voyage planning was crucial to avoid a long swim home.

'Too late. Bizness finished today. 'Oliday a demain (tomorrow)' we were being informed by the Chad Consulate.

'Ou est la maison de le Consul?' We asked brokenly.

'Non, pas possible.' The official sternly warned.

And that ended that. All business was closed for a two day holiday Nor would we be able to take the short cut south round the lake through Nigeria because of our visa problem. More frustrating hours were spent trying to get permission to drive round to the north of the lake. While negotiating with a guide to show us the way, we met up with a weathered Frenchman camping on the shores.

He had been driving around French Africa for three years in an ancient Dodge Power Wagon, together with his family and all his life's accompaniments, including a kitchen sink. His wife patiently settled down amidst swarms of mosquitoes to cook the evening meal and help their 12 year-old daughter with her school lessons. He prepared to set off on his inflatable raft with rifle and fishing rod.

We were looking for a guide, we answered him on his questioning. He gave us the French shrug.

'Too far from de lak, le sable seulement, oui? Alors, too near, 'u are in ze mud, non? Pas de probleme—le geeede non necessaire!'

'C'est ca!'

We got the message. With this cheery bit of common sense that the route round the lake would be obvious, we relaxed for the day, tried fishing—unsuccessfully—what is it about fishing?—washed some clothes and just lay around talking with the French family and their fascinating time out. We watched some Tuareg bring their horses and themselves down for a wash. They swam with them, naked, before rolling them in the sand, re-saddling, re-robing, and riding away.

Setting off at dawn the next day for what our prospective and now abandoned guide had informed us would be a hazardous and arduous week's trek—the Frenchman thought a day—we watched an ominous cloud ahead. The dark brown heaviness descended like an avalanche, stinging sand flying parallel to the ground, building up on the windscreen. We could see no further than 10m. Unable to drive on, we watched Tuareg leading their camels past, only a slit for their eyes remaining exposed in their blue headgear. Our respect rose again for that blue robe and veil, so ideal for these conditions.

After struggling across a particularly large sand dune, in low ratio 4-wheel drive, making several attempts at 'running up' sections, we arrived in Mao, the capital of the Kanem region in central Chad. We found a small eating-place with excellent salad and chicken. Talking to the owner, an elderly Mohammed, about the Hajj trail to Mecca, he explained how it had led its way through Mao in the earlier part of the century. They now simply flew overhead. His view was that the status symbol of attending these days almost exceeded the religious tradition.

Mohammed introduced us to the owner of an ailing Fiat truck we'd come across travelling from Ideles back in Algeria, and had seen several times since.

'Aaahh, merci, merci beaucoup. Le Fiat, c'est bon, non?' He longed for news of its progress.

'Non, pas bon, monsieur. Gear box une grande probleme!' We had gathered that much from the driver.

'Oiu? Mon Dieu!'

He was grateful for this updated report and despatched a mechanic to find and fix it.

Fort Lamy was only ten hours driving ahead, a miraculous reduction on the guide's prophesied week's travelling.

Aiming to mitigate our arriving without permission from the Chad authorities, and to clear our visas for the Congo, we drove into the night hoping to arrive in time for business at Fort Lamy the next day and to tie in with the arrival of the cross lake ferry. Our lights weren't up to it. Nor was our ailing gearbox after all the deep sand. A couple of potholes nearly bounced us out of the cab, punishing the suspension severely. Narrowly missing landing a gazelle on the bonnet finally stopped us, to camp for the night. Nervous of 'shifta' bandits reputedly in the area, we slept with our pangas (big jungle slashing knives) under our pillows.

'Apologeese, ze consul 'az left for ze weekend. Retournez a Lundi.'

So what was unusual about that, at 10.00 on Friday morning!

Open on Monday! Now the whole weekend in Fort Lamy.

We got chatting to a resident over a beer and were advised against seeking permission in arrears for having arrived from the north. The Nigerian ferry from across the lake would disembark a large crowd later in the day. This would be a good opportunity to surreptitiously join their ranks queuing for immigration.

Thanks to the hot afternoon and the obscurantist language barrier that we put up to all their questions, we were at last stamped as 'arrive'.

Next stop, Fort Archembault.

We arrived at midnight, setting up camp in the town square. Awaking to a delightful small town with well-spaced buildings and big trees lining the streets, we were reminded of our Salisbury back home in its early days.

We sought out Claude Vasselet, a professional hunter whose brother we'd met in the Sahara, whose town base was filled with Land-Rovers and desert type vehicles. A house with a large all-round veranda sat in the middle of it. As we were chatting, his wife Lindy, a wild and glamorous Australian about half his age, came tearing in behind the wheel of another open Land-Rover, nearly running us all down.

'Of course, you weell stay wiz us at ze 'unting bateau, oui? Lindy, she 'as prepared it for you,' Invites Claude over a cold frothing glass of beer.

'Great. Thank you, Claude. We've got a bit of a gearbox problem to sort out before we head on, though.'

'Lindy, will you attend to zis?' He looks across at his dashing wife.

Wow! Is she the mechanic as well?

'No worries. Guillem'll get ya roight.'

Lindy got into top gear again, speeding us down to the local Land-Rover wizard who helped us strip the gearbox and readjust our 2nd and 1st gears. Just as we were climbing naked out of the river after a good wash, Lindy arrived to pick us up to go shopping.

Their houseboat was moored on the river that ran between Chad and the Central African Republic. Claude advised against crossing the border behind them into their concession in the C.A.R. and gave us a guide to the bank opposite the houseboat from where we swam across the river.

'Flatties (Crocs)? Noa, they won't bother you!' Lindy assured us, 'Long as ya're quick!'

We stayed on their boat for three days, game viewing, hearing stories about Bongo trophies and their radical clients, and crazy times during the revolution when Claude had been attacked and thrown in jail for resisting.

On our way again, we followed winding forest tracks—the main roads in this part of the continent—encountering frequent police roadblocks. They regarded our military looking Land-Rover with increasing suspicion, often demanding we unload everything, and searching every pot and piece of kit we had.

'Laissez le seat, oui! Ve Eenspect le cussions . . . you 'av weepons?' fiery eyed soldiers and furiously eager customs men asked, again and again.

'Non, we 'ave no weepons.'

We tried hard to remain matter of fact. Reinserting the foam rubber cushions was getting easier after the last soldier broke the zip. We watched some New Zealanders get badly knocked about when these ill-trained soldiers mistook their climbing equipment for weapons.

At Lisala on the Congo river, we met up with an overland company, Siafu, named after the East African travelling ants, moving with three Land-Rovers, and who had experienced similar misery. A New Zealander, Lizzie Hope (little did I know she was to become my future safari assistant) was amongst them.

We'd all had enough of roadblock hassles and decided on the steamer that plied the river from the coast every fortnight, and due to arrive in three days time. We booked to Kisangani (old Stanleyville), some four days steaming up river, cutting out at least two weeks road travel.

Our humour returned. We found our usual crowd of local folk curiously surrounding our camp the next morning. Starting the engine, we dashed for the bush with our hands over our ears, as if it was about to explode—a greatly successful ploy. With the screams of a hundred people echoing down the road, we sauntered back to cook porridge. An old man whose house was nearby was highly amused and offered us pineapples, insisting we park our Land-Rover in one of his outhouses for the next night.

To pass the time we visited a palm oil factory. Straight out of the last century, unprotected belts and wheels flew in every direction. Precipitous steel steps covered with oil, hissing steam pipes and strong hot smells filled the dark corners. By mid-morning, we were downing a beer with the manager and engineer, both of whom were clearly quite content with the state of affairs in the factory.

Their forester friend, Francois, joined us. Apparently, the serious work of the day was over. Many beers later, Francois suddenly jumped up, and, calling for us to follow, leapt into his blue jeep and tore off, making indistinguishable hand signals as he went which we then discovered related to huge potholes in the road.

We thought the forest must be on fire at the speed we were racing.

Following as best we could on the winding plantation tracks, we reached his home deep in the woods, where he pulled out more beers and insisted we were his guests for the night.

He was clearly a master of his trade, and also the mechanic for all the tractors and machinery, using a modified doctor's stethoscope to diagnose his engines. The spare parts warehouse was indicated by pieces of Caterpillar equipment scattered around the house. The following day he showed us some of the timber they pulled out. *Mbangi, mbola, mongola* and the huge *titola*, more than two and a half metres in diameter. He'd been running the operation since 1935, had thirteen children with his Congolese wife, two of whom were taking degrees in Belgium.

Back in Lisala and biding our time with the old man in his shed, the steamer arrived. Three huge barges lashed end on, each some 50m long. We discovered we'd have to load the Land-Rovers and stay on the front one, the ship's 3rd Class, cargo holds covered by big wooden hatches on which travellers bought a ticket that allowed them 1 sq m of deck space. We were to be permitted more, thanks to the Land-Rovers.

The next barge down, 2nd Class, had tin shanties that housed flea ridden bunks in between the cargo holds, inhabited by the mobile river village with all the life you'd expect to find in an African urban village, including the chickens and goats. In the rear, pushing us all, was 1st Class, a motorised barge, housing the bridge, restaurant, bar, air conditioned cabins with the wealthy Congo businessmen, and the captain.

There was only one loading ramp. We manoeuvred the craft, shouting directions via 'callers' to the bridge, about 100m downstream, to fit the ramp so two vehicles (six of them all told in our party) could be loaded between the cargo hatches. Every time the ship moved to reposition, everybody thought it was leaving and the gangplanks we were trying to drive up would be crammed with screaming people fighting to get on board. Finally loaded after an entire morning's performance, we formed a laager with the Land-Rovers within which we made our camp.

Surrounded by seemingly mounds of bodies, goats, chickens, dried fish and roasted monkeys, with associated *katundu,* even make-shift shops, crowded into each square metre of deck space, security was on our mind.

With many hoots of the horn and much palaver and shouting, we finally set sail, some of the passengers clearly still left ashore, in spite of all. As we steamed, at around 6 knots, pushing a substantial bow wave, locals would paddle out in their dugout *mokoros* to sell smoked monkeys (looking horribly like human babies), vegetables, fruit and fish, and anything else they could rake up. *Mokoro* crews, now buying beads, jewellery and the beautiful woven cloths bought up by the traders from the coast, would spend some hours socialising on-board, drinking a good deal of the brews for sale in drums on the deck and sampling other more delicate wares being sold by the coastal women that festooned the 2nd Class shanties.

Come time to leave, their *mokoros* tied alongside were inevitably wallowing in water, flooded by the ships waves. Owners would jump in, invigorated by their erstwhile activities, and enthusiastically bale with any container at hand, even their paddles, often into the *mokoro* next to them. Amidst much shouting and gesticulating, they would be untied, when their bows would drop dramatically, always catching them unawares and throwing everyone off balance. They would jump to their paddles in a furious manner to avoid being caught up with other *mokoros* tied further down, often several abreast, and the formidable bow wave thrown by the ship. Needless to say, casualty capsizes, of which there were many, were left to fend for themselves.

On the second day a rumble brewed on board and we found ourselves caught in the middle. Suddenly, as these things tend to erupt, a man pulled a machete and slashed through a rope holding down one of the Land-Rovers. Unbelievably, our immediate neighbours seemed intent on pushing our Land-Rovers into the river. We were fighting for survival. Thankfully, whistles blew and a contingent of the ship's gendarmerie arrived, with truncheons swinging.

A message arrived from the Captain, inviting us back to his barge to discuss the issue. He received our contingent in his sumptuous cabin with some Dutch gin, together with a former captain turned trader, an interesting Greek, offering their regrets at such behaviour from his 3rd class passengers.

'My appologiees, mes amis, ze turd class pazengurs, zey apparentlee deedn't kno 'ow much you paye for ze Land-Rovers. Zey wur worried you 'ad so much accomodasion space. Now, we 'av explained, and removed ze worriers. All is okay. You 'av no more worries. Be assured.'

Congolese nyangas

**Papyrus canoe on
Lake Chad**

**Ferry up
the Congo
River**

Good to know. We spent a pleasant hour drinking and talking with the trader captains in their mahogany lined wardroom. Escorted back, we found everybody around us very friendly again. The rest of the party described how the Gendarmerie had 'encouraged' order while we were gone. And carried a few bodies away. We now had a guard to ensure a 'bon voyage' for the remainder of the trip.

Stops were made at night when great searchlights mounted on the bridge endeavoured to path-find between the many islands. Other stops were at riverside villages when crowds of people, unfamiliar with the ship's geography, would trample through our space with baskets of fish and roasted monkeys, shouting salaams to those ashore. As dawn lit, large ladies, colourfully attired, sprawled around our camp, castles of *katundu* alongside them.

During the day these ladies would appreciate sitting on one of our vacant camp beds and chatting to us. They would take a great interest in our goods packed in the back of the vehicles, certain they must be for sale. Elsewhere on the boat, two thieves were caught red handed, causing great excitement when one of them jumped overboard. No rescuers. Two of our jerry cans were found by the mate, who assured us the culprit was handcuffed to the guardrail.

All a refreshing change to bumping along dusty tracks and arguing our way through roadblocks.

When we docked early on the last morning, Kisangani's cranes looked alarming. Mangled and teetering on the edge of the quay, close to collapsing into the river. Apparently a drunken driver had driven down the track with his crane swinging round and round, crashing into others. We were going to supervise the off-loading of our vehicles very carefully.

'*Non, s'il vous plait, non* that way. This side, *please!*' shouted Andy, leader of Siafu, as his forward-control Land-Rover hung perilously over the river.

'*Pardon?*' responded the crane director, continuing to swing it in an arc outboard of the ship and the quay. Our directions to the crane man misunderstood, or ignored, the next Siafu Land-Rover crunched into our roof canopy. We counted ourselves lucky for only that.

Back on the road, next stop Uganda.

Chapter 23

Mountains of the Moon

We'd heard gold was a good buy in the Congo, so John and I made a diversion from the Siafu convoy with a mind to improving our abysmal trading record. Our enquiries led us down a dirt road into a village hidden in a valley. Some big guys in shiny suits met us outside 'Jo's Place'. Escorted through myriad rooms in low lighting, partitioned by flimsy curtains behind which who knew what went on, down worse lit steps into a cellar, we meet Big Jo. He sat motionless behind a huge polished desk, with bigger, meaner looking guys surrounding him, shaven heads gleaming in the flickering light of a naked bulb.

'How much you want?' Big Jo doesn't spend much time on introductions.

John and I look at each other. We are not sure how much 'How much' is? We hadn't a clue even what gold looked like.

'Uurh, could we see some, please?' We tentatively ask.

A coca-cola bottle full of gold dust is banged onto the table before us.

We pick it up, feel the weight, pour a little into our hands, smell it. The price is considerable.

John and I look at each other again. How easy it would be to set us up. Stage a road block on the road out of this valley . . . government agents search, find and confiscate . . .

What then?

We commend him on the quality and say we would like to go outside and discuss 'how much?'

Big Jo is unimpressed. He flicks his hand, heaves a grunt, two big boys escort us out.

Climbing into the Land-Rover, me looking into our well-travelled brief case as though searching for money, smiling at our escort, John matter-of-factly starting up and indicating he would like to move the vehicle. Our underpowered Sahara worn diesel landy does its best attempt at a 'wheely', and they don't see us again for dust and smoke as we disappear back up that trail.

Ended the gold bartering chapter.

We head for the Uganda border to catch up with the others, driving hard along the way we'd been shown way. The road got progressively worse. It's Easter, Good Friday. Most people are in church. Towards evening we reached a small town where a military man guards a building.

'Bonsoir, Monsieur. C'est le direction pour Ooganda, oui?' We cheerfully ask.

He looked sympathetically disappointed.

'Non, non, non. Retournez! Oooganda!' He shouts and points back the way we had come.

That 'retournez' word again!

Not only were we on the wrong road, but getting back to the correct one we'd have to back track 80 tough kilometres. Already sore from the days bumping in our hot metal cab, it wasn't easy to contemplate the deep muddy ruts and broken bridges back along the trail. Our stakes were at a sad low as we bartered with a lorry driver late that night for fuel, finally finding the convoy camped by the road in the early hours of the morning.

We'd heard that traffic was sometimes held up for weeks at the mud holes on the road to Beni and the border, where 'truck villages' would sprout, flourishing with shabeens, concubines and everything in between, blocking all vehicle movement. Our plan was to circumnavigate them in a four-wheel drive convoy through the jungle. Ropes attached to each vehicle, our rugged little jeep in the lead, we got through and camped that night below snow capped peaks of the Rwenzori mountains, the famous 'Mountains of the

Moon', so called thanks to their surreal blue tinge that strangely enveloped them in the moonlight.

All next day we travelled through unattractive thorn scrub, designated as game reserve, although no game was to be seen. The Uganda border sat on a watershed amongst hills overlooking a colourful rolling landscape, marred only by a collection of human skulls by the road.

The Uganda customs officials were friendly, in smart uniforms and spoke good English. Could this be the old perimeter of the British Empire, approaching professional? The sensation was soon dismissed as the immigration officer, clearly bored to tears, waxed poetic rhymes with our names.

'A Mr Fynn, with a grin, walked through my door.

I see my life can surely be no longer such a bore!'

Different. After further lyrical extolling of the tourist delights of Uganda, we were happily on our way out the customs house that we had rather dreaded from earlier rumours we'd heard.

Suddenly the mood changed.

'Butten your shert!' A police officer standing outside ordered me.

'I beg your pardon?' I asked in amazement.

A menacing deranged-looking officer with blood shot eyes, hands hovering over a pistol, barred my way. I buttoned my shirt.

The joviality of the immigration officer was replaced by surly military men surveying our equipment. The chief police officer, his shirt barely containing his generous paunch, was counting out bullets in front of us as he handled a rifle. We were summonsed to parade next to our vehicles.

'Keep correctly to our law, mind you own business and be very cautious how you photograph while you are in our country—ignorance is no excuse!' he barked. We knew that included paying deferential homage to his Excellency, President Idi Amin. 'The last king of Scotland' slaughtered more people than Macbeth dreamed of.

'Now you may go. Enjoy yourselves.' He waived us on. Leaving as fast as we could, we would certainly be very cautious with any military we might meet during our transit.

We split up from Siafu, who headed out on their itinerary towards Nairobi, while we wanted to find the gorillas. Driving along the edge of Lake Edward, thunderclouds banked in the sky ahead. Rain began pelting down as we passed a football match, spectators holding up plastic bags and sheets, wild animals quietly grazing nearby.

'We're home, Johno!' This was the Africa we knew so well. Trundling along, our emotions were heightened by elephant, buffalo, hippo and antelope, peacefully enjoying their green munch after the rains.

'Yup. Isn't it good.' The wide grin across John's sunburned face said it all.

We downed some celebratory beers in the Lake Hotel that evening, and got talking with a local rancher.

'Under cattle management, this land yields ten shillings an acre (around one US dollar at that time); under game ranching fifteen. Forty under tourism.'

'Tourism, huh?'

Cogs were beginning to turn as I contemplated the future in Africa.

The gorillas were to be found on the Ugandan side of those legendary 'Mountains of the Moon', as described by Ptolemy in his first map of the world back in the 2nd century BC. Rwenzori, 'The King of Mists' as it translates locally, are the centre of the Eastern Afromontane Hotspots, incorporating widely scattered, but biogeographically similar mountain ranges in eastern Africa, stretching from Saudi Arabia and Yemen in the north to Zimbabwe in the south. It harbors more endemic mammals, birds, and amphibians than any other region in Africa, and stretches in three ancient massifs across more than one million kilometers.

Many of these massifs are volcanic in origin. The Albertine Rift includes the still-active Virunga Volcanoes where more than half of the world's remaining mountain gorillas live. This volcanic and seismic activity was caused by the separation of the African and Arabian tectonic plates resulting in the formation of the Great Rift Valley system that runs from Israel to Mozambique.

The geological turmoil that created the mountains of these hotspots also resulted in some of the world's most remarkable lakes, including Lake Tanganyika (second-deepest lake on the planet, 1,471 metres), Lake Albert, Lake Tana and Lake Malawi. A vast diversity of freshwater fish, some 600 species, is found in them. Some think their waters are interconnected through deep channels in the earth's crust.

Though geographically disparate, the mountains comprising these hotspots have remarkably comparable flora, changing similarly with altitude. Typically, a zone of bamboo is often found between 2,000 and 3,000 meters, above which flourishes the *Hagenia Abisynica* forests, the gorilla country, comprising a dense brush near the ground and an open canopy of trees 20–30m overhead, up to 3,600 meters ASL.

At the highest elevations, in such as the Rwenzori Mountains, Aberdares, Mt. Elgon, Mt. Kilimanjaro, Mt. Kenya, and the Bale and Simien Mountains of Ethiopia, Afro alpine vegetation occurs above 3,400 metres. This is characterized by the presence of the strange giant senecios (*Dendrosenecio* spp.) and giant lobelias (*Lobelia* spp.), so huge they leave man dwarfed as in a goliath garden.

We wanted to see some of this, hoping also to sight some of Africa's glaciers, unusually situated on the equator. Naively ill equipped for such exploration, compounded by our traditional notion that we never needed any such luxuries as a guide, we locked up the Land-Rover, put on our unaccustomed boots, and set off for the clouding peaks above us. After the months of sitting in the Landy, our walking rhythm took a bit of getting into. The path was steep and rose rapidly out of a belt of bamboo into thick forest with 'old man's beard' hanging in haunting drapery, Blue and Colobus monkeys with white mantles swinging alongside us. Rivers rushed in steamy gorges below, turacos darted through dense vegetation, our eyes peeled for long-eared owls and tree hyrax.

Arriving at the climber's refuge, we collapsed on the edge of a precipitous gorge with breathtaking views back down our day's climb. Two smoky hours later, coaxing wet wood to cook our steaks on, we hardly noticed the hard wooden board bunks as we fell into in an exhausted sleep.

Highway between Ethiopia & Kenya

Ruwensuri climb

Siafu looking for a camping spot

In a brisk dawn next day, another laboriously smoky cup of tea while drinking in the magnificent scenery, we followed the path on up to cross an icy river, waded through freezing cold marshes and on to a ridge where another great range opened before us. A waterfall cascaded down a hundred-metre drop across the valley. Vast views of vegetation continued up into the clouds. But no giant Lobelia, clearly considerably higher. Our resources would not see us through another night.

Disappointed in our lack of fitness and preparation, we crashed back down the path at a great pace to make base by nightfall. No game was to be seen following the rampant poaching we gathered had plagued the area during the last few years.

The next evening's camp was just outside the Murchison Falls Park. We picked up a lion calling half a mile to the east, and another to the south. Elephants were browsing a few hundred metres away and came down to the waterhole, clearly visible in the moonlight. Hyenas howled as we sipped our whisky, the stars glimmering against a clean sky. It had been a long time since we had listened to these sounds of the wild. We stashed our *pangas* under the camp beds and slept on top of the landy.

'Couldn't we be on that side?'—on the tourist launch up the Victoria Nile, a large lady, loaded with optical equipment and backed by an equally loaded and sweating husband, whined to the Ugandan coxswain, eyeing the crocs lying like giant lizards on the opposite bank.

'It can be dangerous, and the river is shallow that side, Ma'am' he politely responded. Doing an excellent job, we thought.

'Well, there's nothin' over hier,' she complained.

He obliges. Minutes later, the 10m steel boat heaves, as a hippo hits the bottom, hard. We find we're jammed against the bank, where a 5m croc lies, mouth wide open, exactly at deck level to our open sided boat. The guide extricates us from the bank and manoeuvres back to the other side. Big crocs and their appetites are legendary here. His Excellency apparently made regular use of them to feed on his opponents. The fat lady didn't ask again.

Back on the road in the Park, spotting a leopard in some thicket, I drove in to have a better look, much to John's concern who was sitting on the bonnet staring down into its eyes. We displaced a family of elephant from under a good-looking campsite tree and cooked our evening meal, with them nonchalantly continuing to browse close by. The night was filled with their eating noises and more hyena and lions calling.

Leaving at first light next morning, we stopped further on to cook our porridge, watching eleven lion stalking a herd of buffalo. The buffalo spotted them, the lions' camouflage letting them down in the green plains, and chased them from their ambush positions.

Beside a lake for lunch, two young bull elephants were browsing, moving towards the landy. They suddenly noticed us and made a small mock charge. John, reading on the back platform, jumped behind the wheel and was driving off with me on the bonnet still eating my sandwich. He stopped, sheepishly, a few metres on. The elephant were back to grazing, swinging leg against trunk to pull the grass out, knocking off the soil from the roots like any good gardener, delicately placing the specimen into their mouths.

The campsites improved every night. Next was on a huge river, roaring rapids throwing waves of leaping water, the sun fighting a bloody battle with dark storm clouds over a palm treed island downstream. With deep peace in the surrounding turbulence of nature, we slept soundly. In no hurry to leave the next morning, hidden from passing traffic by a steep bank, we caught up on some relaxing—washing, reading and writing.

Dropping in for tea at the Tororo hotel on our way to the Kenya border, we saw His Excellency, braded up in white uniform, coming out from his white convertible Cadillac parked at the door. Morbidly fascinating. Like staring at a black mamba.

'Fancy finding you here?' We met up again with Siafu on the Equator. 'Thought we'd got rid of you guys.' quipped Lizzie.

'Yah, well. Shit happens.' We laughed, enjoying the coincidence of bumping into them, unplanned. We travelled on and camped together in Nairobi, sending a runner to pick up all our mail at the 'Poste Restante'.

My sister Jane was getting married. She had asked me to 'give her away' in Dad's absence. I needed to fly home for the occasion, the first one in the family to take this meteoric step. John stayed on in Nairobi to wait for me.

We had a great wedding at the family cottage in Nyanga, welcoming Richard Calder, an ex RAF fighter pilot turned accountant, into the family. Unbeknown to us all, the curtain on deeply disturbing times was about to lift on the Rhodesian scene.

Most folk were committed to seeing the political upsets through, and hoped, uncertainly, for a congenial negotiated solution. This was to change into a commitment to fight a long and bloody guerrilla war, by our account defending the bastion of good governance and Christian honesty, by the other side's, fighting for their independence, impatient at the slow pace of democracy.

For me—there was a Land-Rover waiting in Nairobi.

Chapter 24

Ethiopian Thorns

On returning to Kenya, I found John and our army green friend in good shape. He'd serviced her from bumper to bumper, and done pretty much the same to the Nairobi social scene. Time to head out.

Fostering a particular interest in Ethiopia for some years, John had taken part in several expeditions mounted during his time in England to this wild and mysterious land. He had followed the 1868 British Magdala Expedition, which had been mounted by Queen Victoria in retribution against the Ethiopian king Theodorus of the time, who had locked up the British Consul for not delivering messages to his Queen in a timely fashion.

The expedition had set out from India with 208 ships, 55,000 troops, 44 elephants, and included building 20km of railway line and supplying the engine and carriages to move this army through some particularly rough terrain.

It was the first British Army expedition ever to be properly documented, and had carried a camera, for which twenty men and two wagons were set aside to transport. The pictures had to be sent back, in glass plate, to Edinburgh for developing, still held in Oxford today.

Another momentous story he researched was the vanquishing of the Italian occupation of Ethiopia in early WWII. British and South African forces built a road from the Omo river plains, sitting at 600m, through the hitherto impassable Kaffa range of mountains, up to the highlands, near Jimma, south of Addis Ababa, at 3000m. The Italians, great road builders themselves, never imagined it possible. The Allies invaded and took the country through this road.

During his Nairobi stay, John concluded that we'd incurred too few dents on our expedition Land-Rover—it still looked like new. This led to a decision that had us heading out to look for that pass through the Kaffa Mountains, unused since the Allied invasion of 1948.

Loaded with basic provisions we reckoned we might need for a month, mostly fuel, we drove north, past the famous 'flamingo' lakes on the way. Coming over a ridge down to Lake Hannington, clouds of steam rose into the air from the numerous geysers, thousands of the pink birds wading amongst them.

Flamingos filtrate algae, a diet that includes carotenoid pigment (as in carrots), which gives them their pink colour, which intensity apportioned their attractiveness to their opposite sex. Unlikely we could make a similar claim in respect to the red dust covering ourselves.

We spent the night in a camp belonging to John, an African scientist, who was surveying the lake to find the centre of heat for a generator to be lowered into. Amusing and good company, his delightful camp used bucket showers filled with hot water from the geysers. Not a mosquito buzzed as the soda content of the lake dealt with that problem. Nothing survived there other than algae and flamingos.

On through Lake Baringo, to the west of magnificent Mt Kenya, and the spectacular Rift Valley scenery, we set eyes for the first time on the Northern Frontier District (NFD) deserts. The small rains were breaking and we drove through a swollen river up to the door handles, camping on its banks in the moonlight, lulled to sleep with the sound of the rising, swirling water. It came up another metre by the time we went to bed, and had subsided again when we woke in the morning.

Carrying messages continued to be one of our roles, and a great way to meet the local community. We now had one from chief John, whom we'd met back near lake Hannington (now Bogoria), to Major Jesu of the Nginyang Kenyan army base, picking up many more from the Lakori Mission station for the Lodwar mission ahead.

The missionaries gave us useful information about the route, and warnings to cross with caution the main river feeding Lake Rudolph (now Turkana), the Turkwell, which had a reputation for swallowing cars.

The NFD was harsh and dry, its scattered acacia providing scant shade for cattle and hardy herders. The timeless Turkana walked the tracks we were driving, friendly and dignified in manner.

Reaching the Turkwell, we found it in torrent 80m wide, the drift awash. We weren't sure how deep. Walking across, arms clenched so as our feet followed the wheel tracks, we tested the riverbed, the current hopefully strong enough to keep crocs away. Nothing deeper than our thighs.

We prepared the landy by removing its fan belt to avoid the fan becoming a propeller. There would be enough cooling from the water swirling past. Doors came off to allow the river to flow straight through and reduce its pushing force downstream. John went back to the other side to take photos. We trusted they would not be the last of the landy. On signal, I headed out into the river.

Neither of us had forded such a torrent before and I made an early mistake—not to take into account the inevitable drift the vehicle would experience. By pointing slightly upstream, one would crab across on track, a bit like landing an aeroplane in a cross wind.

In no time I was way below the route John and I had carefully waded. Trying to get back on course I was almost heading upstream, a wave of river flowing over the bonnet, not to mention the water streaming through the cab. The front wheels sank into such a deep hole that the vehicle swung down river, floating like a boat, nose down. The engine coughed—John still photographing us disappearing down the current.

Incredibly, with no 'snorkle', the engine kept spluttering, and thanking Land-Rover for their diesel engines that clearly operated under-water, the front wheels gripped again, bringing us back towards the other bank. Like a landing on the Normandy beaches, water pouring from everywhere, cheers from John and me, and the watching naked Turkana greeting our arrival on the opposite side. They were full of praise for the machine that could brave the river that had eaten several lesser machines in the past weeks.

Crossing rivers – African style

Ruwensuri

Turkana River

Omo Mountains

It took us the rest of the day to dry everything out, change oils, strip and clean alternator and starter, drain and strain the fuel tank. Watched closely by our admiring Turkana, we were only too happy we still had it all.

Our camps always attracted an uninhibited crowd of spectators, observing our every move, inspecting every item, curious as to what was in each container we opened. Nothing was sacred, privacy just not being in their vocabulary, even lavatorial excursions. Nor was there any thievery.

A young man carefully scrutinised every knob and dial on our impressive machine, fingering the sand mats and our Sahara goat 'water' skin hanging on the side. Sitting in the driver's seat and swinging the wheel, he experimented with everything short of starting it and taking a test drive.

Suddenly we heard a cry and another, who had been inspecting the front bumper and our good looking rope wound round that, jumped back with a look of astonished surprise on his face. Others crowded towards him. We leapt across. Snake, dangerous insect? Or maybe pressed or pulled the wrong something? Cautiously moving forward again, the tribesman peered into our wing mirror. Astonished to see his reflection. Soon all our spectators were crowding the mirror to get a glimpse of these little men we kept in this small flat thing sticking up on the fender.

We delivered our messages around isolated Lodwar, where Kenyatta, Kenya's first President, had been confined during the Mau Mau rebellion. A Mission station, run by an order of Irish nuns, graciously allowed us to camp in their grounds. One of them, exquisitely beautiful, though declining our advances to convert her to Land-Roverism, joined us to watch a Turkana dance that night.

The women, naked from the waist up, jumped up and down to the men's chanting and clapping. Then a man would dart out and look like he was about to abscond with one there and then, before retreating with much laughter and shrill ululating.

The Irish community were highly amusing, grandly unpretentious and wonderfully generous, sharing their prodigious knowledge about the Turkana and the area. One of the nuns piloted the mission Cessna, flowing robes and all, expertly getting airborne in the heat of the day by bouncing off a convenient termite mound in the runway.

They kindly allowed us to purchase some fuel and we made for Ferguson's Gulf on the Lake, effectively the end of the road system. Slowly bumping and grinding along the alternatively sandy and muddy lakeshore, we gave lifts to the Turkana, who expressed marvel and terror at our great speed, a maximum of 30kph.

At the top end of the lake, we set a compass course for Todenyang, the last Kenyan police post, on the border of Ethiopia. Blue mountains on the Ethiopian escarpment hovered on the distant horizon, cradling our most exciting and uncertain adventure of the entire journey.

There were conflicting stories about what we might expect at the border post. We had avoided official permissions for our trip, fearing time consuming and inevitably expensive sessions with the authorities.

30km crossing the grassy plains brought us to the Todenyang police post, who dashed to their defence positions with machine guns and ammunition boxes, weapons levelled at us approaching. On seeing our un-military attire, one opened the gate, through which we rolled shouting "Jambo" in exchange for salutes from the guards. Formalities were few once packets of tea and sugar were received. Paperwork nil. Noting advice from the captain about the Ethiopian's dubious practices, we drove on across the border in the direction they indicated.

Towards evening we spotted a village sporting a flag pole on the horizon. A jovial captain in huckleberry hat ran the Ethiopian police camp and border post. The officers' Roman features and well-spoken English fascinated me, the first time for me to meet these in Africa.

'We are getting used to you tourists. Two years ago, another expedition with two white men in a Land-Rover came through to explore our Omo Reserve.' They explained after hearing our story.

One of them drew a dramatic flower on the ground with a stone, tracing each petal showing how the vehicle had driven out and around, and back to the centre, and then off again as he outlined a second petal, and back, until finally, he screwed the stone into the centre of the flower.

'They vanished, never to be seen again.'

He described how they found the Land-Rover, deserted, out of fuel. Their verdict on our mission . . . ?

'Very sorry. We don't want more lives on our hands. You may not proceed.'

Not easily deterred, we camped with them, intending to befriend and change their minds in the course of time. We moved the landy to a shady tree to strip and service our starter motor which was still giving trouble after the Turkwell crossing.

'Don't worry, we are quite used to tourists.' They commented again as they helped to push us. We talked with them as we worked, building up much useful information about the terrain ahead. They in turn were fascinated by our vehicle, not having one themselves, and our journey.

lOn the second night, a group of Galla tribes people strolled into camp, dressed only in loincloths with bundles on their head, armed with machetes and knobkerries, accompanied by their cattle. Much discussion arose. We heard they were using 'our' road to move their beasts through the mountains. A guide volunteered to show us the track.

The Police were sceptical, but grudgingly approved. Elated, in the early hours, before anyone changed their mind, we motored out with our man perched behind the seats. Painted face, fine feather sticking out from his mud caked head, with his collection of walking sticks, a stool and a machete, he made something of a figurehead.

Graphically pointing the direction, as if signalling a cavalry charge, big toothy smile from ear to ear, he was clearly happy to be riding with us. Four wheel drive engaged, chains on the front, we left a track in the mud stretching as far back as we could see.

We stopped for the mandatory porridge and mid-morning tea. After enjoying a cup with us, our guide collected his belongings, waved cheerily, and started off back down our track. He had enjoyed his ride, clearly fulfilled his obligations of setting us enroute, and was heading back to join his companions.

We were happy too, to be on our own again, as we had originally expected to be. Continuing in the indicated direction, our RAF map of the area looked as blank as ever. The woodland we were driving through was becoming more and more dense, when suddenly the track we had thought must be the original road became impossible to penetrate further. We backed off and looked for another route to follow. This, too, closed in on us. We reversed and repeated the process further down.

'The flower petals?' We looked at each other.

That deadly flower again. We talked about our options.

'We could try pushing our way through this thorn bush—it may be just a narrow band across the track?' John voiced his thoughts.

'Your call, Johnno. I'm with you, whichever!' I was happy not to be in the chair.

It was an uncomfortable feeling driving straight at a wall of thorn trees, forcing our faithful friend into such hostile territory. John engaged low ratio—the landy pushed, growled and climbed over the barrage. Trees sprung up immediately behind us, sealing off any exit. We couldn't even turn in the tightly packed forest.

We were committed.

The thorns screeched and scraped their way down the side and underneath of the jeep. Anything not securely attached would be ripped off. Leaves, thorns, caterpillars, stinging and crawling insects, angry bees, wasps, even a snake, dropped off the trees and filled the writhing cab to our waists. It was hot. Bitten and stung, we sweated, looking grimly ahead, trying to make out thinner tracts through the trees.

Our unbelievably stout vehicle continued to crawl forwards. Thoughts wandered. What if something broke? Or punctured? It would have been difficult to open the door, let alone fix anything. Nor would we be able to walk out.

After an unimaginably long three hours, we suddenly broke out of it. Ahead of us, as far as we could see was a golden grassy plain, game scattered across, the blue mountains still breaking the horizon, the landy still chugging, in the right direction. A beautiful Ethiopian carmine bee-eater flew in formation with us, swooping for insects disturbed as we travelled. We had arrived in a Garden of Eden, the Omo River reserve.

In this euphoric state, elated with our unexpected expansive freedom, so happy to be out of those thorns, we bumbled through the knee-high grass for a couple of hours, hardly saying a word. Herds of eland and oryx, zebra, distant hartebeest, buffalo and giraffe wandered through the sparse acacia, vultures circling down onto a far-off kill.

Suddenly, we crossed a vehicle track. Backing up, sure enough, a long-disused track headed off at right angles to ours making for some foothills over to our left.

We turned and followed, climbing into the hills, through dense forest, rounding a bend into a small valley. There before us lay a tented military-looking camp.

Uniformed men approached from all directions, apparently surprised to see us, their friendly approach quite a relief. 'Welcome! Where have you come from?' They asked

'England.' We beamed.

'Please, join me for some tea.' A senior man graciously invited us, introducing himself as Daniel, the warden of the Omo game reserve. Welcoming us to his headquarters, he told us he hadn't seen a visitor in the two years he'd been there, and had never heard of anyone crossing the plains through the thorns.

Daniel, gently aristocratic in his bearing, had read Conservation Management at Oxford. A renegade in the political system under Haile Selasse, he was effectively exiled to this wilderness, which he had now come to deeply appreciate. He treated us as royal guests.

We woke in the morning to four punctured wheels. Not too surprising. Pulling out the tubes, we repaired 46 punctures, cutting our patches into small quarters to stretch our supply. The long thorns had somehow sealed themselves in the rubber yesterday. Had one of them deflated a tyre then, we would still be out there.

Our Mr Angel again—in the thorn bush.

Now identified as 'mechanics', we assisted in various maintenance problems. John managed to get their Unimog going again that had sat immobile for years while I sorted out their solar battery charger system. We spent a few exhilarating days patrolling with Daniel in his game reserve. His dream was to see tourist camps develop there.

One evening, we sat on a hill overlooking the vast plains, a leopard coughed in the trees behind us, game and breath-taking scenery filled our view, mountains majestically preened in the last of the sun, the great Omo river splashed silver on the horizon. Overcome with the grandeur of it all, I made a pact with Daniel.

I'd be back. To set up a safari company together and bring people to see this magnificence. With no real idea how this would happen, we were both excited at the prospect. And my safari career was conceived.

Through the Omo Mountains

The Omo National Park, as it is today, 4,068 km² of wilderness, one tenth the size of Switzerland, is bordered by the Omo river, and home to an amazing range of wildlife. 300 plus species of birds have been identified here. Large herds of a wide variety of game roam the great plains.

The river tumbles its 350km way through a steep valley before slowing as it nears the lowlands and then meanders through the flat, semi-desert bush of the plains, eventually flowing into Lake Turkana. Open forests of tamarinds and figs, alive with colobus monkeys and the exquisite birdlife including blue-breasted kingfishers and white-cheeked turacos, run into hippos grazing on the savannah slopes against the mountain walls, where Abyssinian ground hornbills may hop across the riverine trees. The abundant wildlife, spirited rapids, innumerable side creeks and waterfalls, sheer inner canyons and hot springs all combine to make the Omo one of the world's classic river adventures.

However, for the moment, we had a mission to get back on that road, down which no vehicle had travelled in anyone's memory. All personnel and supplies for the Park were flown into the game reserve.

Before dawn broke on the fifth day, we headed out, with fond farewells and commitments for the future. 2,500m to climb, condition of trail unknown. One of the most extraordinary adventures either of us ever lived lay ahead.

The massive mountain range was home to few people other than remote villages along the route. They still wore large wooden disks in their ears and lips, beauty being in the eye of the custom, great hanging earlobes, deformed lower lip and all the front teeth missing when disks were removed. Apparently a deterrent to being sought as slaves.

A policeman had requested a lift to his post in the hills. Two old buffalo bulls appeared in the headlights. His immediate reaction was to shoot them, with his Kalashnikov, a light automatic military rifle totally unsuitable for big game. We spent a few uncomfortable moments restraining our trigger-happy passenger.

Before the sun was up, we'd straddled the Land-Rover on the middle hump in the badly eroded track, all four wheels hanging. We worked in a light rain, building up stones under the wheels, for an hour before we were able to move on. And this was just the beginning . . . the track became increasingly difficult, with steep stony gullies, constantly climbing, strewn with boulders, always muddy. We dropped our guard in his village, all we could do to dissuade him from loading us with more passengers. We settled with carrying the mailbag on to Maji, his headquarters further up.

Progress was slow, constantly in low range gears, seldom exceeding 15 kph. We admired the courage and skill of the British and South African army in making this road through such country. Looking back across the plains as we climbed, we could see the route we'd travelled from Lake Rudolph. The thorn tree belt stretched right across the plain, forming a natural barrier protecting the Omo plains from poachers and tourists.

On reaching Maji late afternoon, a large group of children escorted us to the police station, where we delivered the mailbag. The policeman's astonished gratitude was touching, The track out was down a steep, rock strewn and badly eroded incline, over which we slipped and slid, hitting the landy's undersides too hard and too frequently. We bumped and crawled across a long-disused ford at the bottom, and back up the other side, so steep we strained to see over the bonnet to make out the route through the boulders.

Camp that night, sitting on the tailboard of the landy dead in the middle of the track, ended one of the hardest days driving we'd had, fourteen hours of concentrated mountain trail.

Early next day we continued, with the track climbing up rocky steep hills, testing our driving skills to the utmost. The landy fell, front right wheel deep in a gully, the opposite wheel off the ground. Both John and I were underneath on our backs holding it from rolling over, trying to fit our standard Land-Rover jack.

Fortunately some Galla tribesman on their way to Maji, dressed in their customary loin cloth, added to by long earrings and bundles on their heads, walked down the trail. They jumped to assist holding the vehicle while we hooked up our rope, which others pulled, taking us up the loose rocky hill. Puffing and coughing on our cigarettes, they parted as great friends, having satisfactorily helped a fellow traveller.

We crossed a stream where the track climbed precipitously for several hundred metres, so badly eroded, there was now nothing left except rubble. We'd have difficulty walking up it, let alone driving.

Our eighty-metre nylon rope wrapped around the front bumper was unravelled. We took the bight to a tree further up the hill, each end turned around our front wheel hubs as on capstans. These protruded and seemed designed for just such an occasion. Inch by inch, yard by yard, the wheels slowly turning, regulated on the hand throttle, the landy pulled itself up. Wheel by wheel, boulder by boulder, Johnno and I were outside the vehicle each tending to a front hub, carefully feeding on the rope, under terrifying tension. Avoiding being run over was our prime challenge, the landy grunting and moaning, sliding, rising and often falling back over the wildly undulating loose rocks.

We had pulled everything out of the back to lighten the load. Now and then, we would miss-feed the rope onto the hub, when the taught line would whip off, and we'd jump to the side as the vehicle crashed back down the slope, settling several metres below in a pile of stones that went with it, the grinding wheels going nowhere.

It took us eight hours to climb two hundred metres of track. Exhausted, we counted ourselves fortunate to have made it without casualty. After bathing in the stream we heated up some soup and fell asleep like dogs on top of the landy.

At sunup next morning the slope looked like a typhoon had hit it, our belongings strewn up and down the ascent, boxes, jerry cans, tins and bottles scattered about in the rocks. All this had to be collected and carried up, the trusty rope tied round our waist while the other fed and pulled from a tree above to assist the one carrying.

There was no going back down that slope. We were now absolutely committed to continuing, in no man's land in the middle of this massive mountain range. No sign of another human to ask for help or information.

Often the road was so overgrown that one of us would walk ahead, enjoying the exercise and checking the track, the landy following like an overgrown puppy. Cavernous drops gaped off the edge with staggering views across valleys and wild mountains.

Tiring of walking, we were quietly rumbling along in the waist high grass, both in the cab, one standing on the passenger seat peering ahead, when suddenly the landy dipped into a hole and slid off the edge. It fell, jamming against a tree, teetering on the verge of rolling down into the valley below.

I sat on the door on the high side trying to keep the delicate balance, ready to jump, while John uncoiled the rope and took it round a tree above us, securing the ends to each top side of the vehicle to hold it from rolling. Using the tree as a pivot to revolve around, we tried to pull ourselves back on to the road. We came close to losing it on several occasions, all to no avail.

'Gonna be a long walk out, Rob,' John contemplated as we camped that night. 300km to Jimma, our nearest town.

'We'll be okay for water, just have to decide how well we want to eat?' I was thinking about our heavy, but delicious, tinned stews. The kit would be safe locked up in the back. The vehicle certainly wasn't going anywhere.

Next morning, planning our exit, we were astonished to hear voices coming down the trail ahead of us. A dozen Galla, naked as ever, long haul bundles on their heads, travelling sticks in hand, appeared round the corner. They took one look at us, dropped their bundles and ran, yelling, into the bush.

Clearly, we were the last 'things' they expected to see.

An hour later, we coaxed them back, mainly thanks to our precious oranges, which we rolled down the path, and they retrieved, but apparently didn't know what to do with them. John and I ate one, showing them how it was done. A brave member of their party munched into his, skin and all. He approved, and we soon had them all tucking into more, and sucking on our cigarettes as if their life depended on them. Shamefully, they were our best currency and we weren't going to disillusion them.

They listened intently while we tried to explain what we'd like them to do. We demonstrated tugging on the rope, now attached to the front of the vehicle, whereupon one of them pulled out a big knife and slashed off a length. Oh . . . Not for sale?? We tied the slashed piece back on. More explanations and demonstrations. At last they got the message, pulled on the rope, to great hilarity and jeers amongst themselves, much resembling a 'strong man' competition.

Starting the engine to assist the pull prompted another exodus. Finally we were together, and they pulled us up onto the road with a strength belied by their small wiry bodies. One of them asked for a lift, more excited about riding with us than continuing his journey. We'd encountered this great status symbol before, so laughed with him as he happily climbed in between the driver and the door, wanting to be right in the action. He rode with us to the next village, shouting excitedly at everyone we passed, tapping the top of his head. His Land-Rover, or our heads??

The countryside became gentler, as did the track gradients, although still muddy. Lush green uninhabited hills rolled on forever. The worst seemed behind us. We were in a happy mood. One of us standing on the passenger seat as lookout was now obligatory, watching the road ahead as the driver nudged through the long, tall grass rustling its way either side of the vehicle, like water against a boat's hull.

The engine was quiet, until we came to a hill, when it would growl and groan and grapple with the gradient, emerging at the top like a prize bulldog, when hackles would fall and the motor subside to its workman like tick. Always the smell of grass being ploughed into moist earth and broken roots brought to the surface by tussling tyres. On and on, day after day.

We felt like a migrating animal bound for ripening pastures in some distant land. Strangely, there were few animals. Our sole sighting was a family of warthogs, snorting and crashing through the greenery, aerial tails upright. Fortunately, not too many aardvark diggings.

Tsetse fly played their usual trick of stinging you just as the driving needed full concentration, droning off in time to miss your slap, always at a critical moment, disrupting a crucial limb controlling some vital system like the steering wheel, brake, accelerator or clutch, leaving the driver in dangerous disarray, teetering on the brink of some bottomless gulf.

We stopped to watch the climax of a gigantic meteorological process. A black cloud had been steadily building into a cumulonimbus pillar, its dramatic appearance straining to balance a column of water 10,000m high, darkening the entire landscape. The sombre and formidable accumulation, its base purple-black, totally oppressed the underlying mountains. Our own progress halted like an animal sensing a bushfire, or a stalking predator. We watched the cloud's hatch open, as though the bottom had fallen out, and a solid column of water fall on the mountainside in a density that conveyed a drowning right across the valley. Thankfully, not on our track.

We stayed that night in a policeman's hut in a small village called Jomo, and delivered another letter. His wife served a traditional dish of njera and watt, a pancake with spicy hot relish, accompanied by raw, red hot chilli, eaten like peanuts. We drank too much tej, wine made from honey.

'You what to them?' John was asking in a lazy voice, a gentle smile spreading behind his misted glasses.

'I shoota them!' The policeman emphatically ensured us, a quizzical look almost popping his eyes out.

The officer was telling us, under increasing ease of more tej, that he ran a very tight ship and shot anyone he found drunk, a drunken grin rolling across his own wizened face.

A gentle rain fell on the thatched roof through the night, lulling us to sleep, happily contemplating our not being in our leaky tent.

A beautiful dawn spread across the pink sky, heralding a fine day until the policeman appeared to tell us a baby had died that night from cholera. He and half the village requested a lift to Jimma, the nearest town. On our declining, they stoically accepted the status quo and accompanied us down to enjoy the spectacle of our crossing their log bridge, which they maintained was broken and unpassable. This was not in fact true, but was by the time our 'Land-Rover-crossing-greasy-log' trick nearly toppled us into the water, saved only by a good number of them hanging onto the upper side of the vehicle, the lower side of which had slid off the logs into the riverbed. We left them in a jovial mood eyeing the debris of a now very broken bridge and our slippery progress up the other side of the valley.

The track was often reduced to the width of a pig's path, forcing the lookout to duck down as we pushed through undergrowth, branches and creepers wrapping round everything, including ourselves. The cab was again full of biting, crawling insects and caterpillars. Judging the edge of the road was quite a challenge; we frequently would have to abandon our course and head downhill at an alarming angle, finding our way back further along the track after a recce and some serious 'bundu bashing' lower down.

We passed a village where we saw men carrying soil in bundles on their heads. We decided to do our bit for the community project. Carrying a couple of loads for them in the landy, to their huge delight and amusement, our bonus being an improved road thereafter. We could actually see where we were going and reached a phenomenal 40kph on one stretch.

We met a team of surveyors in a Unimog, the first vehicle we'd seen since leaving Kenya, apart from Daniel's. They informed us of a five-year plan to rebuild the old road. Enthralled to hear of our journey, we all agreed they'd be lucky if it worked out in fifty years.

I recently heard that it was completed in 2002. Thirty years. Not bad.

Their churning up of the muddy patches and hills caused us to slide uncontrollably down the next 200m gradient. Discovering at the bottom we'd lost a wheel chain, we returned to find it being carried on a stick by the servant of an old Amhara we'd passed earlier. He unashamedly sold it to us for some empty tins and an orange.

Later that day we found ourselves driving on a recognisable dirt road, with four-wheel drive disengaged, chains removed for the first time in two weeks, speeding along at a steady 40kph into the night. We treated ourselves to njera and watt and a couple of beers in a restaurant in Bonga, our first town, and rooms for the night in a hotel. A mistake.—we sadly missed the peace of our tent and the hyena calls. In its stead, we suffered blaring music and drunken calls from the bar below, smelly flea ridden beds, and a bathroom from Dante's inferno.

On our last lap to civilization and the town of Jimma, we passed through country quite European in its rolling hills, little squares of cultivation (mostly cereal, coffee trees interspersed) and cows grazing in fenced meadows. Ox drawn ploughs with gleaming metal spikes were cleaned by the clay soil, operated mostly by children, renting the air with whoops and cracks of long whips.

Passing Jimma, we rode into mountainous country again, crossing a deep canyon. We dropped 2,000m from the cool highlands into hot sticky thorn veld, and then back up into the Eucalyptus, all in the space of an hour. We understood better why Ethiopian airlines had set up their amazing circuit of mountain aerodromes and the old DC3's originally operating between them, effectively like a bus service.

Our camp that night on its spectacular edge was breath taking. Another day's driving brought us at last to Addis Ababa, experiencing that anti-climax when you've just completed something momentous, and everyone else is simply carrying on with their lives, quite oblivious of your achievement.

John had several friends and contacts from his previous trips in Addis. Camping in the British Embassy grounds, he was happy to hear the howl of hyena still frequenting the big city. After a few days rest we were off to our next destination—Bahar-Dar and the Simien Mountains further north.

We stopped in with his old friends, Brigadier and Mrs Sandford. The Brigadier headed up the British Army fighting for Ethiopia in the Second World War and had marched into Addis alongside Colonel Stirling of the SAS and His Imperial Majesty Haile Selasse on the liberation of the country. The King had given him this farm in honour of his role. The visitor's book was really a Who's Who of Ethiopia, recording John's stay four years previously

'Sorry old man, can't hear a thing. Lovely to have you, though. Anytime.' He talks loudly across us on seeing John.

'The old home is looking good, Mrs Sandford,' John remarks back, giving the old Brig a respectful nod. It was indeed fascinating that the ageing traditional pole and dagga structure was still in such good nick.

'47 years, and hardly a day's maintenance since it was built.' He replied with a smile on his face.

He explained how they'd carried the termite-resistant red wood in on mules from 50km away. The dagga was mixed with donkey and cattle manure and then fermented for 5 days before application, after which three layers were applied, each following just as the previous coat dried out. The final coat was a soupy broth with a special grass additive which had never been painted and, although weathered, still looked pretty good.

We stopped at the Martula Miriam church, which John and his co-expeditionary, Stephen Bell, had walked into during their last trip. It boasted a famous 5m arch, beautifully built of stone, originally constructed by the Portuguese under Vasco Da Gama in the 16th century. Da Gama had been commissioned to look for the fabled Christian champion, Prester John, and had built several churches around Ethiopia during this quest. Beak discovered this beautiful ruin in 1615, which story John and Stephen had discovered written up in Portuguese annals. They translated it word by word with a Portuguese dictionary and then went to look for it. The first Europeans to see it since Beak, they found his name and date scratched onto a foundation stone on site.

A road had been built since, enabling investigating archaeologists easier access. We stopped for breakfast at an old Portuguese bridge which crossed the Blue Nile gorge below Lake Tana, the source of this great river. There was another famous Church building on the nearby island of Debra Libanos, dating back to early 'Coptic' days. Legend has it that the Ark of the Covenant was hidden there at one time, protected by the Knights Templar. The mysteries of the past permeate Ethiopia from top to bottom.

We camped that night on the brink of a 2,000m precipice, with the Land-Rover parked back on a hill for a 'run down' in the morning as the starter motor had packed up again. Nifty brake-work was a constant demand in this country, chiasmic drops awaiting serious blunders or failures.

This was the Eastern Arc of the Afromontane hotspots, the 'water tower' of East Africa, sourcing many of their great rivers. The people living in these hard and isolated conditions are a legend in themselves. John noted that the village of Martula Miriam was exactly the same as he remembered, except they were now quite used to 'forengis' visiting. We were no longer freaks to be stared at.

On the way back, a storm hung darkly over a little village perched on the edge of the gorge. People were hurrying along the road, bent towards the rising wind, their gabis flowing white against the black sky. Animals trotted alongside, all so frail against the imminent onslaught. Within minutes torrents of water were pouring from the sky and rushing down the stony track. We could hardly see our way, other than in flashes of lightning, when drenched bodies, careening grass and the track, now river, lit up.

Stopping in an eating-house in Debra Marcos, we were warned by the proprietor that 'Shifta' bandits lay ahead, possibly guerrilla fighters in the Eritrean struggle for independence. Driving on for a further two hours into the night, we turned off the road to find ourselves a suitable campsite. Forging a small stream, we bogged down and spent two hours with spades and sand-ladders in the sticky mud extracting ourselves. Engine idling all along as the starter motor was still not working.

Fortunately, neither shifta nor hyenas appeared. The District Governor walked past in the morning and promised to help find our sand-ladders that had disappeared into the mud the night before, which we arranged to pick up on our way back.

Driving mountainous passes towards Gondor and the Simiens, names that seemed straight out of Tolkien's 'Lord of the Rings' which I was reading and feeling much like Frodo on his great journey, we climbed ever higher into the peaks and crags of this wild country. The sun set behind a storm, throwing rays across the sky and lighting up the jagged summits to the west. A sliver of new moon hung over our tent, stars glimmering in the dark blue night.

Adventure at its finest.

We reached the village of Debarak after dark, camping in the jail at the police station. Guides informed us we'd need mules and could expect an eight-hour trek to Sankabur, the Game Park Camp in the mountain reserve. In our tradition, we headed out the next morning alone with our rucksacks, happy to be walking again.

The grand expanse fed our spirits as we followed trails centuries old cut into the sides of mountains, cultivated valleys far below. Some of the ploughers were so young they could hardly reach the handle of the plough. Yells, clicks and ululating songs in high pitched voices intermingled with cracks of whips.

At the top of the range, a blustering wind howled up from the valleys 3,000m below. A flight display developed before us to beat any Red Arrows show. Large black crows came swooping along the crest, wings held in delta shape, making a loud tearing noise at a speed that must have been close to 150 kph. Suddenly, they would shoot up 60m, tumble over and down again, rolling and twisting, before streaking back up. A flip would bear them down across the crest just over our heads, coloured streamers expected any moment, then banking in a huge arc across the gorge they plummeted into the depths with folded wings, only to rise again, pitch forward and stream away like fighter bombers.

Simien walk

Turkana amazed by our wing mirrors

Our path took us down a saddle with the deep gorges either side to four tin roofed huts. Sankabur, at 4,000m. The sun set over the weird shapes of the lower Simiens, followed by the moon rising across the cavernous gorge in the steel blue night. The 18 year-old game scout and his 15 year-old wife with a flirtatious laugh invited us to join them for watt and njera.

He took us out the next day to find the illusive Ibex. We never found them and were content to watch the Gelada baboons, long manes blowing in the wind. Gelada is a species of Old World monkey found only in the Ethiopian Highlands, spending much of its time foraging in grasslands. It is exclusively herbivorous, a grass eater, and has the most opposable thumb of any of the primates, excluding humans. This allows picking apart the grasses with great dexterity to select the more nourishing titbits. It is the only truly grazing monkey.

They live in small harems, often joining together with other bands to feed, forming groups of upwards of three hundred. Although not listed as endangered, only fifty to sixty thousand Geladas are known to exist today.

Walia, or Abyssinian ibex, a member of the goat family, is thought to number only around 500 individuals owing to past poaching and habitat depletion. They have been hunted extensively for their tasty meat and exquisitely shaped horns. Males have very large horns which curve backwards, reaching lengths up to 110cm, which they use for dominance disputes. Unfortunately, they are also valued as mugs and trophies.

Encroaching settlement, road construction, livestock grazing and cultivation are all further problems. The Semien National Park, established in 1969, saved their approaching extinction although they are still in the critically endangered category.

The adult ibex's only known wild predator is the hyena, although young are hunted by foxes and cats. Sporting distinguished black beards, they live in steep rocky cliff areas, as high as 4,500m, often seen standing on their hind legs to get to young shoots of giant heath. Sadly, none of which we were privileged to see, although our game scout assured us he often did.

Our return trip was enlivened by watching a group of small children supervising the mating of a donkey to a mare, which they skilfully manoeuvred together with most effective sucking noises and body manipulation. Not much need for sex education up here.

We met an English chap, about to go to Oxford, walking in a topee and long tweed shorts, hung about with pouches, collecting lichens. He shook hands with us and introduced himself as he puffed on his curved briar pipe. The chickens tied to his mule vied with his muleteer to make enough fuss about moving on as the sun was getting low.

We drove back to Addis through the continuing exquisite Simiens scenery. The gravel road we travelled was like driving on marbles, causing spectacular broadsides on the numerous hairpin bends, leaving us teetering on the edge of yawning gorges, the tyres becoming badly cut up. Added to which the brakes were pulling violently towards the gorge side.

Somewhat taken aback by the strong migration of animals and people competing for the road, in whom there seemed a strong latent desire for each to be somewhere other than where they were, one thing was sure, that at the sound of a Land-Rover approaching, some ancient wanderlust would be stirred which would carry them into the middle of the road, causing you to brake and evade them on the treacherous rolling gravel surface in the last minute.

Hornsmanship was crucial. An immovable law ordains that no Ethiopian donkey shall stop, go, alter course, flinch or in any way acknowledge your horn, nor squeal of brakes, flying stones, shouts, bangs on the door or skidding in swirls of dust. Until the vehicle has passed. At which point the animal will vacate His Imperial Majesty's highway with the utmost speed.

Horses will demonstrate random migration at the sound of a horn, but should these coincide with the path of the oncoming vehicle, they will not be moved to another path under any circumstance. Mules abide by no rules except that they can be guaranteed not to comply with the driver's predictions and are guaranteed to outmanoeuvre him beyond all rational conjecture.

Sheep will disperse across the entire road to form a slalom pattern that invariably ends in an uncontrollable skid. Goats provide similar tests, only the pattern is constantly changing as the slalom is negotiated, causing the driver to break into unusually offensive language. Only after the vehicle has departed, this swirling mass will once again conglomerate and head off the road.

Cattle are a comparative pleasure, usually remaining steadfast, even though they may be blocking the entire track, until at 3m distance, depending on the driver's horn work, they will move sedately off the road.

Pedestrians walking down the side of the road, whether towards or away from you, can be counted on to cross to the other side when you are close enough to be put to your wits end to avoid them. Those walking down the middle of the road play a game of chicken with great daring. After the driver has rapidly slowed to avoid hitting them, they will cross his path, smiling benignly as the driver struggles to regain control. Chattering idlers in a roadside town should be nudged with the front bumper if there's no response to gentle horn work. Unless they are behind a parked bus, in which case they will jettison themselves unexpectedly across the driver's path, frequently landing on the bonnet.

Under all adversity and however blatantly the driver may be offended, it is to be clearly understood that in Ethiopia, it is always the vehicle and driver who are the culprits. The roads belong to the people and their animals.

So it was that arriving in Addis after nightfall, we considered ourselves lucky in having hit only one animal. A mule had broken from its master but 10m in front of us and had cut straight across the road. We could have avoided it had not the master pursued it closely and blocked our obvious path to clear it. We suffered a dented mudguard and broken headlight, but hadn't stopped as almost certainly we would have spent any amount of time in jail, and lost a good deal of our belongings in the process. Knowing we could do nothing more for the unfortunate animal than the owner himself, we ruthlessly drove on.

Chapter 25

Tanzania Troubles

We headed south again from Addis along the Great Rift Valley Lakes and its rolling hills on deserted roads. Much of Africa's volcanic activity is concentrated in these daunting blue-grey ridges of volcanic basalt and granite, often rising sheer on either side of the road to towering heights of 4,000m. The valley floor, 50km or more across, encompasses some the greatest variety in fauna and flora of the world's true wildernesses.

Leaving from a picnic spot, an upright man with an umbrella and revolver strapped to his chest came walking by, his servant carrying a bundle on his head. The bizarre Victorian image in such an isolated spot moved us to get talking, and lift them over the mountain pass ahead, in spite of our being so overloaded. Two days hard driving along rocky tracks and wide open muddy plains brought us to Mega, where we camped in the ruins of an old Italian fort, still in fine condition and beautifully situated overlooking the plains of the Northern Frontier Districts.

Following a little-used old wartime track down the mountain at sunrise, we mused over the historic happenings from our 800m vantage point above the plains, and how the Italians had sat guarding this while the Allies were making their way up the pass we'd followed from the Omo River. The trail was slow, boulder covered and overgrown, where the only indication of the road was a different coloured grass, treacherous aardvark holes hidden amongst it.

Ahmed

End of a long day

Passing from cattle to camel country again, we spent a long hot day driving the gravel plains and lava swells towards Marzabit, the oasis National Park in the midst of desert. We could see the well-forested mountains from afar as we drove.

We didn't search too hard for an entry gate on reaching the famous reserve of Marzabit, working our way up to the highest crater holding Lake Paradise. The dry flat landscape far below stretched north towards the Somali Republic. Immediately below nestled a perfect circular lake, about 800m across, rimmed by lush green grass leading into deep forest mounting the steep sides of the crater. A point opposite made a gap shaped like a rifle site, formed by the outpouring of lava those eons back, through which game now meandered in to drink.

We made a superb campsite amongst the trees on the edge of the crater-lake. A mighty elephant slowly passed us, its tusks burgeoning low and sweeping up again, almost crossing at ground level. He had to lift his head to walk, carefully manoeuvring his trunk around his gigantic tusks while eating. He waded into the lake and spent most of the afternoon in this dignified bath, clearly happy to have the weight of his tusks supported in the water.

At nightfall, vehicle lights emerged in the gap and bounced round the lakeshore. Alarmingly, an armed patrol jumped out, surrounding our little camp. Then the warden came across and explained that we should have booked and paid for an armed guard to be where we were. Dangerous gunmen frequented the forest intent on killing Ahmed, the famous tusker and pride of the Kenyan National Parks, whom we had been watching that very afternoon. Mzee Kenyatta, the president himself, protected the big bull. The warden kindly allowed us to continue with our camp for the night, leaving one of his men for security.

Sadly, political poachers shot Ahmed a few months later.

Back on the trail for Nairobi, our ailing exhaust finally broke. We growled and blared our way across the bush and onto the main road south. The noise was fantastic. We couldn't even hear our own horn, conversation out of the question.

We stopped to climb Mount Kenya in search again for the giant Lobelia, sans guide, losing the path in thick cloud. Disorientated, we thought best to head straight down the mountain, only to find ourselves in a Tolkein style moss and lichen covered forest. We waded through greenery up to our chests, an eerie mist wafting past and shrouding the view. After a confused ramble, we finally and somewhat embarrassingly made our way back to the forest rangers hut, whose guide we had earlier spurned.

Thundering down the road to Nairobi, people cringing on the road-side, we prepared to spend a few days working on the Land-Rover, readying it for the last long haul home. Routing through the fabulous Amboseli and Tsavo game reserves to Mombasa on the Kenyan coast, we camped by mistake on a golf course, only discovering this when a ball bounced off the landy in the morning, accompanied by irate remonstrations from the golfers.

The Tanzania border discovered that John's driving licence registered him as being born in Rhodesia, our politically incorrect destination carefully concealed to this point.

He told them it was the name of the house his mother had lived in London. Ignorance being bliss, we sailed through, first stop Moshi to refuel and continue on our way to Lake Manyara and the Ngorogoro Crater.

A man in a shabby suit approached us, looking the windscreen over which was lying folded flat on the bonnet, enquiring where our commercial licence was. I indicated it on the dashboard shelf. He drew our attention to the law that required it be displayed. I slapped it onto the windscreen.

'Okay?' I looked at him.

Introducing himself as some kind of inspector, he said it wasn't okay, cleverly deducing that it had not been displayed for the time we had driven from the border, 20 minutes back. We had committed an offence in Tanzanian law. I was to please accompany him to his office.

'Johnno, I'll be back in a tick, you right to finish the refuelling?'

Irritated, I brusquely followed him up the stairs in the Service Station building, where a huge fellow behind an equally huge empty desk gave me a ponderous lecture on how Tanzanian law worked, and, like everywhere else in the world, breaking it had consequences.

Trying hard to maintain my sanity, I asked him what the consequences might be for our heinous crime.

'Anywhere from 200 shillings, to 20,000 shillings' he carefully alliterated. This latter was close to the value of the Land-Rover.

'And where might we lie in the scale?' I asked in disbelief.

'That will be for the court to decide.' He priggishly informed me.

'Court?! When is that?'

'Maybe two, maybe three weeks . . .' He settled back into his armchair.

I didn't need to think too hard about what he was waiting for. Johnno walked in at that moment to see what the hold-up was, and had it all laboriously explained to him. We were in shock and not at all sure how to proceed, never having entered the arena of bribing. Meanwhile, the Land-Rover was to be impounded and we were under arrest. On remand.

Escorted under armed guard to a compound where the Land-Rover was to stay, we were then to be taken to the cells. Seeking a solution to this twist of events, we suggested to our guard that we all go down to the hotel for a beer, which he readily agreed to, telling us of the brands he liked most.

Plying him with pints, I excused myself to go to the toilet, and made a bee-line to telephone the British Embassy in Dar Es Salaam. I managed to give them a passport number and our whereabouts before it clicked off for the fourth time.

Nothing more to be done.

Slowly sinking deeper into our chairs with our beers, I could hardly credit my eyes, when James Goodman, who'd been at Bristol University with me, suddenly walked through the doors of the hotel. I remembered that he lived in Tanzania, his father farming here.

'Hang in till I get back, I think I know who's behind this,' his dad who was with him smiled wryly after listening to our story.

An hour later he reappeared with a letter allowing us to accompany him back to his farm. The guard clearly knew who he was and happily agreed, enjoying another pint. By the next day he'd spoken to the High commissioner in Dar, who asked the Consul to speak to the Secretary of the Treasury, asking him to have a word with the Moshi District Governor—who would discuss with the local Administrative secretary the possibility of speaking to the Regional Finance Officer—who would connive with his subordinates to encourage 'Fats' to give the tourists back the keys of their Land-Rover and allow them to continue as a demonstration of goodwill by the people of Tanzania to Her Majesty.

Next day, we met the shabby suit man and 'Fats' in their office, together with James and his dad. 'Fats' could not have been more effusively friendly, apologising how easily mistakes can be made, and how welcome we tourists were in his country.

'Tanzania needs you!' he guffawed, his huge belly heaving.

In Africa, nothing's over until the fat man sings.

We'd had a close shave, and wondered how it might have ended had not our friend walked through that hotel door. Thanks Mr A.

Lake Manyara Hotel stands on the edge of a cliff overlooking the lake 300m below. Wandering along in front of the hotel, we came across a big garden. Could our little tent be accommodated in it? We knocked on the door of the house, to be met by a man in a bathrobe—slightly embarrassing.

'Of course!' he replied, and before we knew it, his wife showed us their bathroom and kitchen, and laid out towels on the garden furniture.

'Make yourselves at home.' The Kellys called to us as they went off to manage the hotel, leaving two complete strangers with the run of their home.

After cleaning up and cooking, we reckoned we deserved a further treat after all the Tanzanian abuse, strolling over to the hotel for a Tia Maria and a reefer of hash we'd bought in Mombasa. This turned out to be far stronger than any we'd yet tried, and before long we were in fits of uncontrollable laughter, much to the amusement of the young waiters around us.

To even greater embarrassment, our hosts appeared from the dining room to chat, making polite conversation and enquiring what we were up to, all seeming to us most hilarious. Our slow and incoherent answers, which the other of us would repeat in an inane draggy voice as they gyrated before our eyes, were impossibly crass. They no doubt left us to rush straight to their drinks cupboard and inspect the damage. No mean feat of navigation later, we found our way back to the tent.

Profusely apologetic the next morning, we breakfasted with the Kellys, who politely maintained they hadn't noticed anything odd. We thankfully were able to explain a little and tell of some of our adventures, and the need to let our hair down. They kindly sympathised and invited us back on our returning their way.

Off to the majestic Ngorogoro Crater, it's magnificence an added balm to our souls, we at last set course for the final run home.

"Ad enuff!' A legend I'd once seen blazoned onto a Queen's Guard's tee shirt aptly summed up our feelings.

Our driving skills were stretched in a different manner as we joined the famous 'hell run', the road used by heavy traffic hauling through to Zambia and Malawi from the coast while the new railroad was under construction. The only maintenance apparently received on the gravel surface was an occasional dusting by a tractor towing thorn trees.

A bolt dropped out from our swivel pin on the front axle, losing all the oil. An old Italian on a mission station, equipped with 19th century's technology, manufactured a new one for us in his workshops. Oil was also pouring from the main crankshaft bearing seal, and we lost our spare spring from its lashing on the front bumper. Old army-green friend was definitely coming to the end of its journey.

We rocked into a truck stop at the end of a long day's tough driving, covered in grime and dust. It was a typical roadside bar and restaurant where you could buy anything from live chickens in a sack with their head sticking out, *sadza,* the stiff maize porridge and staple diet of southern Africa, with vegetable or *nyama* (meat) relish, local beer, 'strong stuff', to a variety of marvellously available fat 'mamas'. All we wanted was a meal and a beer and somewhere to wash before heading down a bit further to find our night's campsite.

Leaving after an entertaining few hours with the pub's patronage, we unfortunately backed our Land-Rover into a lamp-post carrying all the electricity cables for the village. Immediate darkness, followed by sparks leaping all round us as the overhead wiring fell about, brought cries and exclamations from the blacked out pub. A menacing crowd emerged. John looked at me, grinned, and hit the accelerator. Wails and shouts escalated behind us, some chasing us down the road.

'Pay-back time.' We couldn't help thinking.

Just before the border next morning we came to a pod of twenty lorries parked on the road. We drove round them through the bush to find two 40 ton rigs stalled on a hill. We sailed through an empty border post, one happy step closer to home.

The Malawi border accepted our long expired European insurance policy, allowing us to make the refreshingly cold Nyika plateau for the night. We were arriving too late to pay the entrance fee at the gate, and leaving too early the following morning. We settled the matter by carrying a letter from the guard to post in Blantyre. Arriving in the capital celebrating their independence and Dr Banda's newly announced presidency for life, we joined in. Anything for a party at this stage.

Our last project was to see the Cabora Bassa dam being built by the Portuguese on the Zambezi. This enormous hydro-electric scheme, equal to Kariba in output, was in its infancy. The company's headquarters in Mozambique's Tete mistook us for consultants they were expecting. So they organised us to connect with a military convoy travelling next morning to the dam site through territory occupied by Mozambique and Zimbabwean freedom fighters.

A young Portuguese engineer met us on the edge of the impressive Cabora Basa gorge, absolutely sheer for hundreds of metres, where we watched huge lorries looking like dinky toys tipping vast quantities of rock into the riverbed. Going down into the gorge on the precipitous road carrying gigantic machinery, from which we had to take refuge on what seemed very tiny lay-bys sticking out over the gorge, or cut into the cliff, we entered a tunnel through the rock face. Built to channel the Zambezi while they built the dam wall, we understood it would become the turbine race in due course. Huge machinery moved like monsters in the murky dark, while a slender swaying footbridge crossed the gorge 12m above the water on which teams of African workers carried concrete in buckets on their heads.

The engineer finally twigged we weren't the visiting consultants and unceremoniously escorted us off the site. We gave three crack-looking commandos a lift to their camp, figuring they'd beef up our security on the way out. Only to be told that vehicles with soldiers were specially ambushed.

Buying demijohns of Portuguese wine in Tete, which bustled with macho soldiers eying the girls and drinking duty free beer, we set off on the final leg for the Rhodesian border.

'Well, Mr John Francis Wedgewood Fynn,' said the first white immigration officer we'd seen since leaving England, 'and what are we going to be writing about?'

John had 'journalist' in his passport.

I was not allowed in, not being able to prove my residency, which we'd been so careful not to carry on the trip down. We had to phone family in Salisbury, suffer tedious officious checking and rechecking before finally being permitted entry, cringing at the arrogance of our own border man.

Not quite the welcome we'd been looking forward to.

Nevertheless, tarred roads, white lines, no potholes, friendly waving locals and BSA policemen courteous and smart, even cold cokes in the service stations, certainly was.

25,000km behind us, home and family just down the road.

We put our hand on the hooter as we drove up the last hill to No 27, our RAF flares streaming red smoke. Canvas roof and windows off, demijohns of wine strapped to the front bumper, our well used sand-ladders rattling on the front jerry cans, trusty rope tied round the spare wheel on the bonnet, washing up basin nestled inside that, floor covered in cream of tartar pods from the Zambezi, bits of wood from the Congo jungles. Everything covered in mud and dust.

We'd arrived on Ness, my sister's, 21st birthday.

What a homecoming party!

Chapter 26

Malawi Gold

We now had to climb back into the real world and get on with making a living. John headed for Zambia, where he took up a successful farming career outside Lusaka, although, years later, the socialist policies of President Kenneth Kaunda drove him off his land.

Zambia today has turned full circle with new policies and governments progressively developing and growing their economy. Zimbabwe's demise has been Zambia's gain, in tourism, agriculture, and renewed vigour. John is back there, working as an international agricultural consultant.

In July 1970, I became a site engineer with Roberts Construction on the Pelindaba nuclear research station outside Johannesburg.

'Why did you do that?' asked the contractor after I'd told him about leaving the Navy. 'And now you're going to do what?'

I was telling him about my plans for Ethiopia while he sympathetically shook his head—'This one's a real nutcase' was the thinking bubble clearly establishing.

I left Johannesburg after 6 months to take up a position in Malawi on the Sucoma sugar estate installing the irrigation system for a 2,000ha extension. It was back in the bush, on the Shire river, where I found a lovely Mauritian girlfriend, Odette, the daughter of one of the managers. I took with me my beautiful golden Labrador, Frodo.

We three did most things together, travelling at weekends up to Mount Mulanje to visit a former Navy mate, Colin, who was working on a water purification scheme for the UN Children's Fund.

Colin was building a 40ft sailboat, *Nyanja*, in an old tea factory warehouse. He planned to sail her home on the completion of his contract. The timber was cut from the mountain to fit the shape of her hull, pit-sawn and carried down on the shoulders of the timber merchants who worked the high altitude forests.

He was getting married. My wedding present was Nyanja's keel—two and a half tons of Malawi Railway line welded into position.

'Well, that should stabilise the nuptial bed!' murmured Anne, his lovely Danish bride.

Constructed on a low loader, he launched it by demolishing one side of the warehouse to remove it, and driving it down and into the sea on the Mozambique coast, floating off at high tide and sailing back to England.

The irrigation company's MD came up to inspect the project. I lined up an aeroplane from the local club to fly him in. The entire hierarchy of the company had been wiped out in a light aircraft accident a year earlier, and a blanket ban had been stipulated for directors in small planes. In deference to my navy training and he being an ex RAF pilot, he agreed.

Arriving at the airport on Monday morning to pre-flight the aircraft after a particularly whacking weekend, I was in a strange state of mind. My attention span appeared limited to seconds. I went up to the control tower for a briefing, and walked out not having absorbed a single word.

Feeling very anxious, and battling to make the simplest decision, I met the boss's international flight.

'Nice to meet you, Rob. I'm really looking forward to seeing how you've handled that No 4 pump station intake.' He was straight into the job, as expected.

I picked up his case off the conveyor and abruptly walked out to our plane, fighting the mental agony of knowing something was dreadfully wrong with me.

We climbed in, started up, and I called for taxi instructions. All I could pick up was the runway to use. I started to taxi round the perimeter of the airfield, looking at the numbers marked on the ground at the end of each runway. To my great relief, I found them, and expressed this to my boss in the seat next to me, who, by now, was beginning to look at me in a strange way.

I called for take-off, couldn't decipher the response, stowed the microphone, and opened the throttle. Boss gripped the side of his seat and started to curl up his legs as if preparing for a crash. I was fully engaged in trying to read my instruments, which to my considerable concern were indiscernible.

A blur of movement ahead appeared as a large aeroplane landing straight across our take off path. Much squawking was filling the radio, all of which I ignored. I still couldn't read the instruments—seeing them clearly enough, but unable to make out what they were recording.

Shaken in the turbulence of the large aircraft, we were airborne, the stall warning immediately screaming. I pushed the nose down to pick up flying speed. Our awful predicament was rapidly dawning on me. I was in command of an aeroplane, without any ability to assimilate what the instruments were telling me, and had no idea how to deal with it.

I frantically sought a solution, not daring to say or do anything, but simply fly straight ahead. Then, we were flying over the escarpment into the Zambezi and Shire valley, the dry veld stretching into the distance. I could make out the great river, when suddenly, I spotted a patch of green on the horizon.

'The estate! It's Sucoma ... there, do you see!' I pointed excitedly, like a child seeing for the first time. The boss quietly nodded.

Instant relief for me. Solution found—simply fly towards it and land. No more problem.

The boss, valiantly attempting to converse, convincing himself this wasn't happening, pointed out features he recognised. Ignoring him, I concentrated every effort on getting there and landing.

'Maybe we could fly around a bit to have a look at the pump stations, Rob?' He suggested.

I simply pointed the aeroplane straight at the end of the runway. I noted the airspeed was much higher than it should be, but had no idea how to correct it.

Hold the nose on the end of the runway. Cut the throttle. Hang in. No distractions. Please!

Wheels hit the threshold. Far too fast. We bounced back into the air. On the third bounce, well over halfway down the runway, determined I wasn't taking off to fly round again, I stood on the brakes. As the wheels hit for the fourth time, the tyres burst, collapsing the undercarriage, and we slid on the aircraft belly deep into the surrounding sugar cane.

When all the noise stopped, amidst thick dust and a strong scent of sugar, I calmly undid my straps, opened the door and walked round to the luggage hatch. Retrieving his suitcase, I casually made my way back through the swathe we'd cut in the cane.

People were running towards us, the boss was shouting, and I collapsed. Soon afterwards, in the company sickbay under concerned medical surveillance, I had no idea what was happening to me—nor could focus on anything—other than vaguely remembering the serious party at the week end and fearing I must have been spiked there.

Cerebral malaria? Some weird tropical River bug? A week of tests and consultations with a psychologist followed as I gradually recovered normality. The diagnosis was uncertain and put down to a mysterious disease of the Shire valley.

The boss also recovered, and as a huge measure of his generosity, I was allowed back on the job. But not to fly.

Shwoo, Mr A, you sure had a job back there. I vowed never to smoke Malawi Gold again.

Meanwhile, in Ethiopia, where I was still planning to head back up to, everything hit the fan. His Imperial Majesty King Haile Selasse was toppled in a revolution headed up by the cruel Mengisto (now in asylum here in Zimbabwe), and the kingdom was in chaos. Daniel and the Omo Game reserve vision were out the window.

My contract ended and Frodo and I packed up and headed home, sadly saying goodbye to Odette.

What next, I wondered? Which is where we started in Chapter 1—please read on to see the extraordinary destiny that lay ahead.

Chapter 27

Esmerelda

'What are the bullet holes in the bows, Jim?' I asked.

All this background stuff was good preparation for building up Old Kaz. And I was learning much about the curved balls. I knew nothing about the business world, or hiring and firing. Good guiding and management is our constant challenge in the safari world staff, and we had guys keen to get a foot in the door by offering to work for their keep regularly landing on our shores.

I had a soft spot and considerable respect for ex British serviceman. A former paratrooper, Jim, met me in Kariba one day. His capable, casual manner, a contradiction I'd come to know and enjoy in my Navy colleagues, drew me to him.

There was nothing and nobody worth mentioning that Jim hadn't done, met or been to. He quickly learned the ropes of safari camp life and I counted myself fortunate to have him onboard.

After a few weeks of repairing tents, water pumps and Land-Rovers, he offered to do the run to Kariba to collect our clients. 'Be a nice change,' he proffered. I questioned him about navigating the lake passage, where haze often obliterated sight of land, which he had only made once before, in the opposite direction, when he arrived.

'Do it with a blindfold in the dark, mate!' He assured me.

'Okay Jim. Take it easy, and don't forget the empties.' We needed to return our used beer and mineral bottles to exchange for full ones.

'No worries. See ya later.' I watched him expertly drive my boat, with no compass, over the horizon. After longer than I was expecting, he finally returned with our guests, whom I happened to know well. Busy greeting them, I didn't check the boat, but noticed Jim's raggedly torn shirtsleeve. I got a nod and a smile to my query about how his trip went. Walking and talking with my friends up to camp, they were curious about Jim and his cool handling of the rough conditions he had encountered on the way across to fetch them.

'Funny . . . he didn't mention that. It's been pretty calm on our side?' I noted.

My eyebrows rose when I heard he'd arrived in Kariba with a boat full of smashed bottles and crates. I went to investigate, and found what looked like bullet holes through the boat's foredeck.

Jim now explained he'd taken a 'small detour' on the way over. He'd mistaken the Zambian town of Siavonga for Kariba. On driving into the harbour, he was summoned by Zambian soldiers to motor towards their position. Only then did he realize his ghastly gaffe.

All credit to him—he pretended to have engine trouble while he pondered his options. Stepping back into the driving seat, he opened up the 50hp with everything it had—and headed for open waters.

A fusillade of gunfire followed from the Zambian soldiers. They were shooting well. Fortunately, the AK rounds mostly hit the crates of empty bottles behind his seat, a couple going through the foredeck and out through the bows, one clipping his shirt sleeve.

Good for the red berets.

'Do you and Rob really want this Fothergill Island, Sandy?'

Dr Colin Saunders, a fatherly figure and chairman of the National Parks Board, was on a visit to outlying Parks camps. He was concerned about the survival of our young family on their own in such a remote station with a guerrilla war waging around us. And Kazungula Safaris was still where is wasn't supposed to be.

'We sure do, Colin. But we can't carry on in this tented camp site any longer. We'll be under water next rainy season.'

A Government Minister had an eye on Fothergill as part of his retirement package, stalling all our efforts to move there. With some help from our friends, and the deteriorating tourism market, suddenly tenders were called for to develop a lodge on the island.

We were the only one to tender. In a record-breaking three weeks, the tender was granted. Financing the tender was something else.

'We have a Hotel Levy fund, diligently collected for years, which is designated for tourist development.' Mike Gardner, Chief of the Tourist Board, was tipping me off. 'Nobody has ever used it.'

'Would Fothergill Island stand a chance?' I asked.

'Why not?'

In March of 1977, a soft loan was duly approved to finance the purchase of materials for building the lodge. What wouldn't buy a match in the latter year inflation crisis, Rhodesian $30,000 was made available, valued then at only a little less in US$.

I had been planning for the last four years to make the move. The moment we had the green light, Sands and I, with now two small children, moved across with our nucleus building team. It was incredibly plucky of her to undertake this wild move, with us and our staff living in reject tents from Old Kaz while we built ourselves pole and dagga huts. Water was carried up from the lake, cooking done on open fires, washing on rocky ledges in the shallows by the shore, and work from sun up to sunset, our only communication with the outside world being the old-fashioned 'Lake Navigation' radio. Sands and I loved, talked and shared, closer and in more harmony than we ever had.

In standard optimistic fashion, the new Fothergill lodge was to be ready to move into by November—five months away. No pressure. We just felt so privileged to be living on our own desert island, as it were.

People passing on the lake would see the structures going up, sticking way out above the scrubby trees. They would call in to see what was happening—nothing much else was developing in the escalating war scenario.

'Aren't you lonely out here?'

'Would you swap your office for this?' We'd smile. They'd smile back and nod, understanding.

I was seeing for real why capitalism works. Ownership inspires one to lengths nothing else can. No ways would I have worked like this for a salary? The challenge was how to inspire the workers to feel the same involvement.

Michael Bhunu, our chef's son, was a newly fledged carpenter. He and I headed up the team, wielding hammers, saws, and *demos* (traditional axes ideal for shaping and joining). No power tools or fancy instruments.

'Ask nobody to do anything you aren't prepared and able to do yourself,' was our motto. This was no hire and fire market. As a worker, once in, you were in, unless something very awful cropped up. Michael and I were out there with the guys under the sun, hour after hour, day after day.

In between measuring, checking designs and physically working out and translating my roughly drawn plans onto the ground, we were training men to use tools they'd never seen before and jobs they were amazed demanded such attention to detail.

'No, Zack, no . . . if you use a saw like your mother does her bread knife, you'll be back in her kitchen before the elephants drink today!' I'd hear Michael threatening to send them to their worst humiliation if they would not learn well.

'Aah, suure? Aaieewa!' Everybody would laugh at Zack's expense. Humour always made light of the tough work, and we made sure there was lots of it.

Structures were built to last, so different to their scanty huts back home, it wasn't easy for the guys to get their heads around what we were asking them to do. I was design and site engineer, project director, quantity surveyor, head carpenter, instructor and labourer, all in one. Very clear how the lodge should blend into the bleak landscape, I had a vision for every part of it and how each future guest would have a view and experience of a lifetime in the new Lodge. It was fantastically creative and rewarding to see it happening before my eyes.

Working off an old table—that served alternatively for baby bathing and office in our mud hut, files in wooden beer crates on the floor, Sands continued to run the books and ordering of supplies. The Salisbury office closed after Lizzie left to go home. The Lake Navigation radio, dependant on the weather and how well the aerial stayed clamped in the tree, canoes were used for carrying paperwork back and forth between the camps.

On top of her many administrative chores, Sands was a fulltime Mum, electing not to have help with the family chores. Mistakes in this primitive environment could be costly. Cooking, mud hut keeping, washing nappies in a daily safari down to the lake shore, little Cath in her 4-wheel drive push cot, *kutundu* dumped on top, Neen helping push with all her might through the sand was all part of Sands' role.

The workers' wives, who all had their own children, and bore their seemingly permanent pregnancies valiantly, would offer to assist Sands with ours. One of them lost track of their toddler one day, unnoticed until cries were heard from down one of the 'long drop' latrines. These 4m deep holes were capped with a concrete slab, suitably 'holed', roofed and enclosed with a surrounding wall.

The entire work force rushed to the rescue, shouting directives to the toddler. He was instructed to fit the noose that had been dropped to him around his arms and chest so he could be pulled out. To no avail. We were soon stripping down the walls and lifting the concrete slab to let the father down into the hole. After a good wash and disinfect, no one seemed worse for the experience. A sobering reminder to keep a closer eye on the children, of which there were at least twenty in the staff village. Sands was henceforth a touch wary of our willing but bush-bred Tonga mothers and nannies.

We woke with the sun and went to bed with it, resting several hours in the midday heat. At the end of the day we'd take our evening stroll to the shore for a family relax time, enjoying the spectacular sunsets, and bath in the lake off rocks where we could keep a lookout for crocs. Dinner was back in our mud hut under paraffin lamps.

Life was never better.

Setting up Fothergill

Mr Hook

Thatching the dining lodge

Brick-making

Sands & Neen off to wash in the river

I again used local material where I could in the buildings, searching out knurled old tree trunks lying at the water's edge', suitable for the uprights. Our test for their solidity was if they took less than half a morning to cut through with our big two-man saw, they were rejected as too rotten.

Big trees were scarce, thanks to that bush-clearing. The upside of that exercise was having open waters, free of 'sticks', around us, providing good trolling for tiger and trouble free boating on our game viewing trips.

'I smell cattle dip, Rob?' commented a farmer friend who'd dropped in. He picked up the scent of arsenic, well known to ranchers for dipping cattle against ticks.

'Well, don't shout about it." I cautioned him.

Our accommodation was being constructed in traditional Tonga style, slender sticks tied between the main structural poles to form the wall, which would then be covered in *daga* (mud) and roofed with thatch. It was a cool and tested Zambezi Valley structure. The snag was the termites loved them too.

I'd come up with a treatment to render the sticks termite resistant. We'd cut them green and stand them in a drum of cattle dip until the leaves turned brown, signalling the arsenic was now drawn through the branch. It worked wonderfully, although no doubt environmentally suspect. Alors, Afrique!

In building our new Fothergill Lodge, I tried to retain the atmosphere of the tented camp we all loved so much,but without tents blowing away in storms, leaking flaps and holed canvas. My commitment was to still feel part of our surroundings—natural air-conditioning, no doors or windows—these were simply openings in the structure, sealed against strong winds by drop-down reed mats. Full walls were avoided, the hut open in every direction to take advantage of any breeze. This meant big overhangs on the roof to keep out the rain. Cold was not an issue.

Bathrooms were open to the sky. Liberating, albeit a little disconcerting to the ladies enjoying a midday shower that were in line with the aerodrome take off path. Not to mention distracted low-level pilots.

It was a different kind of lodge, which attracted equally different kind of visitors, and we all liked it that way.

The island vegetation was scrubby, hardly a tree taller than a man—thanks to years of elephant trimming, and the original bush clearing operation to remove all trees for future fishing grounds before they were flooded. Monstrous D9 Caterpillars pulling battleship chains attached to gigantic 4m diameter water-filled steel balls had ruthlessly cleared the huge areas. Somehow, Fothergill had been classified as a fishing ground.

The result for us was no trees—we desperately needed shade. So the focal point of the Lodge, a large double-storied thatch Gazebo—dining room downstairs, 'look out' bar upstairs, was the priority major structure to go up. Its design became the forerunner of many safari lodges that sprouted around Zimbabwe after independence. It was the only one of its kind when we built it, with the best of magnificent in old colonial ambience. Clint Eastwood chose it for his film '*White Hunter, Black Heart*'.

I was only too aware of my limited building experience, and not a little concerned about my ambitious plan. I had carefully built a scale model from grass stems in the Old Kaz camp, critiqued by Sands, who was great on décor but not so good on structural engineering. Trying to picture in my mind just how this mammoth would actually be constructed, I placed and glued each piece of grass, imagining the size and weight of the pole, and how we'd handle putting it in position. The main trusses would weigh close on a ton, to be handled manually.

Twelve heavy seven metre poles, the largest I could find anybody to supply, were man—handled into the vertical in two parallel lines, half the labour force struggling to lift each one. To hold them in their correct position while they were 'dindered' (compacting the earth to secure them in their holes, using sharp iron stakes) was another challenge. The tops were sticking six metres straight up into the sky, like a Zimbabwean nuclear missile site. These were lined up by eye by my standing way back, hanging in one of our scrubby trees, shouting instructions to the work crew as I levelled them with the lake horizon.

'Bufflo, Baas!' a man was hollering at me.

'Nooo, not below. On top! *Pezulu,*' I shouted back.

'Bufflo, *Nyati, Baas, ya pasi* (beneath you)!' he furiously gesticulated.

I slowly turned to find a big dagga boy eying me from 3m away. He'd been attracted by all the gesticulating from my tree and had come to investigate. My little tree suddenly became even smaller and spindlier. All went real quiet. The old boy gave a snort, and trotted off. No question who was the boss around here!

The rest of the structure had to be built around these uprights, and only when we had completed that sufficiently to get up to those tops and place the 'wall plates'—the poles that run along to support the roof—did we discover what a brilliant job we'd done. The accuracy of man's eye.

This became our warehouse where we would stack all the materials arriving, their ordering and delivery a mission in itself as all movement on the road was in armed convoys. These waited for no one and did not always get through unscathed. The slow lumbering transport trucks were easy targets, only travelling once a day on the main routes.

Fritz Dolleman, a successful Chinhoi farmer, visited us regularly in his professionally homebuilt steel houseboat. He offered to lend me his fourteen ton truck and trailer to transport a particularly big load of poles, typically generous of the farming community. I went with the driver to supervise the loading. Newly 'treated', it was difficult to gauge the weight of the poles. Heavy was all we knew.

The main road to Kariba wound its way down the Zambezi escarpment in a dramatic cliff-hanging trail, the original access road slightly improved since the dam was constructed and a major feat of engineering at the time to get the road through between rainy seasons.

'Juz give us a bulldaozer to foller me, man, and make sure the beer is cold, hey!' volunteered one of the old engineers from the renowned Rhodesian roads department in conjunction with the water department, responsible for the dam. Surveying the timeless elephant paths that criss-crossed the hills, he established a track that formed the basis for the road, still used today.

It is testing for any heavy vehicle driver. I loved driving big trucks and asked the driver if I could have a go. It has to be one of the most harrowing drives I have ever made. The brakes were ineffective with our heavy load on the steep gradients, vital gear changing all that kept the vehicle speed down. No veer off 'truck ramps' if I slipped up. The convoy was forcibly stretched, one of the military vehicles tearing along with me, the other big trucks left growling their way slowly down behind us.

We screamed down the narrow winding road with precipitous drops over the edge, 20 tons of poles behind us, Mr Angel clearly riding with us in the over-loaded fourteen tonner, ensuring nothing came up the other way. There was no chance to stop and hand over to the real driver, who sat riveted in the passenger seat, even more terrified than I was.

Our newly built Gazebo, apart from our living room, became our administration centre and warehouse, where more valuable and potentially removable material was stacked around us.

By paraffin lamp over dinner one evening, I heard a scuffling down the other end of the cavernous building. Picking up a lamp, I tiptoed down to investigate the intruder, suddenly finding myself standing next to an equally surprised hippo. We both jumped and hippo shuffled off. Nothing too unusual about that.

Next evening, same noise, same time. I cautiously re-investigated, expecting and indeed meeting friend hippo again. We looked at each other curiously, and quietly went our separate ways. Every evening thereafter, for the next three years, Esmerelda, came visiting at dinner time.

She became so familiar that I could walk slowly up and greet her with a hand shake to her tusk, when she would open wide her huge gaping mouth, breathing hot sweet hippo breath over me, shaking her head up and down. As construction progressed she adapted to the new situations, arriving as we sat down with our guests for dinner under the stars, to graze quietly, well, noisily actually, on our cultured lawn. Diners would have this gigantic mouth chomping next to them, and occasionally a huge grinning jaw would rest on their table, collapsing it under a hippo head weight of +200kg, leaving a wobbly looking table and guest.

She also took to visiting the harbour at the end of the day when the boats from the afternoon's activities were being rowed ashore from the jetty for the night's parking. She would slide quietly astern of a boat, open her mouth over the engine, and give it a gentle push to help it on its way, the paddling boatman on the bows chuckling with delight as he slid up the bank. In between assisting the boatmen, she would frolic about, lying on her back in the mud, paddling her stumpy legs in the air to the cheers of onlookers gathered for our daily cabaret.

This clearly had its risks and we were at pains to warn everyone that she was indeed a wild hippo, and that they should avoid approaching or feeding her. Sands was a good, and bad, example in this respect. When she noticed Esmerelda approaching during dinner, she would quietly collect her plate and glass of wine and make smartly for the stairs leading up to our 'look out' bar. Most of the guests took this as their cue to do the same. A mass exodus would follow, leaving just me and my immediate dining companions who I'd managed to restrain, and one hippo, all peacefully continuing our meal with the peanut gallery audience above us.

A group of German visitors arrived, celebrating a birthday, for which they'd specially brought a keg of beer. We consumed this in one evening. We were regaled the next morning with stories of weaving young men finding Esmarelda asleep on a sandpit near the path on their way home and deciding to take pictures of each other reposing on her, which they showed us. Whether she was asleep, or plain tolerant, I don't know, other than they were plain lucky young men.

She must have been the most photographed hippo in the world. One day, we received a letter from a lady in Canada who had just read about and seen pictures of Esmerelda in a Toronto newspaper. She related her strange story of how she had been working on a rhino project in the Matusadona two years before. Her favourite evening activity was to sit on the high ground at a point behind Fothergill and watch the sun go down.

'One evening,' she wrote, 'an extraordinary spectacle played out before me. A big cow hippo started running up and down the shoreline, enraged and bellowing. Catastrophically, it ran on to one of the many sharp, spear like stumps that stood amongst the grass, impaling herself, where she died in roaring agony.

'Aghast and dumbfounded, I walked down to inspect the carcass and seek the cause of the commotion, which I never found—maybe a croc after her baby? What I did find was the baby hippo nearby, which after a while overcame its shyness and approached its now dead mother, and me. An adoption process took place, and I walked back to the camp with a baby hippo following.

'We now had a no options camp pet, whom we named 'Hey You'. We had to feed 'her' mealie meal (the staple diet of everybody in Africa, including Hey You). This rapidly became a somewhat hefty and unexpected increase in the food budget. I encouraged the cook to add grass in an attempt to wean the young lady off the mealie meal. No ways. Mealie meal was tastier. One day the cook, whose grass cutting duties were becoming quite onerous, suggested we pour the mealie meal onto the grass! Reducing its quantity daily, we finally persuaded Hey You into being a grass eating hippo.

'She would walk with me, and we swam in the lake together, her keeping the crocs at bay, I hoped! She was a great companion. We bade a sad adieu after six months, returning again three months later to check on her. We boated round the bays I new so well, calling her name. There was a particular hippo that seemed quite friendly, but we didn't want to presume on the reunion, in case it was somebody else!'

Our Canadian friend posed the question whether Esmerelda might be their 'Hey You', describing that 'Hey You' loved chocolate mousse, and could we try her on it? We didn't, but I did notice a particularly brown set of hippo teeth. It was possible, and I passed on her best love.

We called Esmarelda 'her', as that's who we thought she was, until one evening we were amazed to see 'her' with a full and unashamed erection. It is very difficult to sex a young hippo, their genitals being completely hidden. Poor Esmerelda, in this delicate state, was greeted with hoots of laughter from all her onlookers.

Soon after this, clearly the beginning of her manhood, she came unwittingly into competition with two territorial bulls, who chased 'her' off Fothergill to Long Island, some 5km offshore. There she seemed to settle down until a sad episode with some campers ended in her being shot dead, so often the tragic end for wild animals that become too familiar with man.

Flotilla from 'Old Kaz' to Fothergill

Bulldozing a runway

Esmerelda

Painting a lodge

Happy family

Chapter 28

Fothergill Frolics

We had taken bookings for 7 November, 1977. Timing was critical. Our cash flow was tied to a smooth transition from Old Kaz closing end of October and the new Fothergill Lodge opening a week later.

No worries. There's a civil engineer in charge.

But Murphy was there, as always. Boss Jim was despatched to the other side of the Lake to collect Mopane poles, returning so loaded that she sank on her way home rounding the point in heavy weather. The tractor sank up to its axles in the fine soft sands off the beach when the driver took a short cut with a load of stone. The lake level was rising, and we had to stop everything to get it out. Two days. Materials didn't arrive after convoys got shot up. A Land-Rover engine seized when somebody forgot to check the oil. There was just too much to do with not enough trained leaders, nor contingency plans.

Our fifty workers were on a steep learning curve. Drawings and plans, tolerances and deadlines, plumbing and electricity were about as far out of their scope as the space race. So there wasn't much delegation allowed.

'I want to be a waiter, Maam.' Tyson, our longstanding woodcutter and general labourer, was thinking ahead and ready for promotion.

'Good, Tyson, you can join the training on Saturday afternoons.' Sands was eyeing up who might work in the running of the lodge.

With her patience and talent to teach, the staff were fortunate to have such dedication and commitment.

Also conscious of the wives and children and their need for education and learning new skills to earn, women culturally not being acceptable in the workplace, Sands would find time to hold ladies' classes—hygene, motherhood, domestic crafts, knitting and toy-making. She planned for their wares to be on display in the future lodge shop. It was a great motivation for each lady's quest for independence, and deeply appreciated by all.

On cue, at the end of October, we closed Old Kaz and started the move across. Every craft that could float—rafts, jetties, rowing boats, canoes—even the hulk of a former yacht which we used as our worm farm, were roped in. We had purchased the diesel twin-engined Tuna, another famous operation Noah boat, formerly run by my old friend and rival, Jeff Stutchbury, which took on the role of tugboat in the operation.

Our gallant armada, tied in line astern in good naval fashion, stretched to over half a kilometre. Tuna slowly towing the whole fleet over the seven kilometre voyage, we trusted for fine weather en route. We wondered how many times had she done something so similar in the past, except with animals rather than loaded katundu? Once at Fothergill, we'd offload onto the harbour shoreline and head back for another trip. Our foreshore looked like the Normandy beaches, only without bagpipes, or anybody shooting at us—other than time.

To transport the four game-viewing Land-Rovers, I'd made a raft equipped with heavy loading ramps. On the first tow, landy raft tied straight behind Tuna, the remaining armada astern, we slowly built up speed.

Without warning, the raft's bow-wave suddenly started to push the nose down like a submarine entering its dive. I immediately pulled off power, but Tuna's heavy steel hull, heavily loaded, took time to respond. For a terrifying moment the Land-Rover roof tilted towards me, about to slide off the raft deck and disappear into the depths. God smiled, and to my infinite relief, it slowly, so slowly, surfaced again, water pouring out everywhere.

Mr Angel does it again.

The day our lodge was scheduled to open we still had much stuff strewn around the harbour. The pine floor in the upstairs bar was only half completed, no plumbing connected, nor any accommodation completed, the kitchen nor bathrooms functional. The place looked like, and indeed still was, a building site.

Promptly at 0900, a long standing client, Trail Garvin, arrived in his boat for the fishing holiday he had booked months previously. Trail, ever-gentlemanly, walked up the path from the jetty, shaking his head and apologising for obviously getting his dates wrong. Reassuring him, I took his suitcase and Sands organised a breakfast of bacon and eggs which he and his party ate amongst the building materials stacked in the dining room. Assuring him all was well, we asked if he wouldn't mind going off fishing for the rest of the day while we got his room ready. He looked around with a smile, went back down the path to his boat, and went fishing.

Our staff watched this interaction. I'd been saying for weeks, without effect, that we needed to finish and have the camp habitable by today. One of the great attributes of African people is a huge respect for preserving dignity, for not bringing 'shame' on one's household.

This now kicked in.

The entire labour force turned into an army of ants. Shouts, demands, responses, encouragement and humour echoed around the camp. Nobody walked anywhere. They ran. Tools flew up and down, lunch and teatimes were cut to minimum, no energy was spared, no one rested. During the course of the day, every job was completed that needed to be. The sites in the camp that were to be occupied and utilised were swept and finished off. Thatched roofs ran down to the eaves. Building materials were tidied. Paths cleaned, beds made, mosquito nets hung, water flowed in the pipes, generator hummed and lights glowed for the first time on Fothergill Island.

Trail stepped off his boat that evening, and walked slowly up to the lodge. His head didn't stop shaking while his smile simply grew wider, as did ours.

We needed a pool. Lake dips with the crocs were not being widely accepted.

'You gotta mix and lay all the concrete in one go, Rob, or it'll leak,' Our swimming pool buddy instructed. Fifteen tons of concrete, mixed by hand, all in one go.

I ordered Chibuku, the local opaque beer, a meal in itself, and cokes. These were lined up on the day, in clear view of the gaping hole in the ground where the swimming pool was to be. The understanding was that they would only to be touched on completion of throwing the concrete.

Starting as soon as it got light, the entire work force pulled in. Two teams competed against each other, allowing one team to have a break while the other worked, alternatively jeered and encouraged by the 'off' team. Tea or lunch breaks were to be taken in the 'off' shift. I expected to be at it the whole day, lining up paraffin lamps for extending the operation into the night.

'*Eweh*! You want to be back in your mother's kitchen???? Swing dat *foshel* (spade) man!' Zack, earlier threatened the same punishment for misusing the saw, berates his work mates.

'Zack, your mother's sadza stick has more energy than your *'foshel', No?'* The men hit back.

Hapless individuals were mocked for their lack of motion, or praised for their prowess, African style, in the best of humour. Zimbabwean work songs rose in their timeless rhythm from the huge hole. It was a real good team-building day—just as well, I expected it to be a long hard one.

By midday, lunch time, seven hours after we'd started, the job was done and the beer being drunk. What is it that we've missed in motivating our work forces so? Free cokes and Chibuku beer?

In the early hours of one morning, waking me, Sands is asking 'Why are the chickens making that noise?'

'Probably an owl sitting on the roof,' I drowsily reply, willing her to go to sleep again.

Our vegetable garden and chicken run, heavily fenced in with 3m high wire netting to ward off the animal kingdom, was close to our sleeping hut. Positioned so best to keep an eye on our farming effort. The dawn chorus from the chicken run was our most reliable alarm clock.

Sands wasn't having any of it, and nudged me again. I grumpily agreed to investigate.

The heat of October in the mud walls of our hut made it like an oven. So we slept naked. In this stark attire, we jumped off our bed and crept round the kitchen, armed with a torch which I planned to turn on at the last moment to surprise whoever was disturbing our farm yard. Perhaps I'd reckoned our attire would do the rest?

Sands, close behind, almost moulded into me, as a women tends to be behind her man creeping naked in the pitch dark through wild Africa, worrying about her chickens. Switching on the torch as we rounded the kitchen corner, a great black-maned lion growled and leapt away, straight into our fence, boomeranged off, nearly falling on top of us, and then bounded off into the dark.

'Oh, so that's what it was,' trying my best to sound real casual. I wouldn't have a wife on the island for much longer if this was going to be a regular occurrence.

'Rob, I want you to put a proper door on our hut, today!'

I didn't argue.

March 1978, our official opening, camp mostly tried and tested. All the dignitaries of the tourist trade and associated government chiefs were invited. We had just completed the airstrip by driving a grader through the mopane scrub from one side of the island to the other. Aeroplanes disappeared from sight twice on their take off run in the undulations. But, we had an aerodrome—a boon in the light of the dangers on the roads. Now to be used by our invited promotional guests, a critical audience, yet generously enthusiastic in their support for our newly opened lodge. Many other tourist establishments were closing due to hostilities.

With the camp about to burst at its seams for the first time ever, we were still working feverishly to make it habitable. I will never forget looking up, covered in cement and tar, still working on the drainage system in our last built accomodations, as the first aeroplane did a low fly over the camp prior to landing.

Leaving Sands to meet and greet, I issued rapid instructions for what still had to be completed, tore off for a shower and change into my smart new uniform.

'We are not the first, nor the last, to be in a war,' feeling somewhat Churchillian, my opening speech began. 'But we are the first to be dining in a full lodge on Rupert Fothergill's Island.

'Nothing in our precious country stands other than through the toil, sweat and persistent perseverance of those who've dreamed and believed. Thanks to them, this little land-locked country in the middle of Africa holds its own today. Opening our Island lodge at this time is just a part of those wonderful dreams and beliefs.

'Thank you all, and especially my hard working team, for standing by us in our dream. Sandy and I welcome you to our official opening of Fothergill Island.'

Many of the construction team were standing there, newly trained as chefs, waiters, and bedroom hands, whose dedication and preparedness to be cuffed and taught had made this day possible.

The Tourist Board themselves had gone to unusual and creative lengths to keep the industry afloat in the extraordinary wartime conditions. One of these was to assist in providing the basic income that establishments needed in order to keep operating. This guaranteed our essential income even if no tourist arrived. Provided you agreed to stay open. The guest list was submitted monthly for scrutiny and computation for payment, proportionate to the deficit in one's break-even requirements. These brave decisions were continued in the face of mounting casualties, including the shooting down of two Air Rhodesia Viscounts on their scheduled service into Kariba.

These flights had to climb over the Zambezi escarpment, the range of mountains running along both sides of the valley and lake. The two planes were hit with heat-seeking missiles as they sought altitude after take-off. One exploded in the air, all on board killed. The other was skilfully force landed in a small clearing after two engines were destroyed and caught fire. Unfortunately, a steep *donga* (gully) lay across the middle of its ground run, breaking up the plane and killing the pilots and forward passengers. Three of the survivors trekked out for help, while the remaining thirteen rallied and nursed their wounded under the shelter of a wing.

Fothergill official opening

Smith's visit

The harbour

Visitors made welcome

Tragically, a group of Joshua Nkomo's terrorists, the Soviet backed wing of the Nationalist movement, saw the plane go down, came in and shot the survivors. SAS men were para-dropped in to the wreckage to find a butchered bundle of bodies under a tree. A small boy with teddy in his arms, an old man with $10 in his top pocket, an air-hostess holding a blood soaked flannel. The three who had gone for help managed to lay low and escape, and tell the tale. Several of our regular guests, all friends, perished on these flights on their way home after staying with us.

The Dean of the Anglican Cathedral in Salisbury, in the commemoration service to those who had died, deplored 'The Deafening Silence' of the outside world in his stirring sermon—as did we all.

Our patriotic fervour to see our country through all this was high. Not so much because of political motivation, but simply because we loved our land with a passion and would defend it against any destroyer. We didn't see Ian Smith as a high flying glory seeking politician, but one who believed, as we did, that the freedom and prosperity our nation enjoyed was worth fighting for. Akin to the allied response to Hitler's aggression.

We all knew there were flaws in the system, but believed the foundations were good, and we'd get the building sound, with time and patience. We took the Nationalist's political blustering on both sides with a pinch of salt. But none of us accepted the barrel of a terrorist rifle as a negotiating tool.

The PM's Spitfire pilot nerve and his down to earth way of dealing impressed us. His political obstinacy and stupidity did not. No question our 'indigenous' people needed more say in government. But, for all the injustices, on both sides, there was a right and honourable way of doing things, and they needed to be sought and given their chance.

Whites were learning how deep the indignities of the past were felt by politically motivated blacks, and to what lengths they were prepared to go in righting these. Many were opposed to the government's intransigence and departed the country in protest.

Nevertheless, Smith, a charismatic leader, held sway. A personal eye opener came when he visited Kariba to unveil a plaque in commemoration of Rupert Fothergill. A last minute decision was made to come across the lake and see our new camp on the island, named after this famous conservationist. In typical low key security style, the PM, confident of his safety, needing no fanfare, stepped nonchalantly ashore.

'Good afternoon, young man. Would you show me around and tell me how you are getting along over here. I'm interested.' He engaged in his clipped Rhodesian accent.

We talked as we walked, just him and me, the security dudes and accompanying government ministers following at a discreet distance, him intensely concerned with the problems of our surviving out here.

'This is a big one.' He sympathised as we surveyed the waves breaking over the leading edge of our camp on the lake shore. I was explaining how the lake-facing front of the camp was being seriously washed at the new high water level and how I had built my chalets here on the peninsula to form a protection for our harbour. Before we moved camp, in good engineering fashion, I'd built gabions (rocks enclosed in wire mesh and a well-proven method of safeguarding wave erosion) to protect the front. What I hadn't anticipated was the rocks I'd used, that looked as hard as concrete when collected, dissolved after a time in water. The oversight was about to cost me my chalets and my harbour.

'What's your plan here?' asked the PM.

Hearing my response that it was beyond my budget, rubbing that stubborn chin, he remarked quietly. 'We'll have to see what we can do then.'

We walked on. I did not pay great heed to his remark. What was a Prime Minister of a country at war going to do about my little camp being washed away? They left after a good lunch and a nice outing.

Mid morning the next day, an aircraft circled and landed, unannounced. I went up to find a Ministry of Lands pilot, an engineer, a Natural Resources Board man, and a fourth from the Prime Minister's office.

'We understand from the PM there's a Natural Resource in trouble here. He said you'd show us the problem,' the pilot explained.

'I think I know what you're talking about. Follow me, gentlemen.'

I took them down to the ailing waterfront to ask if that might be 'the trouble'. They nodded, took detailed measurements and notes, discussed ideas over lunch, and left.

Three days later the car ferry 'Sea Horse' arrived offshore, loaded with sixty tons of rock blasted from the quarry in Kariba, dumping it to form a breakwater in front of the crumbling cliffs. This process continued each day for a week, after which the breakwater stretched the entire length needed to protect the peninsular. The operation would have cost more than building my whole camp. It survives to this day.

On 3 March 1978, history was made. An internal political settlement was signed between the Smith government and the three black opposition parties then operating in the country, combined to form the United African National Council (UANC). The external nationalist parties under Joshua Nkomo and Robert Mugabe refused to participate and remained at war.

The coalition government was to steer the country towards black majority rule, and peace. Ninety percent of the voter's roll turned out to elect Bishop Abel Muzorewa as Prime Minister of the country, renamed Zimbabwe-Rhodesia.

The British called it 'a step in the right direction'. Not quite the resounding support we needed. Possibly the biggest gaff in British diplomacy over our country. Condemned outright by the warring nationalists, they vowed to escalate the war.

Sadly, the end we looked forward to was not in sight.

Chapter 29

Pretty Python

Tough politicking.

Somehow we carried on outside it all, life full and rewarding, an optimistic outlook our essential ingredient.

Dick Pitman, a young and adventurous British journalist, pitting his wits against the odds of starting afresh in our strife torn country, arrived to stay for a weekend. I was impressed by his determined and inquisitive approach to get on the inside of the story. He asked if he could build a traditional hut to live on the island while he wrote. Liking his preparedness to give anything a try, his impecunious position being a direct result of that, we agreed he would work his keep for half the day while he wrote during the other half.

It worked well. He knew boats, was passionate about being in the wild and its conservation, had a cheerful disposition and we enjoyed a mutual love of flying. After he produced his first book, *You Must Be New Around Here*, he made enough to buy a white short-wheel-base Land-Rover, which he called White Elephant, his only possession in the world besides his typewriter.

I had to visit the police station in Kariba one day.

'Why don't you take White Elephant for a run'? Dick suggested.

After pushing it up and down the yard at Kariba harbour for ten minutes, cursing its obstinacy and thinking it would have been quicker to walk, it finally spluttered into life, belching black smoke and vibrating like a wet dog shaking itself dry.

The police post was perched on the edge of the Kariba Gorge with a fierce climb to get up there. Determined not to have a repeat performance of starting it again, I parked in a suitable position for a quick getaway on the downhill side, leaving the engine running and handbrake on while I dashed in for my brief business with the charge office.

I hadn't been there two minutes when a constable appeared at the entrance enquiring whether I was driving the white Land-Rover.

'Uuh . . . yuh, that's me' I replied hesitantly. Road tax out of order? Maybe it was stolen?

'Is it in the way?' I asked innocently.

'Ahh no, it just went over!' he nonchalantly responded.

I dashed out to hear a kawomp . . . kadunk . . . clumpety clunk coming from over the edge of the Kariba Gorge precipice. I tore to the side to see White Elephant sixty metres below, neatly wrapped around a *mopane* tree with its front bumper and bonnet half way up the trunk, the engine breathing its last clunk . . . clunk.

Feeling quite sick, I ran down the hill to Harry Maun, our friendly garage mechanic. I explained I'd wrecked Dick's landy and had clients waiting in the harbour for transfer to the island. Would he please retrieve, repair and send me the bill

After a morose journey over in the boat contemplating what I was going to say, Dick was waiting my return on the jetty.

'How did she go, Rob?' he enquired with his inimitable smile.

'Let's go have a whiskey, Dick,' I replied as casually as I could.

'What? But it's only lunchtime!'

He looked paler by the minute while I related the story. He needed more than one whiskey, and took several days to recover, assisted by stress medication from Janet, our resident nurse.

He got his revenge. One afternoon, needing a break from camp, he borrowed an island Land-Rover and my rifle—I cannot imagine why I should have lent him that, even knowing how nothing beats a quiet walk in the bush to calm your soul. He parked the landy on an old termite mound, handbrake on—the usual flat battery—heard this bit before?—and was standing in the front of the landy surveying the scene through his binoculars. When the hand brake slipped. The landy ran forward, pinning Dick under the front wheel. Unfortunately, he had my trusty old hunting rifle hanging on his shoulder. With whose barrel he proceeded to dig himself out.

Our first alert to this crisis was a slapperty slap as the Land-Rover arrived back in camp on a flat front wheel. Dick climbed out covered in dust, clothing torn, in no mood to answer questions. My twisted and broken rifle lay on the seat. Had he been attacked by a large and cantankerous bull?

The story emerged later with another smile and another whiskey. On him this time.

Good friends to this day, he went on to launch The Zambezi Society, dedicated to the conservation of the great Valley. His latest book, '*A Wild Life*', is filled with the humour we all enjoyed so much back there.

'Robin, I don't mind the noise of the reed mats in the wind, or the mosquito net blowing in my face, but I do object to floating around in a wet bed!'

Grace Goodwin, a favourite fisherwoman client and highly polished English teacher and godmother to our daughter, Cath, had spent a night with an umbrella up over her bed, dodging leaks in the new thatch.

'Sorry about that, Grace. I'll have Lymon up there to look at it while you're out fishing.'

She would be out for the entire day in our open boat, on her own with the gilly, coming back for Cath on one of her afternoons, while husband, Tony, read or joined us on game drives. The boat broke down on her last trip and we only found them several hours into the night—still fishing. As many of our guests became, she was part of the family.

A missionary who had spent the evening before extolling the virtues of prayer and faith as the best weapons against fear had a lion kill outside his chalet one night. The pride chased a buffalo herd straight through the camp. Our missionary spent the night listening to the pride eat and fight over the carcass two metres from his bed. Only a low wall topped by a reed mat separated him and his wife from the grizzly feast.

We learned of their ordeal when the kitchen porter brought them morning tea, promptly dropping his tray and running for help. Chasing the lions off, much to their chagrin, we pulled the buffalo carcass out of camp to ensure our guests' slumbers the next night. Our missionary assured me he had slept well after pushing the dressing table against the doorway. His wife looked less confident.

Our lodge had become a favourite among the hard pressed farming community. They lived on isolated homesteads facing guerrilla attacks and ambushes as part of their daily existence. Fothergill was one of the few places they could come to, put their rifles against the wall, and relax. They were always treated as special guests in need of care and attention.

Sands would welcome the weary travellers with her charming smile and inviting laugh. Nothing too much trouble. Her grandmother taught her to cook and her fare was the envy of the lake. She made all the uniforms and bedspreads and supervised the catering, housekeeping and reservation teams. Staff and guests loved her.

Pregnant with our third child, she had to spend most of her troublesome term in Salisbury. Rachael, or 'Chop' as she was to be called, derived from lamb, thanks to her role as one in our annual Christmas pageant, was on her way.

I had decided, without Sands knowing, it was time for a house. God knows, she deserved one, having lived the first six years of our marriage in tents and mud huts. In typical Fynn safari style, the whole downstairs lounge was open to the bush and lakeshore. Upstairs bedroom and office had a 360 all round view, from where I could keep an eye on the camp, the shore and aerodrome.

In between 'call ups', trying to complete the lodge and my home with Sands away, I pretty much left the running of camp to our team, led by highly efficient Janet Conway. A theatre nurse for most of her life, she ran the camp in as ordered a fashion as her hospitals, not to mention her coping with the odd medical emergencies.

I was quietly sitting in our pub one evening when I overheard two lady guests talking next to me.

'Who is the manager around here, anyway?' the one asked.

'I really don't know, except that every time I've asked, he's always building his house! I think that's all he does. Must be a mansion!'

I had to smile and suitably embarrass them by introducing myself.

Rach popped out three months early, no bigger than a slab of butter. I had only just had time to build our home. The house, ready as, was a great homecoming for Sands. The staff, as always, were on the jetty to meet her and the new Fynn-ess, dancing and ululating.

Sands would be quite nervous on her own when I went away on all too frequent 'call-ups'. Having been such a daring young lady, I was surprised, but put it down to mothering three young children in this wild place. When I came back from one call-up, I found she had stretched chicken wire across the steps leading to our upstairs bedroom, 'to ward off wandering lions', but in such a manner that it now literally looked like the chicken run.

'You want a door on the stairs . . . ?' After all these years of tents and mud huts with rickety old doors, or none at all, I had become familiar, even attached, to our open style living. I tried to understand.

A great Mum, in the midst of our exacting lifestyle, Sands always had time for our children. Her seamstress skills produced all their clothes, and there would always be little goodies to munch at home, tucked away and called 'seekies'. On our weekly supply run which arrived on the local 'tramp steamer', every member of staff and their families down in the harbour, off loading, checking inventories, greeting those arriving, and sending off those going on time out, a regular feature of all the excitement would be three little girls sitting on a rock, tucking into a tin of Milo and condensed milk, Sand's treat to them in the absence of any other on our island home.

As the children grew, to ease the scrum in our home upstairs, I converted a building into their own room that had been built as stables for horses we hoped we might get but never did. Positioned next to our house to facilitate watching over possible lion activity, it served the purpose well. Rustic in nature, as all the buildings were, windows were simply openings covered with chicken mesh.

Moving to the new house

Reception & Sands' office this way

Neen's dog, Jess

Relaxing one evening over dinner on our front lawn, children tucked up in bed, a blood-curdling scream from seven year old Karina suddenly rent the night air.

'Snake, Daddy, Snaaaake!'

I leapt to the door and switched on our generator driven lights to find a huge python curled around her bed, clearly seeking out her Jack Russel that always slept with her, fortunately inside the mosquito net. Gavin Ford, our new guide, whose herpetologist experience, and all other botanical knowledge I might add, was far superior to mine, was called to assist. We gathered Mr Python into a pillowcase, to be dropped off on next morning's game drive.

After assuring the girls how nice and friendly pythons were—although they love eating Jack Rusells—I settled everybody back into bed, a little worried that Neen would be troubled by the experience of waking to find a snake's head just next to hers.

All that was alleviated the next morning when excited Neen related the story to our guests over breakfast, as was her daily habit. Her morning news bulletin, given to each table as she circled the dining room, was one all looked forward to.

'Hello. My name's Karina. My mum and dad own this camp. And, do you know what happened . . . ?!' started most days for newly arrived guests.

This day she recounted how beautiful the snake looked that had been on her bed last night, what lovely markings it had on its head, and that she'd be drawing it in school that morning.

Cath and Rach listened intently, all having had a good look at Mr Python too, and agreed. What this all did for guest's confidence in their own sleeping security, I wasn't sure. No ways could we block up all the openings into their chalets.

We initially educated our children through a most efficient government correspondence school developed for the farming communities. It incorporated lessons on radio, delivered with an 'out of the movies' schoolmistress voice that would take the children through little dances and exercises, drawing, handstands, making models, and stories read in breathless tones. The children loved it, as we did too, taking every opportunity to listen with them.

**Fothergill
School**

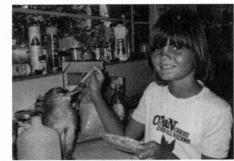

Hours of parental supervision, falling mostly on Sands, the huge and heavy plastic yellow envelopes of homework had to be assembled fortnightly, posted off and received back after marking. Children and teaching parents are a hard combination, and there would be argumentative and sometimes infuriatingly uncooperative attitudes.

Finally, we decided to build a school and employ a teacher. One of our guides, Richard Whittaker, who was a trained teacher, took on the duty.

Richard's teaching and disciplinary measures were delightfully unconventional, filled with humour and motivational fun. I was driving out early one morning on a game drive, our first 'sighting' was the teacher running down the track being chased and pelted with elephant dung by the pupils. I found out later that he'd set up booby traps of flour bags that fell on their heads when they opened the classroom door that morning, his hiding behind the bushes given away by his sniggering. He is a fine member of Harare's independent school teaching staff today.

Thereafter, various lovely teaching ladies who liked the idea of living differently and needing to 'get away', came and went, with varied approaches, from strict ruler beatings on the hands, to granny loving persuasion, to out and out 'do what you like as long as you do it loudly and strongly'.

School started at 0600 and was normally all over by 1000, with a little homework session in the cool of the late afternoon. In between, the children explored. This could mean training frogs, racing beetles, teaching chickens acrobatics, fishing, canoeing, game drives with Dad, or 'helping' Mum. It was a wonderfully free existence.

Neen was the leader of the gang, with Cath a competitive understudy, little Rach following in the rear, agreeing with everything her sisters suggested, trusting them implicitly. They were an inseparable team, known as The Fothergill Pirates by my family in town.

Island dress, spotlessly clean at the beginning of the day and looking like chimney sweeps within hours, consisted of pants and a 'T' shirt, the latter discarded as the day warmed up. A common sight was three off-white bottoms walking down the path, the Lodge's logo of a paw mark clearly displayed, often with a fourth brown bottom, a warthog's, tail high, our latest family addition, all in formation. Always set on another mission, studying a new insect or reptile. They lived in their own world, where school never stopped.

Neen had adopted an orphan monkey found on a game drive, probably having lost its mother to a predator and somehow escaped. It never let her go, clinging onto her neck every waking moment. Neen was protectively jealous of her charge. Cath and Rach would sneak in a cuddle with sleeping Monkey in its box cot when Neen wasn't looking, quickly to be admonished by surrogate mother once discovered.

'When are we collecting grass again, Dad?' Neen asked.

'Monkey needing a holiday?' I enquired.

Thatching grass was cut from vleis inland, where marshy ground allowed it to grow long and strong, before buffalo and elephant ravaged it. Loading thatch is quite an art, which I needed to instruct the team in. We would camp out on these trips, exploring the area for future game viewing potential while the guys cut and combed grass.

Days off would be sailing the old 'Fish', Dad's boat he'd tried so hard to sail in Sofala, to National Park camps up the Ume River, on the other end of the Matuse, where we catered for ourselves, enjoying family time, game viewing, walks, fishing and reading—everything but looking-after other people. Neen discovered what red chilli was like, insisting on spooning large dollops into her soup after watching me.

'Plosions, Daddy! Plosions!' She sputtered as she stuffed tomatoes into her mouth to cool down. The others noted the effect—another lesson from big sister.

Cath never stopped sweeping and cleaning, and Rach did whatever Cath did.

The break from planning, advising, hearing about another problem that needed dealing, and thinking for our sixty strong working force and similar number of guests was a joy Sands and I hugely needed and appreciated.

Back on the base . . .

'Hello . . . yes, this is Fothergill Island reception . . . yes, I'm sure we could . . . sorry, excuse me a moment . . . Karina, take the monkey off that postcard stand . . . because I say so! . . . Hello, sorry about that, as I was saying . . . Ooh nooo . . .' Sound of crashing postcard stand . . . 'Look, I'm so sorry, could I phone you back?'

'Eveeeer!' Sands wails.

'Madaaaam!' echoes back.

Ever, employed to assist minding the children, arrives and packs the team off.

Mother, teacher, housekeeper, caterer, bookkeeper/receptionist, wife and friend to all, Sands' time was cut out. Fothergill was a particularly gentle environment as the African bush goes. But poisonous insects, spiders, snakes and stinging, biting bugs were around, as were the entire Zambezi line up of monsters and meanies.

The isolation didn't add to a mother's peace of mind. It seemed the more children, the more nervous she became. I watched my Tarzan girl strangely transform into this worried Mum. Child-care discussions filled the radio-telephone waves, and frequent trips across the lake were called for to visit the local hospital. Kariba had some of the best medical care in the region in those days.

Only once did we scramble the aeroplane for our children. To fly Cathy to Harare. She'd been hanging upside down from the thatched passageway connecting the kitchen to the dining lodge by her knees. And dropped onto her head. She went a little funny—Janet diagnosed concussion, possible brain damage. Fortunately, it was established as minor concussion, and we all went shopping instead of visiting her in hospital.

Cath was the family comic, keeping us in alternative fits of laughter and exasperation. Cap back to front, front teeth pegged in a big smile behind every action and remark, she would dress in green overalls when 'working', her cheeky little face inquisitively peering into everything going on. She called herself the 'bobo' (from *bobijan*, Afrikaans for baboon) mechanic.

A strange illness overcame her when she was two years old. She was diagnosed in Salisbury with lymphatic lymphoma, cancer of the lymph glands. They started chemotherapy straight off, giving her a 50/50 chance of pulling through.

A little cottage was found for Sands to live in town with the children, constant medical attention demanded. Our smiley little island girl was subjected to nightmare treatment, bloating to embarrassing proportions on cortisone, losing her hair and self-confidence. And gradually transforming into a whimpering nervous wreck.

She would have to visit the hospital weekly for the chemo and radiotherapy, submerged into a tunnel, strapped to a sliding bed. The look of terror as she disappeared into that machine, pleading with her eyes not to be subjected to this, was a shocker.

We took stock in our bewilderment and headed for Cape Town for a second opinion. The Red Cross children's hospital, one of the finest in the world, looked at the slides from Salisbury. They asked us to leave them for a week to be studied further.

On our return, they called a misdiagnosis, concluding that this was a subtly similar virus and very easily mistaken for leukaemia. They advised ceasing all chemo treatment immediately. Salisbury insisted they were correct and that if we followed this advice, we'd be endangering Cathy's life.

I simply could not bear to watch the trauma of the treatment any longer. We followed Cape Town's advice. Cathy fully recovered and has her own family of three children today. I recalled Sands saying how one of the radical Christians had met her with little Cath, blown up by cortisone and hairless from her treatment, in a supermarket one day in Harare where he had laid hands for God's healing on her, loudly and dramatically. A bit embarrassing at the time, but wow, what a good thought.

While we were away on this trip, my mother Maasie, at 62 years old, insisted on coming to the rescue and holding the fort on Fothergill. She relied entirely on gut instinct, carrying on in all spheres 'As we always do, Darling'. The best of British.

It was the hot season. On a balmy night, one of our guests had pulled his bed on to the veranda of his chalet to enjoy the cool of the evening and sleep under the stars. Unbeknown to him, or the staff, there was a sickly lion roaming the camp that night. He woke up to find the lion tugging at his arm. His cries woke his wife who screamed so loudly the lion let go, gave a good roar and loped off into the dark to find a less cantankerous prey.

'Don't worry, it was only a lion attack. Hot tea and cakes are being served in the dining room, and the bar's open. Do come up.' Maasie walked through the camp, reassuring all.

Her remedy for most things was brandy. Which she insisted the unfortunate victim of the lion mauling should have in copious quantity, and in which she joined him.

The lake was rough, as it often was in the early hours of the morning. The anabatic wind blew into the valley from the high veldt as it cooled through the night. The boat trip to Kariba and hospital had to be delayed. When our guest finally got there, the medical staff waited four hours to sober him up before they could administer the anaesthetic and operate.

John Stevens, the Matusadona warden, came down the next day in a helicopter that was fortunately doing some game capture work in the Park. He found the lioness lying up a few hundred metres from the lodge and shot it from the air with a single bullet in the back of the head. In the disechtomy, he found an emaciated liver that would have seriously curtailed her hunting ability.

Chapter 30

Don't Mess around

It was time to introduce guide licensing, something all agreed was necessary for the professionalism we sought. The starting point was clearly for all existing operators to be licensed. Examinations were waived, and for the field approval we were each to be sent to a Parks warden, who would satisfy himself of our ability.

I had not hunted dangerous game extensively, preferring to observe and photograph them. But was reasonable handy with a rifle and knew where to shoot if I had to, as was every young man who went on call-up. I accompanied some professional hunters for further experience, volunteered for 'Parks' problem animal control, adding valuable understanding as to how to deal with a charge. Satisfying myself of my own proficiency, I applied for the field test.

I was sent to Johnny Bunce, warden of Marongora, a station at the top of the Zambezi escarpment above Mana Pools. He was a man of few words, as was the way with many of the old 'Parks' staff, and dubious of the bush skills in the new breed of safari operators who had not done their 'time' in Parks. After a quick briefing of what was expected, we headed out before dawn to shoot an elephant.

As the light touched the treetops, we picked up the spoor of a breeding herd. Following it for miles, without a word amongst us, the pace was fast. Johnny and his scouts were testing my stamina. Four hours of tracking at just less than a jog, we found the herd. And walked straight into their midst.

As would be expected, the matriarch responded and charged, herd closely following. Johnny stepped aside, bowed and with a wave of his hand.

'Over to you, young man.'

Not wanting to take out the matriarch, I shot the cow next to her. Almost simultaneously, Johnny's rifle cracked in my ear and the matriarch went down next to mine.

'Don't mess around.' he says as we sipped our tea under the tree while the scouts hacked out the tusks. 'You always have to take the leader, or they won't stop.'

I was upset at the waste, but he was quite right in assuming the matriarch would have kept coming. Two down—my fault, not his.

Next day we found a herd of 200 buffalo in thick *jesse*. I managed to take out one of the bulls, wondering who would find our remains if a charge was sparked from the rear. Buffalo crashing through this undergrowth in which we, and surely they, couldn't see more than 3 metres. I've since learned a thing or two about their behaviour, and the extreme unlikelihood of such an occurrence.

It didn't help the nerves back there, though.

Thankfully he didn't insist on lion, and I went home after three days, approved as a registered professional hunter/guide.

We had been carrying rifles on our walks from camp for some time through a special concession agreed with National Parks. Fortunately nothing went amiss to question the validity of the arrangement. We had been lucky. Within weeks of being given my licence I was thankful our casual arrangement had been formalised.

Game walks around the island were one of my favourites, strolling through the short panicum grass on the wide plains along the shoreline for the first few hours of the day. The majestic Matusadona range unfolded in the early morning light, streams of grazing impala quickened into action on our approach, becoming tumbling rapids, leaping in the air, bouncing and cascading away. An almost spiritual time, often deep in the silence of our own thoughts, and simple appreciation of the surrounding beauty, I couldn't think of a better way to start the day.

**Fothergill
established**

We would stop, observe and absorb the strange ways of this wonderful world. Herons crawking on the shore, fish eagles whooping from their lonely sentinel on skeletal trees, old bull elephants in their 'club members only' groups, swishing mud and sand off the grass roots, or systematically pulling another *mopane* tree to shreds, munching and grinding their daily 200kg intake of fodder, which action occupies three quarters of their life.

We might crawl on all fours up to a herd of buffalo blackening the shoreline. Heads high, sniffing the air and snorting, the young following the older and braver, three hundred heavy bosses would focus on our little group lying low in the grass, and move cautiously in. Sometimes to within metres. As we stood to move on again, there would be an immediate stampede, crashing of horns and pounding of hooves in the dust. Then they would stop and turn, bellowing their objections, studying our departure. Sometimes the lions were hiding and observing all this, waiting for their opportunity.

One morning, on the last lap strolling down the airstrip, smelling breakfast cooking, we spotted a breeding herd of elephant in the scrub mopane, next to the shoreline plain. We hadn't seen any previously, so diverted to have a closer look.

Approaching to within 50m along a game trail, a gentle breeze coming from the herd, we positioned ourselves nicely downwind. My clients lined up to take photos, the lake in the back ground, a herd of impala warming in the early morning light. A perfect picture. I cautioned everyone to be particularly quiet, recognising the pointy-tusked matriarch as one for having a short fuse.

One of the party coughed, that awful tickle rising in his throat just when he knew he shouldn't let it out. into their own room Without the slightest hesitation, the feeding matriarch, not having heard or seen us up to that point, lowered her head and charged straight for the sound, her herd of two cows and three youngsters close behind her. I yelled for everybody to run back up the path, bringing up the rear myself. A portly couple were not making sufficient speed. I could hear the elephants crashing through the trees, closing the gap. Another couple decided they'd be better off running away from our slow moving group.

Things were getting chaotic.

Glancing over my shoulder, trying to chivvy the portly couple along, I saw the matriarch break through onto our path.

Twenty metres behind me.—in full charge, head down, clearly intent on skewering somebody.

We were not going to get away. I stopped, turned and fired.

She fell crumpling onto the ground at my feet, my boot caught under her head. As we moved away, the rest of the herd gathered round her, trying to resuscitate their leader. Giving us a chance to regroup and retreat.

Mortified at having to take down such a gallant stalwart, who did her job of protecting her herd so well, and had lost her life because of our clumsiness, I was sombrely unresponsive to the excited chatter and questioning of my clients as we made our way home.

Somehow, breakfast had lost its flavour.

Chapter 31

In the Sticks

The political front was as turbulent as ever. Talks were arranged in the drama of a train parked dead over a line marking the border between Rhodesia and Zambia on the Victoria Falls bridge, suspended 120m above the boiling waters of the timeless Zambezi. The nationalist leaders drank themselves into a belligerent mood. No progress was made.

More talks followed in Geneva, London and Lusaka, and on board Royal Navy battleships in mid ocean. The Rhodesian Government and nationalist 'freedom fighters' held out, dug in for a long war of attrition, each certain they would have victory. Finally, all succumbed to the enormous international pressure.

The talks on HMS *Tiger* in mid Atlantic, and again on HMS *Fearless* in the North Sea, and then in Lancaster House in London, arbitrated by the British Foreign Secretary, Lord Carrington of Margaret Thatcher's Government, brokered a cease fire, and an agreement to hold elections. A new constitution gave reserved seats to the Rhodesians for ten years, with a blocking minority over certain sensitive issues.

In April 1980 the Union Jack was re-hoisted, under a British appointed Governor, Lord Soames (Winston Churchill's son in law) and then lowered for the last time on African soil. The new Zimbabwean flag in its vibrant red (for the blood spilt), green (for the land), black (for the majority people) and yellow (for the gold) bore the communist star and the soapstone bird, the trademark of Great Zimbabwe. The bespectacled, impeccably dressed, erudite Robert Mugabe was sworn in Prime Minister amongst frightening stories of brutal and flagrant intimidation.

Twenty percent of the white population packed their bags without hesitation and left. Salisbury became Harare, street names and towns changed to other African derivatives. A new era had launched.

Mugabe showed unexpected statesmanship as he brought the warring factions together in reconciliation—in retrospect, a clever sleight of hand. The world was taken in, as we all were at home. Nine hundred million pounds of pledges, and an influx of aid workers poured in. The economy boomed, growing by 24% over two years. Great strides were made in re-establishing education and health care after the deprivation of the long war years.

Commerce, industry, and tourism took off. The erstwhile negative worldwide publicity now worked in our favour. People streamed in to see this little country in the middle of Africa that had held out against such odds for so long. Our Fothergill Island boomed with it.

We built up the lodge accommodation to hold a total of sixty, bringing in big earth moving equipment to level our airstrip with the kind assistance of a large tobacco company who needed space for their twin engine plane. We increased our boat and vehicle fleet, and bought our first aeroplane, a four seat Cessna 180.

I exploited the load carrying capacity of this aeroplane, and the later, bigger C206, a six-seater, to a degree that I'm sure Cessna would have been surprised. Richy, my pilot brother-in-law, called it the 'Faga Futi' ('put more') airline. I didn't have a commercial licence and stretched the law by flying my own clients and including the cost or their flight into our accommodation charge. Fortunately no incident arose to put this grey area to the test.

I was thrilled to be flying again. It sure beat bouncing across the water in spine-crushing waves in my open boats. As with every pilot in every plane, each flight is a learning curve. Consistently reminded of the adage 'There are no old, bold pilots'—it seemed to take me a little longer than most to get old and lose the bold.

I took off in somewhat of a hurry one day, having just topped up the engine oil in my pre-flight check. As we got airborne, the windscreen blacked out with oil. I went round and landed, peering out the side window. I'd forgotten to put back the engine oil cap—thankful for small solutions and big mercies. And closed cockpits.

'The new Jonsen, she's gone, Saah!' Patson, one of my boat drivers reported.
'What do you mean, 'gone', Patson?'
'Dropped off, Saah. Buggered. Dispaired. Saah.'
These Johnsons were the first brand new outboard engines I had ever owned. Three spanking white 25hps. I'd put them onto our two small fishing boats and 'Kunjiri', our warthog looking canoe catamaran. We were all so proud of the shiny new machines. I would keep walking down to the harbour just to see them on the back of our newly painted craft.

Patson had forgotten to check the security bolts and chain before leaving harbour and one had bounced off the transom on the first big wave he hit. Listening to his explanation took stringent self-control in my avoiding a strangulation charge.

A unique and peculiar feature of Lake Kariba is 'the sticks' as they are known by boat cox'ns. These trees had been submerged, green and still growing, as the lake flooded. The sap over a period of time had now been replaced by salts in the water. An early petrification process, making the wood as hard as steel underwater. They would break off at, or just under, the water level, becoming a serious hazard to boating. Every cox'n has to know where they are and treat them with great caution when approaching the shallows.

Certain very hard trees continue to stand tall, forming an eerie, grey landscape of knurled and twisted shapes, artistic in the early morning and late evening light. In addition, they make great perches and nesting sites for birds, both them and the broken stumps making a food-laden habitat for fish.

'The
Sticks'

Fortunately, the lake around us had no *Bilharzia (Schistosomiasis)*. This disease originated in the Nile and has crept down through African waters over the century, decimating populations, lethargy and general ill health being the early symptoms. Long term, it attacks the vital organs of the body, even the brain, leading to an early death. It is very simple to treat these days with an excellent cure developed in China, relatively inexpensive. Treatment not so available in the rural communities—it has reaped serous devastation throughout the continent.

Absorbed through the skin from water in the form of a microscopic worm, it enters the body unnoticed, breeding in the bloodstream and invading the body organs. The water in turn is polluted through infected human urine carrying a different microscopic worm that, on release, has to find a specific snail in the water to invade and be hosted. The infected snail in turn emits the human seeking worm back into the water. Who knows which came first. This water-born creature can only swim vertically and so is carried laterally by current alone, in the lake not far.

The cycle is broken if either the infected snail or humans are absent. Hence *Bilharzia* is not found in fast running rivers absent of vegetation, or cooler waters such as mountain streams uninhabitable by the snail, or in wilderness areas where no human has polluted the water, such as our National Park shoreline.

This was just as well since we found ourselves frequently swimming, both intentionally and unintentionally. The boat journey to mainland Matuse was a short hop during the rains when we could not drive across the flooded causeway. On one trip, with a very full boatload destined for the Land Rover parked on the mainland, we motored into a big sea running outside the harbour, acceptable as we were driving with the swell. What I didn't notice was that every time we surfed down a wave, my view blocked by the crowd sitting on the front seat, a good deal of water was being shipped over the bow. Nor did I notice this water was collecting in the stern under the back seat as I carefully steered the boat through the high sea under as much power as I dared to keep the bows up. Throttling back to negotiate our channel through the sticks, a wall of water swept up the boat, instantly turning us 'turtle' (upside down). Mr

Angel in attendance as ever, crocs lying low as they normally do in a big swell, everybody splashing about inside the hull and around the wallowing craft, all managed to hang on till we washed ashore.

Guests rallied round, retrieving bits and pieces, including our tea in a floating waterproof cold box. After turning the boat upright, bailing it out and pulling it ashore, we warmed up with a cup of tea. And continued with the game drive. A great memory is of John and Eileen Rayside, both in their late sixties and regular visitors from Harare, in their underwear on the roof of the landy, sipping their tea, drying out.

Chapter 32

Chief Chikwenya

We had always talked of extending our operation into the magical Mana Pools National Park on the Zambezi River east of Kariba. John Stevens, warden of the Matuse, promised that if we could secure Chikwenya, a beautiful area on the downstream border of the Park, he'd leave 'Parks' and join us to run it.

Mana is one of the most beautiful and unique parks of Africa. 1500 sq km bordering the great River, a highly productive floodplain loaded with game, cathedral like forests of the great *Faiderbia (Acacia) Albida*, or winter thorn, their nutritious pods a major food source for just about everybody through the dry months. Declared a world heritage site in the 1980s, it is the only Park I know of that allows visitors to walk unescorted, at their own risk, amongst what are known as 'dangerous game'. An easy entry point for incoming guerrillas during hostilities, it had been closed as a fully operational war-zone for the last eight years.

National Parks agreed to permit a commercial camp on each border of the Park, offering us the choice owing to our successful operation on Fothergill. Preparing our design for Chikwenya along the lines of the much loved Fothergill chalets, we ordered materials and headed down into the valley with a convoy to open up the camp for the 1982 season as soon as the rains abated.

Rob Fynn

'We won't find much in the way of roads. There's the airstrip, a few tracks which will have washed badly at the river crossings, and that's about it.' John warned.

He knew the area well having spent his early 'Parks' training years at Mana. He also reckoned it would be a good idea to sweep for landmines before we drove in.

'So who's going to do that—the leading vehicle?!' We joked, but it needed thinking about.

'Don't worry, I'll get the army onto that.' Fortunately, John seemed to know who to talk to. The excellent strategic sand airstrip needed the same treatment.

Loaded to capacity, carrying all the provisions and materials we'd need for a month, we drove in with our families, consisting of John's New Zealand wife, Nicci, and their two daughters, Briar (4) and Sarah (2), and our three, along with another good farming friend, Lindsay Crawford, who kindly volunteered his 14 ton truck and trailer, and Nigel Biss, our maintenance manager and one of the finest mechanics in the country. A good guy to have around on this kind of trip.

We camped at the bottom of the Zambezi escarpment the first night, having trundled through the day from Kariba, invigorated by the breathtaking view of the valley as we came down the escarpment. It had been a 'No go' area for so long, those of us who hadn't seen this beautiful land for many years were much excited about getting back here.

The following day we hit the first riverbed. Down went Lindsay's big lorry and trailer. Deep into the sand. We offloaded. Hours of digging and winching later, only partially reloaded, we headed out again.

'Hey, Lindsay, you got lead-plated wheels, or what?' We joshed as we sank down again.

'Stop wimping, and dig!' responded Nigel. Good humour and camaraderie carried us well as the process repeated at every riverbed, until we were travelling with a virtually empty lorry, having offloaded more kit at each crossing, the trailer abandoned long back. While guys did what guys do, pulling on winches, chopping trees to make sand mats, hooking up vehicles to tow others, and digging, the mums organised picnics and played with the kids, having a whale of a time in the sand and exploring the river beds.

We finally arrived at Chikwenya on the third day, wading through long grass to get a glimpse of the river. I was reminded of the Boers making their great trek north from the Cape, when on arriving at a river some 100km north of Johannesburg, they saw hills that looked like the pyramids, and assumed they'd reached the Nile. The river bears that name today, and the town that grew up was named Nylstroom.

Also feeling a bit like we'd crossed the continent, our site was on the confluence of the Zambezi and a sandy riverbed, the Save, which bordered the Mana floodplain. Magnificent views spread across the rivers, plains and mountains beyond. And maybe the Pyramids behind them! It was an amazing undiscovered paradise.

John escorted Lindsay's lorry back to his trailer and went on to fetch a 'heavy', a 4-wheel drive 'Parks' Bedford, to pick up the materials we'd left scattered along the route, and to assist the lorry out. The 'heavy' broke down on the way back and John had to walk 20km in the dark to our camp, armed with only a stick. A 'Parks' guy.

We found a special 'dining room' site under the canopy of some big evergreen Natal mahogany trees, *trichelia emetica,* which looked across the floodplain and constant stream of game to and from the main river. Deciding it didn't need a roof, nothing could beat those magnificent branches overhead even if it did mean the odd bird poo landing in the soup, we planned the rest of the camp around it.

Our accommodation huts were open, as on Fothergill, other than a stout mesh from the top of the low wall to the roof as protection from the prolific predator population around here. John warned us they had a reputation. With good strong doors and metre high walls, the occupant enjoyed a good view out while lying in bed, albeit as from within a cage.

We used as much local material as we could. Ample sand lay in the dry Save, and the land cruiser would race along the riverbed, workers hanging on like side-car racers, getting up enough speed to enable the heavily laden vehicle to climb up the steep banks back into camp.

We worked long hours, determined to open for the latter part of the season. The rains normally came in November, when the camp would close and be packed away until the following April.

'Do you need some help there, Rob?'
'Sure do, Ness. Thank you, and bring some fresh stuff!'
My sister Vanessa was on the HF radio from Salisbury, asking if they could join us for the school holidays. Together with her husband, Davey Peech, and their two young children, Luke and Rececca, they drove in to help us build. And bring supplies. The children would all sleep on mattresses in the back of vehicles at night, while we slept on the roof-racks, constantly wary of those strident lions.

At the end of a day's work, we'd walk through the magnificent surrounding woodlands. We were fascinated by the elephants who would stand on their back legs, reaching upto five metres into the tasty *Albida* with their trunks, pulling down branches bearing their delicious 'apple ring' pods. Adept at giving a tree a good shake in just the right place for a shower of pods to come cascading down, they would then 'hoover' them up with those dextrous trunks, leaving a share for the ground animals after they moved away.

Leopards would lie on the great branches that extend parallel to the ground, intact only because they were above trunk height, and would wait for an unsuspecting impala to browse the fallen pods underneath them.

One day, John was out looking for a suitable piece of gnarled wood to make a basin stand. Unwittingly, he was standing beneath a leopard. When it could no longer handle John's close quarters, the big cat dropped from the tree three metres from him and bounded off across the plain.

The open savannah between the great pillars of winter thorn stretch as far as the eye can see, impala flowing like golden streams, bunched eland, waterbuck and kudu beautifully blending, zebra in their outlandish camouflage, rare rhino like slow motion boulders with spears sticking up, rainbow coloured lovebirds flitting from ground to trees, trumpeter hornbills wailing their plaintive cry, kestrel and falcons hurtling through like fighter-bombers, the bigger raptors patrolling above, on the lookout for some action from the laidback kings. It was such a privilege to be in this stunning niche of nature.

Reopening
Chikwenya
after 8 years –
convoy setting
off & stuck

Camp
hidden
under river-
side trees

Briar & sister in wheelchair

We opened for guests in July, having built the camp from scratch in four months.

'Sorry about that, Minister.' John apologised in embarrassment.

'Oh, don't worry' she said, charmingly 'Worse happens in the donkey carts at home!'

Our Minister of Tourism in the new government was delightfully approachable. She'd come down with the head of the Tourist Board and leading travel agents for our opening ceremony. Her seat in the land cruiser, only a short while back crazily careering filled with sand, had sprung loose as we lurched up that riverbed rise, landing her bottom up in the back of the vehicle, legs sticking in the air.

John and Nicci had never dealt with tourists as clients before and were a little nervous. Nicci's easy going New Zealand manner coupled with John's naïve charm and great knowledge of the bush were a huge success. We confidently left them to it and returned to Fothergill.

We'd all worked flat out for years, under tough conditions, and Sands was poorly. Her doctor advised a good holiday. It didn't seem the right time to be going, it never was, but the doctor was adamant, as was our staff.

We headed for the Wild Coast of the Transkei in our little red bus, the children's name for our Renault 4 station wagon, reminiscent of my own early family holidays in the Morris Minor.

Way off the beaten track, in St John's Port on the Wild Coast, a message came through the local store.

'A 'Janet' phoned you. She said important to call her back. We've got a number for Fothergill Island in Kariba.'

My stomach tightened as I headed for the store and called. She would never have phoned other than for a big emergency.

Down at Chikwenya, a lion had mauled John and Nicci's daughter, Briar. They were at Harare's Paryrenatwa hospital, fighting for her life. Janet insisted we stay on, saying they were coping fine and that there was nothing we could do by coming back. Uncertainly, we accepted her advice and stayed on.

Yura de Weronin, an elderly Russian gentleman guide, as solid and reliable as the Siberian winter, who was with us on Fothergill, took over at Chikwenya. I gathered John had come back from an early morning walk, and was shaving up at the manager's house, some 50 metres upstream along that dry Save riverbank. Four year old Briar had been with him, questioning what he'd seen on the walk. She now decided to join Mummy preparing breakfast and ran off along the path that followed the riverbank back to camp. This passed a dense stand of *Vetiveria*, 'adrenalin' grass, which hides everything and had been earmarked for slashing, though was not yet cut.

John continued shaving, when he heard the unmistakable grunt of a lion from the path Briar had just taken. He called. No response. He fired two shots into the dense grass with his double .470.

A pride of young lion broke cover, one of them carrying his daughter.

An excellent shot, he continued firing at the feet of the lioness carrying his little girl. After some 50 metres, the lioness dropped her and ran off. Briar was alive, lungs punctured, unconscious. Nicci had been on her daily routine radio call to Fothergill when she heard the shots. They scrambled our aircraft with SRN Janet on board. John sent an SOS on the radio and another plane picked it up, two aircraft now racing to save Briar's life. Nicci and he were on the airstrip with Briar and their younger daughter, Sarah, to meet the first aircraft that landed. It was ours. Two hours later they were in the intensive care unit of Harare's Parirenyatwa hospital, a fine institution at the time.

They fought for her unconscious life for three weeks, Nicci and John camped alongside her in the hospital. Infection set in, her lung remained collapsed. They discovered her spine had been severed. Thanks to excellent care and much prayer, Briar lives. A paraplegic ever since, she drives her own specially adapted car, has been through university in Perth, Australia, and is now married to Dom Passaportis, a long-standing Zimbabwean friend, and with a child of their own. She is one of the bravest, most cheerful and beautiful young ladies you could ever meet

The family never returned to Chikwenya, setting up a top guiding and tour operating business—John Stevens Safaris—from their home in Harare, with John continuing as a much sought after guide. The Briar Stevens Trust was established to assist in her welfare and treatment. Both still exist to this day.

The Steven's family, together with Briar, on one of their medical trips to London, were invited to No.10 Downing Street to meet with Margaret and Dennis Thatcher. Ushered into the reception lounge, they were offered a glass of sherry while they awaited the Prime Minister's appearance. John, who doesn't smoke or drink, knocked over his glass.

Should he go over to the drinks cabinet to refill the glass, and be caught red-handed as the Thatcher's made their entrance, or be found by them with an empty glass, either way giving quite the wrong impression?

Nothing of the sort was perceived, of course, but for John, the super fit, conservative conservationist and long-standing professional guide, he laughs it was one of the most appalling dilemmas he'd faced in his entire career—'Give me a charging buffalo, anyday!'.

Driving back a week later, we visited Sand's relatives in Durban, where Kuis asked casually as he read an excerpt from his newspaper.

'What do you think about this, Rob?' An accident at Mana Pools. where an elderly Russian guide had been killed by an elephant.

No names in the article.

I picked up the phone and Janet confirmed the tragic news. Dear old Yura. In an uncannily similar circumstance to Briar's accident, he had returned from an early morning walk and was on his way to the manager's cottage from the 'dining room'. Watched by guests he made amusing gestures to chase away an elephant calf that was snuffling the *albida* pods outside his house.

The elephant mother, nicknamed 'Spot', due to a weathered bird guano on her back and whom we all knew well, was browsing some fifty metres away. Upset by the perceived threat to her calf, she came charging across the newly cut grassed area. Yura appeared to take little notice of the charge, in spite of the head down and trunk curled in classic serious charge mode, continuing to wave his old bush hat at the calf. In the last paces of the charge, he reached for his rifle which was all along slung over his shoulder.

In full view of the guests, he was hit in the throat by a tusk and then pounded into the ground with her knees and head. Nobody could do anything, and by the time Spot hurried away with her calf, there wasn't much left of Yura. Most bones in his body were broken, his jaw was hanging, and his sad blue eyes told the story to the traumatised guests that he was ready to go. Which he did shortly after.

We hurriedly packed and headed out on the three-day drive home.

One of the oldest professional guides in Zimbabwe, always with a story for every occasion, we remembered how dear Yura had held a theory that you could have a 'trust' with an animal you got to know.

'I don't like you moving that old dagga boy, Rob.' He once ticked me off after moving an old buffalo friend of his.

'Sorry Yura. I was concerned about the old boy's familiarity—remember it wasn't long ago that dagga boy killed two guests on Spurwing Island when they walked into him on their way home one evening?' I reminded him.

We'd moved an ageing buffalo bull from Fothergill that had taken to sleeping in camp near the paths at night as a protection for himself against lions—for us, an accident waiting to happen. I had asked 'Parks' to dart him and take him a long way off, which Yura was convinced would upset the old chap and that he'd be back to take revenge.

Yura had been a lonely old man in his latter years, his pretty younger wife having left him, and we'd heard him on several occasions say that he'd like to go with his beloved animals one day.

We paid our deep respects. John and Nicci were still on their vigil at the hospital and Briar was stable, thank God.

I flew straight down to Chikwenya once we made Fothergill, to find the weary and fearful staff demoralised and ready to pack up camp.

'The Chief's *mudzi* (spirits) are not happy, Bwana Rob,' Robert, our head caretaker told me.

'Settle down, guys. We're going to get on top of this.'

I tried hard to re-enthuse the team and settle their fears.

I didn't know much about *mudzi*, but I did know the guys were very unhappy. Old Chief Chikwenya's grave was in a big baobab behind the camp. It had been a shrine to the locals who'd lived here before the Park was established. The staff was convinced that his *mudzi* were the negative influence over our camp.

I was to fly back to Kariba the next day to collect our first guests after Yura's death, against the staff's wishes. Although I understood their misgivings, I was in the 'climb back onto the horse after a fall' thinking.

We talked and agreed we'd see the season through for its last couple of weeks. They also asked that we deal with Chief Chikwenya's unhappy spirit.

'Lets call on God to help us—come pray with us, Bwana.'

We prayed together on the banks of the Zambezi.

I hugely admired their fortitude and loyalty. They'd been through hell, left on their own to hold the fort after two ghastly accidents, isolated and bereft of their management, with no nearby help until I had arrived. I wanted to stand with them in every way I could.

Deeply contemplative, I went to bed in the manager's cottage that night, the enormous landscape of the Zambezi flood plain lit by a full moon. What else was hiding unknown and mysteriously in this African bush? I was eerily conscious of the double tragedy that had unfolded metres from where I slept.

In the early hours of the morning, I awoke to a strong foreboding, feeling and even smelling some horrible presence. Lying in my stretcher, positioned along the wall and level with its top, from where the wire netting continued to the roof, I opened my eyes to see a huge lion's head inches from mine, the slit yellow eyes staring into mine, warm pungent breath reeking over me.

Heart pounding, I leapt up, shouting at it. The great head continued to stare steadily, unmoved. I lunged towards it and shouted again. This was definitely not a configuration of leaves. Finally it turned and limped unhurriedly away, I now noticed it dragging its badly wounded hind leg.

I groped for my rifle, desperately wanting to shoot this clearly dangerous animal before it moved away too far. By the time I found and loaded my rifle, the lion had disappeared into the shadows, its awkward gait fading in the dry leaves. Towards the camp. I didn't have a strong spotlight, and no way was I going out alone after this animal in the dark with my pathetic little flashlight.

I am not normally fearful, but that night I was gripped with a horror verging on panic I have never experienced before or since. Rooted to the ground, fiercely worried about my staff and how secure they would be against this marauder in their tents, I prayed like I'd never prayed before. Thankfully, no cries for help tore the night apart. Peace at last fell upon me and I went back to bed, rifle now beside me, to fitfully see the remainder of the night away.

At first light, I followed the spoor down through the camp, where the lion had stood for a while contemplating its next move, before padding into a thick reed bank by the river. I raised Parks on the radio. Our old friend and long-time Mana Pools ranger, 'Dolfe' Sasseen, was on set.

'Dolfy, we have a problem here.'

'I'll be round straightaway, Rob. Don't do anything till I get there.'

The staff, thankfully, had not heard nor seen a thing the night before, but were greatly concerned to hear my story. We had another reassuring prayer session together. I left them preparing camp and awaiting Dolfe while I flew off to collect our guests.

Arriving back three hours later, having briefed the clients, we were urgently signalled by the staff.

The lion was close by.

We crept through to the 'dining room' trees, to find it lying in the sand of the riverbed, right there in front of us. A thrilling arrival for the guests who sat awaiting the drama to unfold—not quite so for me, hugely aware of how critical it was to deal with this right now.

Dolfe was out in the park looking for it. Mindful of his strict instructions, I alerted him on the radio. He was on his way back requesting I sit guard over the lion. I certainly wasn't letting it slip away again, whatever Dolfe asked.

His Land-Rover bumped into camp after 20 minutes, lion still basking on the sand. Escorting him straight to the view, he whispered.

'I need to get closer. I'm going to walk along that gully by the river, out of sight of the lion, and creep up onto the bank nearby where he's lying. Cover me from here, Rob.'

I understood his need to get closer. The lion was a good 80 metres off and our heavy hunting rifles were not great at long distance shots.

As we watched him and his sergeant crawl along the gully, the lion abruptly lifted its head. It had clearly sensed their approach. Suddenly, it took off at a frightening speed across the sandy riverbed towards them, on three legs, grunting as only a charging lion does.

We could hear the sergeant alerting Dolfe, who was a touch deaf from too many rounds going off too close to his ears during the war years. The lion disappeared over the bank in a determined charge.

A single shot rang out. And then silence.

Cautiously making our way to the scene, not sure who we'd find alive, a white-faced Dolfe and his wide-eyed sergeant stood there, the lion lying dead at their feet. Dolfe had only seen it as it came over the bank, in a flying leap straight at him. He managed a brain shot, dropping it in mid-air.

'Must have been Jesus behind the sights, Rob. I've never shot like that before!" A strong Christian, I'd not seen him shaken or disturbed by much, but he was trembling over this one.

Chapter 33

Tusk High View

Jesus?

Behind the rifle sights?

Pulling the trigger?

The Christian story was a new and deep penetration in my life.

I'd always believed in God, but had little idea of who or how He was, or is. Brought up as an Anglican in church schools, this close intimate relationship with Jesus seemed almost kooky? But Dolfe wasn't the kooky kind.

An order of Anglican Nuns had brought Sands up in an orphanage after her alcoholic father had committed suicide, her Mum simply unable to cope. Their wise, strict, loving faith had been a great foundation stone in her life. But she didn't talk about it, at least not to me. There was a lot she couldn't share with me, or I with her. Our Achilles' heel.

In recent months, committed Christians, quite independently, had homed in on us at Fothergill, almost commando style, challenging my spiritual stance, and questioning what I was doing about it. I found it unnerving, intrusive and offensive. Belief was a private affair between God and oneself. Thank you.

Sands went along with it, quietly. Again, no discussions. 'Let sleeping lions lie' was my approach.

One night I had to go out looking for a boat that had not returned from fishing. We still didn't have enough radios to go around. This often meant searching for hours in the dark.

I had discovered from Dad and his stories of commando operations in WWII that white is the most effective camouflage on water at night. It blended into the reflections. So we knew to look for the darker shadow of a boat against the trees, not the white hull itself. Spotlights only blinded us as we searched the black waters, and we'd found it more effective to look with one's natural night vision in the starlight. The negative being that the lost party couldn't see us searching.

That night we combed the shoreline where they had reputably gone fishing. Our routine was that if we didn't find them after a couple of hours, we reckoned they'd be okay for the night, tied up in some creek for a balmy night under the stars, cox'ns and clients all briefed beforehand, and we'd head home. I'd go up with the aeroplane at first light and find them. The water in the lake was good to drink, they'd have a cold box and food on board and would survive the adventure till morning.

We were about to head back when I spotted a glow in the dark. A cigarette burning. They show up at amazing distances at night. Sure enough, there was our boat.

'Sorry about that,' I apologised to John, our fisherman, on the journey home.

'Not at all, old man. It's good to see you and I was quite comfortable. Got some lovely tiger bites after dark. And I'd prayed, and knew you'd find me.'

I was dumbfounded. He hadn't seemed the praying kind at all, one of the last to leave the pub each evening, knocking back G & Ts and smoking cigars together with his dynamic and amusing young wife, Amanda.

Intrigued, I asked them to join us for dinner at home the following evening, something I never normally did. Our nights off with the family were sacred.

After our meal and lively discussion, Amanda asked if she could read something from the Bible to me. I happily agreed and she read the scriptures from John's Gospel that established the divinity of Jesus as the Son of God.

'Who was in the beginning, and was with God, and was God, and without Him was not anything made that was made". John1:1. And on . . .

I listened with intense interest. Although I'd vaguely heard them all before, I was now hearing something very different. That the great creator God was really interested in little me, my daily needs, and sought a personal relationship.

Wow, it seemed a mighty small call for a mighty big God. Well, we could all do with some of that. But didn't He have more important matters to deal with?

I had a thousand questions, contemplating again the frailty of man and my confused attempts over the years to get my mind around this all-knowing God who didn't seem to mind about the devastating mess in this world that He had created.

But it was beginning to resonate that if we were to enter this eternal 'Kingdom of Heaven' the Bible talked about, and understand more, *we* needed to *do* something. It wasn't going to just happen because I'd been baptised and went to a church school.

Pensive and attentive, I wondered how I'd missed the enormity of all this. I was profoundly moved, not wanting to miss the show for another minute. I wanted a front row seat.

I sort of understood about us all being sinners. In comparison with God, anyway. Except maybe the Queen! An inkling of the spiritual battle raging between Good and Evil was dawning, and what the outcome was likely to be. I wanted to be on the winning side.

'It is a bit like 'Royal blood'. If you haven't got it, you can't have it, other than marrying into it.' Amanda said. 'Jesus is asking us to repent from our old life and ways, and receive His offer to join His family, becoming a child of the Father God, to be adopted by Him.'

And all this forgiveness of sin stuff . . . Did I really have such a great deal to repent of? I hadn't murdered or raped anybody, nor stolen anything significant—couple of shoplifting jobs in younger days . . . And, yeah, admittedly some fairly hefty clangours in my 'lady mad' days that I tried desperately to forget . . . And . . . Oh dear, the more I thought about it, the more I saw.

Amanda seemed to know my thoughts.

'You'll know what you need to repent of.' She explained. 'Step aside, give over to Jesus. Honour Him as Lord. Let go all that image and pride and self-importance. And let Him forgive you, in that loving way that only He can. And forgive yourself.'

A tall order for this go-get-it-if-you-want-it, think-it-through-but-leap-off-the-cliff-if-necessary, dare I say. arrogant young man. Just step aside and hand it all over to Jesus? But I was really taken with the idea of that deep forgiveness I knew I needed.

I began to sense what she was talking about. All those broken relationships for one great big everlasting good one . . . I also knew there could only be one captain of the ship. Jesus was sounding like a good one, and this whole discovery was vastly different to the boring old religious stuff I perceived hearing before.

Yes. I wanted in.

I prayed, asking forgiveness for my self-centred life and for Jesus to take control and instil a right attitude within me. Simply, honestly and earnestly. Right there and then.

Surprisingly, it was not a heavy, dutiful sacrifice. More like giving and receiving a hugely pleasing, releasing gift. Like there was nothing I wanted more.

I understood that I was now 'born again'.

Oh, my Gosh!

Jesus first used this term 'born again' in John 3:1-15 to Nicodemus, an elder of the Jewish religion who, as a group, were offended and mystified by His teachings. Jesus had explained that if anybody was to enter into the Kingdom of God they needed to be spiritually born again, opening their eyes to the revelations He was preaching in the spirit. Without which they were walking blindfolded.

Shwoo!

I woke up next morning, my world changed. Literally. It all looked different. Everything was brighter and sharper and deeper and clearer.

A little confused, but feeling an indescribable joy, I knew I had an amazing new friend, totally dependable, to lean on and look for back up in the battle, and to thank for the good things life brings.

'Believe on Him and you will be saved,' I'd read in John 6:40.

I understood how the Scriptures had been studied more deeply than any other literature on earth, by thousands of scholars over the years, and what was included now were universally accepted as God breathed. Fundamentally, intrinsically right. I hugely looked forward to getting to know them and seeing how they were weaved into the tapestry of our universe and our lives.

'Ask in my name and you shall receive,' I'd seen the night before in John 14:13. As we headed out on my early morning walk, I prayed a quick list of the game I wanted to find. Leopard was at the top. They were rare. It would be a good test for God.'What are you looking at, Rob?' my clients asked, lining up behind me.

We'd arrived at the first fork in the dry riverbed. I was standing, waiting for divine direction, feeling not a little foolish.

I heard nothing.

After a few minutes of this embarrassment, I moved on, making a feeble excuse about a Red-faced Mousebird that had flown into the bush. I was the only red-faced one around there. All we saw that morning was a tortoise. Which I hadn't even asked for.

Clearly I'd got something a little topsy-turvy. Maybe I shouldn't take this too literally. Yet Amanda and the scriptures we'd looked at said to do that. I had a lot more to learn about what 'In His name' meant.

A little muddled, but nevertheless totally committed, I was eager to learn more. The ardent inner fire that drove me to want to experience everything life had to offer locked me in to know and to live out this miraculous promise of God's. It was the ultimate challenge, ultimate gamble. One's own life as the stake.

Put in the vital ingredients, it seemed then, faith, scripture and prayer, wait for them to bubble up and, 'Hey Presto', God would appear and grant every wish! This grave misunderstanding was regrettably how I kicked off, and is taught in some churches to this day.

I have come to know and understand better now, but that was to come at great cost. I am learning that anything of worth is costly. The quiet trusting faith and patient searching of the truth I've come to know now are part of this priceless rock of peace which we only seem to really find with toil, time and a fair amount of trouble. The easy times are great, but no learning comes out of them.

A dramatic event broadened my understanding.

My game walks into the Matuse varied in their locality. At the end of a long and busy Christmas season, I headed for my favourite, Croc Creek, nestled in the foot of the Matusadona Mountains and at the mouth of the Kanjedza River, a dry course that wound its way through the Mopane plains. The lush riverine vegetation livened up the landscape, attracting game and bird life.

We left early from Fothergill by boat with our packed breakfasts. I had with me a lovely family from the Swiss embassy in Lusaka, including Granny, the Reverend Coles and his wife from a small county church in Sussex, together with my trainee guide, John Bradshaw, who was still recovering from being blown up by a landmine in the war. John, today, is headmaster of Springvale school.

Not far into the walk, we came across one of the biggest conglomerations of breeding elephant I'd ever seen in the Matuse. More than one hundred.

'We're going to have to move out of their line of scent, guys, and smartly,' I explained to my group.

They nodded. Trust the guide.

The breeze was pushing in from the lake behind us. We needed to get downwind. Elephant breeding herds are probably the most dangerous animals to encounter on foot. Their protective instincts are ferociously developed. The slightest whiff of man can turn a peaceful gathering into an angry, killing rampage. We aimed for a small plateau I knew of open ground a few metres above the Kanjedza spring, with a great view back down the river, and nicely downwind.

I headed into the *jesse* thicket parallel to the river, hightailing it with my team for the foothills. Thirty sweaty minutes of adrenalin pumping walk, crouching and dodging thorns, buffalo and goodness knows what else in the dense vegetation, brought us to the little plateau.

Worth every drop of blood drawn and thorn-scratched, a panoramic view opened below us. The great herd stretched towards the Lake, buffalo, eland, waterbuck, even rhino dotted amongst them. Marabou storks and vultures wheeled, indicating there might be a 'kill' down there. We'd find it on our way home. All agreed to spend the rest of the morning soaking it in.

Not five minutes after we'd settled in, I heard a sharp crack behind us, a branch breaking, further up the hill, downwind. Nobody else paid much attention, but I instantly knew it was an elephant browsing. Almost certainly an 'Auntie', as we called the defending cows, posted as scouts on the outskirts of large breeding herds. The wise thing to do would be to withdraw, move further up the hill and hope to find a higher vantage point. Get more scratched, pant a lot more, probably lose our lovely open view, but, at the very least, put ourselves downwind of this elephant.

I didn't do a thing. Tired, too tired, from the long and continuous stint of guiding through the Christmas holidays, idiotically, irresponsibly, I continued to sit there without saying a word to anybody, hoping the problem would quietly disappear. Which, of course, it never does.

Minutes later, the peaceful group of four cow elephants we'd been watching, calves at foot, drinking from the spring just below us, looked up the hill in unison. Straight at us. I knew they hadn't seen, heard or smelt our group. Auntie behind had given our position away, transmitting our threatening presence in that low frequency communication they are known for, inaudible to the human ear and penetrating kilometres through the bush to other elephant.

'Okay, guys, it's only us. Don't get in a tiz now.' Our cover broken, I was gently letting the mums know where we were, hoping to avoid any last minute surprises. As often as not, they will move away on hearing human voices. On the other hand, they well might chase us off.

Looked like they were 'on the other hand'. A mini charge broke out up the short slope towards us. Shaking and lifting their heads and trunks as they came over the ridge, ears out, they were testing the ground—typical fear-inducing elephant tactics, always effective, but not too serious at this point.

My group huddled behind me as we backed off, trusting as ever that the guide had this one under control. I shouted back at the ellies, always a good deterrent in close up contact, my rifle ready.

They stopped, swaying on their knees, waving their trunks in an attitude I knew was a focused consultation.

'What do you think, Gals, shall we take them out, or leave them to it? He's got a gun.'

We stood our ground, my elephant warning shouts growing in volume and profusion. They would either charge now, when I would reluctantly have to shoot the leader. Or, they'd run away.

Thankfully, they turned and ran off along the ridge.

Wiping my brow and turning to reassure my team that all was under control, I was greeted by a terrifying sight. A big, well tusked, determined cow elephant in full charge, head and trunk tucked in, coming down the mountain straight for us, was leaving a swathe of flattened trees and grass behind her.

She was coming in for the kill.

My team broke into a very understandable panic, bomb-shelling in every direction. Granny grabbing children, husbands clutching wives, every person on red alert escape mode. I knew I had to get to the place where the elephant was going to break out of the *jesse* surrounding us before she picked somebody up.

Dodging fleeing bodies in between us, screaming like a banshee, I got ready to shoot.

She broke out of the bush, all feet forward, skidding to a halt. Have we a 'stand-off'? Might she also turn and run, after stopping? The last thing I wanted was to shoot our valiant old, grey friend. In the pandemonium, my rifle up and pointing at her head, we collided, knocking me back and causing a pull to the trigger by mistake.

The round harmlessly grooved her forehead. Our world stopped for a millisecond following the deafening report, and for an embarrassing moment I was standing next to a large angry wild cow elephant with an empty rifle. Bad position to be in. The big hunting rifles require each round to be individually loaded.

I leaped behind a nearby *mopane* to do just that, finding my trainee, John, shoulder to shoulder behind the same tree. Mrs Ellie was coming round. She knew who the troublemaker was. John ran off. In my frantic reload, the cartridge breached. Eject. Reload, walking backwards, watching elephant closing. I stumble in reverse over a rock, fall onto my back, dropping everything in the process.

In an instant, the gigantic, roaring, slobbering, rough haired amazon was on top of me. Her strong scent, so peculiar to elephant, filled my nostrils and whole being.

How uniquely extraordinary is our mind in these desperate critical moments. I experienced the sensation I'd had years earlier in the Tiger Moth, where life's journey flashed past in an instantaneous movie. I even had time to think how tough it was going to be for Sands to carry on alone and bring up the children.

'Go on! You ghastly beast, you!'

Back to Earth. The Reverend, bravely standing a few metres away, was reacting in good British manner, faithfully hoping he could shoo the elephant away. I wished he'd move further off and get himself out of the danger zone. Apparently, in his anxiety, he pulled the trigger on his cine camera now and then, maybe praying it would turn into a ray gun? I still have those short bursts of film, showing the elephant coming round the tree, my backing off, and then falling out of the picture, when the elephant seems to leap like a cat after a mouse, landing on top of me.

I remember clearly and loudly calling on the name of Jesus. He was likely the only one who had any influence in this jam. His trusty Angel was not sleeping on duty, as the miracle of my being here to write this story is surely proof.

Theatricals out of the way, I switched into high-level survival mode, trying to escape through her back legs. Anything to get out of the turbulent front-end action, where rolling and scrabbling, ducking and diving, crawling and cringing in desperate avoidance tactics seemed destined for disaster. She was doing her best to kneel on me, tusk me, throw me, anyway she wanted me. A grand old tussle, my aghast team of hiding walkers reckoning afterwards it went on for about two minutes. A long time in hand to trunk combat.

I don't recall blow for blow, but two incidents remain clear in my mind. The first when she must have tried another skewer job with her tusk, which ran along my shoulder blades while I was scrabbling on all fours, scooping me up through my shirt collar. Hoisted 3 metres above the ground, hanging by the scuff of my neck from the tusk, an angry elephant eye glaring next to me, all I can recall is how good the view was from this vantage point.

My shirt collar finally broke, dropping me to the ground and back into the fearsome 'dodge-'em-big-feet' game, desperately still trying to get out through those hind legs. Her dragging back tactics were gaining ground, clearly leading towards a terminating squash any moment.

Next remembrance was a tight squeezing around my waist, I couldn't breathe. She had me in her trunk, from where I expected to be shortly flying through the treetops, or pulped against a *Mopane* trunk. Then, I found myself with both hands on her tusk, wrenching my way out of her grip, like some parallel bar exercise in the gym.

An impossible feat. Elephants pick up 300kgs of log with their trunk. And superman Rob gives her the slip? I don't think so.

In actuality, I had reached the point where I simply had nothing left to do anything. Adrenalin all used up, like I remember in those wearisome rugby scrums or long uphill runs that just never stopped.

'Be nice and quick, old lady . . . Now, that's where you needed to be, Rob.' I was thinking to myself as I looked at a dense *caparis tormentosa* thorn bush through her back legs, but having not an ounce of oomph left to do anything about it.

I'm not sure what happened next. Whether Mr Angel gave me a flick, or Miss Ellie did with her trunk, I flew into that spiky bush like a human cannonball, thrust deep into it, thorns in my mouth and face, arms pinned back, waiting for the *coup de **grace***].

I waited . . . and I waited . . . and I waited.

But nothing happened.

Slowly and painfully I extricated myself. There was no more Mrs Ellie. She'd run away. Unheard of, normally squashing their victim into strawberry jam.

Well, she'd gone.

I could hardly stand I was feeling so weak. Euphoric to be alive. I pinched my arms to see if I was really there. Or was I in heaven?

'No, still here, Rob.' I saw the shattered radio and my mangled rifle in the dust. And Rev Cole scurrying out from behind bushes with his trusty camera pointing at me. I lifted my hands to say a big thank you to Jesus and his Angel, just amazed to be still intact.

'Are you okay, Rob?' a tremulous voice inquired from behind another bush.

'Yup. Thank you. Absolutely fine!' I responded, sitting there in this happy daze.

Then a shrill voice alerted us.

'Oh Noo! Gran's broken her ankle!'

I tried to absorb the boys' news.

I staggered across. Sure enough, brave Vera was lying quietly, her ankle sticking out at right angles. She, too, had fallen over a rock.

The boat was four kilometres away. No radio.

There was no option but to carry her back between us.

I was wearing long, strong khaki shorts, British army style, which I took off and made a stretcher with, a log running though each of the legs. My equally long tailed shirt preserved a modicum of decency.

Us four men picked up a corner apiece, Vera's daughter cradling her legs as she walked in front. Mrs Cole walked to the side consoling and encouraging. The two boys carried my rifle, walking ahead as advance couts. I couldn't do more than 30 metres at a time before needing another rest.

It was a long walk back, interspersed with good drama.

'Buffalllooooo!' . . . 'Rhinoooo!' the boys would cry at various stages from the front. We would unceremoniously dump Vera on the ground, the rifle thrust into my hands as we grouped together in a 'Custer's last stand'. In the direction the boys were pointing, an animal would be quietly grazing in the distance. Everybody calmed, we'd sit for another rest, and talk.

So many questions.

'What did it feel like?'

'Were you afraid?'

'Why did God let that happen?'

'Why did you miss?!'

And we'd talk about it all over again. A band of adventurers who'd shared something big. And survived.

Finally back in the boat, I collapsed with Vera onto the deck and John drove us back, me popping my head up now and then to give directions. A crowd was gathered when we arrived at Fothergill, overdue as we were and alerted by another boat who'd seen us and reported I was drunk!

Admittedly, I looked a mess. Torn clothes, covered in blood, deep grazing and bruising, hardly able to talk with my mouth hanging open on one side where thorns had gashed it, having difficulty breathing from the bruising of the trunk hold on my rib cage. Vera was still lying in the bottom of the boat looking particularly white with makeshift bandages and splints on her leg. We did make a spectacle.

'You're dying!' Sands gasped in horror as she walked up to me.

'Sands! It's okay, Hon.' I slurred, somewhat shocked to hear her say that, but knew she had a dramatic tendency. But, good heavens, I'd helped carry Vera back over 4 kilometres to the boat, didn't she know?

To prove how *okay* I was, I announced *I* would be flying Vera and myself to Kariba hospital.

'I'd go anywhere with you young man, but *you* are *not* flying us to Kariba!' responded Vera.

'Don't be bloody ridiculous, Rob!' One of our guests who'd flown in with his own plane insisted he'd fly us over.

Vera's ankle was set, and I had the most wonderful saltwater bath of my life, in a huge old-fashioned hospital tub. I lay there a long time, deeply tranquil, in wondrous gratitude, having confirmed that not even a finger was broken.

Mr Angel had come through pretty good on this one.

Looking like I had Mercurochrome chicken pox, mouth with six stitches, but otherwise feeling good, a huge sense of relief and peace pervading my all, I spent a couple of days resting up.

I wanted to get back walking as soon as possible and allay any subconscious fears lurking within—that old 'falling off the horse' remedy again. Out on the Island Walk a few days later, where I knew each old stately bull elephant by name, I felt I was on trusted and familiar ground. But as I approached my old grey buddies with my small group of clients, as I had done countless times before, anxiety welled up inside me. I could smell that elephant scent again, remember the rough hide and those piercing eyes. I had to steel myself to keep going.

'C'mon, Rob, you can do this.'

And then it was over. Once again we were oohing and aahing, close up to a wild bull elephant, watching him eat his morning fill, breaking off selected branches, stuffing them into his cute pointy lipped mouth, crunching deliciously, letting off vast quantities of wind, dropping mounds of dung, and urinating enough to flood a termitary. Savouring every second, I knew that I knew and loved them so well.

The Parks investigation exonerated me, and my professional guide's licence was still intact. An amusing epilogue was the diplomatic community in Lusaka, frequently phoning to ask, 'Eez it ze camp where zee geede fought ze elephants? Yah? Good, zen ve vould like to book in for ze valk vis him!'

Chapter 34

Angels and Aeroplanes

'You what?!'

The most miraculous part of my elephant escape was Sandy's story. And this is where kooky and cooked get close. Hoping to avoid being either, I listened.

Sands was big into fortune telling in her earlier days. She'd frightened herself on several occasions, even seeing peoples deaths before they happened, so on meeting my scepticism, had dropped it altogether. On becoming a committed Christians, she'd understood the difference between Godly prophecy and plain devilish 'fanookery', and truly put it behind her.

Until I went under the elephant. She now told me her story, for the first time, it having been deeply buried for all the reasons for all the years.

On one of her modelling trips to Bulawayo, she'd met an old witch with a crystal ball. The uncanny truth she revealed of Sands's past was unnerving, but tantalisingly she led her on to tell of the future. Sands, in the throes of divorce, heard about a new man arriving into her life from overseas, describing me, whom she'd never met. I was travelling across Africa at the time in the Land-Rover.

The old lady went onto describe our future relationship, even to the point of calling it 'turbulent', our subsequent marriage, our children, and how we would live in a remote place by the water, surrounded by animals. And then she drew a sharp breath, hurriedly ended the session, and packed her ball away under its cover.

Sands knew there was something more and insisted on knowing the end. Reluctantly, the witch explained how the new man of her life would be tragically killed going about his work, and how she would be left to carry on with the business, and bring up the children, alone.

She'd had put this away, never wanting to remember it again, until that day. As she told me, I was amazed at the accuracy of that satanic prophecy, and how closely I'd missed going under, truly owing my life to my new covering from Christ, and his gallant Mr Angel. Had I not made that decision with Amanda, I had little doubt about the different outcome there would have been on that 'elephant day'.

My new found belief was pretty much my whole life now. I focused as much as I could on what my role might be in advancing the 'Kingdom', feeling fulfilled and good doing it.

'Praise the Lord! Hallelujah, Brother! Glory to God, I hear you're a saved man, Rob!' The word got round surprisingly quickly.

These devoted Bible believing 'Born again' Christians emerged like the wildebeest on migration. Persistent, persevering, uncompromising. A whole new world was homing in on Sands and me, which amazingly I was happily encouraging.

Sands took it all in her stride. I discovered she'd been 'saved' for a while, but she knew me well enough not to push it. We set aside one of our chalets for fulltime Christian workers. Free of charge. It was known as the PTL (Praise The Lord) chalet. The joy to see these selfless folk, often overworked and stressed out, on a holiday they likely could not have afforded, and watch them leave, refreshed, revived and ready to go again was the best reward of all.

Meanwhile, they would offer to teach and minister to us while they visited, to which sessions all were invited, guests and staff. We supported mission organisations in our area with accommodation and transport on land, water, and in the air, privileged to work closely with David and Janet Cunningham of Scripture Union, setting up a youth camp for kids on nearby Long Island.

A true 'desert' island, one kilometre long by a half wide, edged by white sandy beaches scattered with driftwood and a few shady trees in the centre, it was the perfect campsite. We put in a pump, storage tank and simple plumbing, in equally simple structures. If a gust of wind blew too hard you could easily be left standing soaped up in the shower, exposed to the world.

Wire netting was strung in the water to make a croc-free swimming area. Each morning on camp, I would swim round with goggles and snorkel, shooing away 'flat dogs' which had come in during the night—all they had to do was walk round and slip in from the shore. They would struggle to get out from under the netting and disappear in a swirl of sand, which of course meant they could equally do that in the other direction.

No worries. We would then declare the pool safe to swim in, followed by an avalanche of bathers who would enjoy it for the rest of the day. Everybody loved it.

Miraculously, nobody got eaten—Mr Angel never off duty

I had not read the Bible in depth before. I was impressed by its simple beauty, amazed by its variety and perplexed by its complexity. That the prediction of Christ and how He would be birthed and then die for us being found as a thread from one end of the Old Testament to the end of the New, prophesied thousands of years before He came, and that a mathematical pattern relating to the numerical value of the old Hebrew letters, and later Greek, which the writer would have to have known the end when he wrote the beginning, is awesome.

'For that which I do, I allow not; for what I would, that do I not; but what I hate, that do I . . . Who will rescue me? . . . Thanks be to God, through Jesus Christ our Lord.' Paul writes in Romans 7. What a total wrap up of Christian theology, but quite something to get one's mind around.

One of the great discoveries for me was that God did indeed have a host of angels, clearly of the highest calibre and more than enough for each one of us.

My exhilarating appreciation of the 'Good News' was not quite so exhilarating to family, friends, staff and guests. With the usual intense insistence I had for everything I pursued, and with regrettable insensitivity to their own personal spiritual persuasions, I sent most of them paddling in the opposite direction.

'Rob, please, can we just drop Jesus and the Bible out of this discussion.' In my determination for them to 'see the light', I fear I was a painful old fashioned Bible thumping record with its phonograph needle stuck in the same groove.

I tried every trick, stopping at nothing. We had never had a film show on the island. I heard of one on the Christian circuit, 'Armageddon', about the great prophetic war ahead, starring and directed by the musician missionary, Jimmy Swaggert.

That should shake them up!

I arranged for projector and reels at our house one evening when no guests were in camp, asking all the management staff to join us.

After a jovial dinner and a few drinks, everybody was keen to see the mystery movie which I had refused to reveal. We sat out under the stars at our house. Within minutes of it starting, Jeff Stutchbury and his wife Veronica, who were now running Chikwenya, stood up, muttering something about 'Charlatan!'(Jimmy or me, I wasn't too sure), and headed for the lodge.

After ten more minutes, Sandy and I were the only ones left watching. The rest excused themselves, some politely and others not so, drifting back to camp to have their own party.

Whoops!

I didn't hear the end of that for a while. Thank God, some of them paddled back.

The flying operation with the Chikwenya camp now open kept me in the air a good deal, to my great delight. The control tower at Kariba watched me take off ond day with such a heavy load that, after getting airborne, to pick up flying speed I had sunk behind the trees into a valley off the end of the runway..

'God damn it Rob, I thought you'd gone in!' The controller was not amused when he called me up on the radio to see if I was okay.

'Hey, relax. I'm still flying, aren't I?'

'You won't be for much bloody longer if you frig around like that.'

He had a point, which thank fully sunk in, reinforced by several other incidents. One evening flight back from Harare, night fell sooner than I had expected. A heavy haze from bushfires had extinguished the evening light prematurely. On top of that, an untimely headwind had retarded our progress. A night landing on the island was likely to result with an elephant tusk up our whatnots, or an impala wrapped round our hotpots. Heading back to Harare was out of the question as I had no 'night rating'.

Searching the remote area we were over for a landing spot, I noticed an airstrip immediately below. We'd been flying over nothing but bush for the last thirty minutes, expecting nothing less on this stretch until over the Zambezi escarpment and onto the lakeshore. I landed in the fading twilight. A farmer arrived in his Land-Rover, headlights on, bumping across the bush road.

'Good evening, can we help?' he eyed me suspiciously. There'd been rumours of clandestine cross border flights and landings on remote airstrips by political insurgents.

'So where'd this airstrip pop up from?' I couldn't wait to ask.

Alex Van Leenhoff of Montezuma farm explained how he had recently built the strip for an aircraft he planned to purchase. Appreciating his hospitality, I didn't forget a private toast to that doughty Mr Angel for putting me over the spot at exactly the moment needed.

Finally sense over the legal implications prevailed, and Mission Aviation Fellowship, MAF, became a part of our Fothergill family. Originally established by ex WWII airmen who wanted to give something back to humanity after the destruction they had witnessed, these volunteer pilot/engineers were prepared to fly and maintain their single engine planes in the most remote and rugged conditions, trusting in their faith and considerable expertise. We offered them a base on the Island, and an income for ferrying our clients.

Jon Cadd and his wife, Cher, arrived, flying whatever mission work was needed in the area, fitting in our operations between those demands. They were an amazing team. Cher manned their HF radio base on the island whenever Jon was in the air.

'Hi Hon, we're at flight level One-a Zero, upside down 'n nothin' on the clock, loacashun 5 miles doo north of Siakobva. How ya doin Babes?' I would hear Jon reporting back when I flew with him.

Jon Cadd & Mission Aviation
Fellowship (MAF)

MAF blurb would return from Cher, including reports on how the kids and dog were doing.

'Roger that, love you tooo, call in One-a Fiva,' John would answer, and on we'd drone until the next report in fifteen minutes time, superbly navigated through the African skies in an aeroplane one had very confidence in.

I watched John's meticulous attention to detail, eyeing up the weight of every item being loaded, going through his flight checks like his life depended on them, which of course it did. Knowing how many hours he had under his belt and the impressive attention he gave to his flying, I tightened up my own disciplines.

We had some great years with them until the local 'professionals' chased them away. 'Ma jearous!' as we say in Shona. Our plane was a backup, seldom needed, and a most convenient access for us as a family to the outside world.

We had enrolled Neen into a little farm school called Rydings, converted from old tobacco barns, in the Karoi farming district. Several hours by boat and road were now swapped for a twenty-minute flight over the mountains. The only drawback was poor Sands' inherent fear of flying, and Rach's periodic projectile vomiting from the back seat.

'Oh No-o-o! Rachael!' would regularly chorus from the middle row seat.

'Hold your horses gals, we're nearly there!' My invariable response—the show had to go on.

The great boon about flying the route to Harare was the Kariba power lines, always there to follow, whatever the navigational difficulties. One weekend, we'd planned a 'fly in' from the Mashonaland Flying Club. It was cancelled due to weather. My cue to fly the family out for a weekend break.

Once over the escarpment I found the cloud base at tree top height. A good excuse to enjoy some low flying, following the power lines. Climbing over some high ground, I ended up in low cloud over treetops, again . . . Determined not to risk climbing through it this time, I made a tight turn watching a tree through the mist just beneath my wing tip, concentrating everything I had on holding this position while we worked out how to fly out of it.

'What's the reciprocal course to fly back out into the clear, Sands,' I called tensely, not daring to take my mind off this critical flying even for a second. That tree was awful close to the wing.

'What's that?' she shouts back. This was not the moment to be getting into a maths discussion.

'The reciprocal! 180 degrees of the course I flew in on, which was 070. C'mon Sands!'

Sorry Babes! Bit rough on you, considering I couldn't even work it out myself.

Nothing like adrenalin to sharpen the tongue, and mental arithmetic. She had it in a flash and we flew back out of the low cloud. Rob wiping his brow, and apologising, Sands rolling her eyes.

Chapter 35

No Uniform

One of the most tragic turns in our life's journey hit us in 1981. Sands, my fit, lively beautiful energetic young 33 year-old wife and our young children's ever caring Mum took seriously ill.

It started with a tick bite. Picked up while on our first Scripture Union youth camp at the Kyle dam, central Zimbabwe, where the girls and I were singing a ditty, much to everyone's amusement as I could never remember my lines.

> *The cows in the field, they chew their cud all day,*
> *And as they do they have a smile and give their milk*
> *away . . .*

And on! That's all I remember now—not much more than then—the girls of course having the whole five verses off pat.

The tick bite developed into a deep vein thrombosis in her leg, from which all kinds of blood circulation problems followed. And then a serious asthmatic condition which required frequent visits to specialists in Harare, returning with buckets of pills and puffers.

It was the beginning of a long traumatic downhill slide in her health and suffering, and in our relationship, which carried on right through to her recent departing to be with her precious Jesus—thirty years later. We each had radically diverging approaches as to how the sickness should be treated. I was for a herbal 'feed and exercise the body correctly and it will look after itself' approach. Sands, whose prerogative it was since it was her body, had other ideas. Modern medicine was the answer. Uncountable visits, whose number only vied with the expense, to hospitals and specialists in Harare, Johannesburg, Cape Town, the USA, and finally New Zealand and Austarlia, never got on top of it.

There was no precise diagnosis. References were made to lung diseases, heart conditions, blood disorders, allergies and reactions to various possibilities, including the Island, the Zambezi valley, and me! She could no longer lead an active life. Chronically dependent on friendly, and sometimes not so friendly, doctors, by phone and regular trips to town, she stacked her bedside table and body with medication, all of which had side effects, which needed other medication to counteract.

Our lives became an agony of drama, disappointment and disagreement.

I knew nothing about ill health, never having had to deal with it. I tried to be pragmatic and supportive of the physician treating her, assuming he, at least, knew what he was doing. As I saw the devastation caused by his drug treatment over the years, I wasn't so sure and more strongly urged Sands to go the alternative route. The physician did not support this. Sands, who was often at a loss as to what to do, ended up more determinedly relying upon him and trusting my gut-feeling doctoring less and less. Probably because she knew how little I really knew about it.

Watching and living with the torturous deterioration of my vibrant, valued wife was acutely distressing. Valiant mother of our children who loved and needed her was laid unbearably low by pain and suffering. And I was not coping. I'd landed in another world where I had no experience, insight or recognition.

Then an unfortunate mishap complicated our unhappy situation even more. Following a hysterectomy deemed to be helpful, Sands developed a worse asthmatic problem with added circulation difficulties in the leg which had suffered the deep vein thrombosis years earlier.

We sought a second opinion from a specialist surgeon we'd heard about in Cape Town. We were always hearing about another 'miracle' doctor who would save the day, who was always further and further away, and more and more expensive.

He proposed an operation that he was developing which, in his view, would solve her problem. In lay terms it meant removing a vein considered unnecessary in her right leg, and reinserting it across her pelvis to carry the blood from the left to the right side of her body. He explained how her womb, now removed, had acted as the major blood-reticulating vessel for her damaged leg before the hysterectomy, and how this proposed operation would dramatically improve her circulation from the current 'dead' leg, having lost the former route.

'So what would you like to do?' He asked, establishing the cost.

What on earth did we know about it? The complications that might set in, the implication of more surgery in an already ailing body, the myriad intricacies we had no knowledge of, nor the recovery process—really, what did we know about all that to make this weighty decision? It seemed downright unfair to ask.

Sands herself hated the idea of another operation, and I was left with making the decision. The Harare physician was opposed to it, to his credit. I had listened carefully to all the surgeon had to say, whom after all we had come all this way to see, and he gave the operation a 50/50 chance of working.

'What would you do if it were your wife?' I asked him.

'I'd do it,' He said, looking me straight in the eye.

'That's good enough for me,' I replied, appreciating his directness.

It didn't work. The induced vein collapsed during the premature flight home from Cape Town. Premature as the surgeon requested her presence for surveillance for 6 months—she left after two, both of us deciding it looked good and missing her in our home back on the island, convinced all would be well recovering there rather than on her own in Cape Town. She was met by ambulance at Harare airport and went straight into emergency surgery where they undid all the intricate work the Cape Town specialist surgeon had just performed.

The aftermath was that Sands was left with chronic lymphodaema in that leg, where the blood simply would not pump back efficiently to the heart, resulting in a limb that swelled to elephantine proportions, her biggest physical hindrance and frustration to the end.

And I had made the decision for the op, and encouraged her to come home early.

Our prophesied 'turbulent' relationship hit a typhoon low. Fundamental principles I held of life, coupled with my faith, laid a deep commitment in me to support Sands through whatever. Her long-term sickness and the huge complications of the physiological and psychological impact needed special support, I knew.

But wasn't doing too well.

I fasted for 40 days, seeking divine understanding. But didn't hear a thing.

Preachers, healers, counsellors and Christian friends prayed, called on our God and rebuked Satan. We attended course after seminar after special service.

Nothing changed.

'But we've prayed Daddy . . .' our children would plead, simply not understanding—as nor did we.

'I know.' I'd say, which I didn't. 'Hang in there, darlings . . . Jesus knows . . . Mummy'll be alright.'

But she wasn't.

The tension of expectation, and awful disappointments, the heartrending delusion and insinuations of spiritual failure from some fellow church people were demoralising, *in extremis.* Sands and I fell into severe depression. I never realised the extent of it at the time, nor was it identified by any of our counsellors of doctors, until much later.

'You may not take your wife back to Fothergill. If you ignore this advice, I will no longer take responsibility for her condition.' The specialist announced.

'I see.' I actually didn't see at all. 'So you think we should make a plan to live elsewhere?' I couldn't imagine how or where.

'No, I mean as from now, your wife may not go back. If you act otherwise, I will no longer attend or advise her.'

Sands was totally dependent on this man. His order meant our leaving our home, our life, our everything. There and then. She was not even permitted to go back and pack.

We were refugees in Harare.

Wandering the town, moving from one house-sit to another, we eventually made arrangements with Maasie to move onto her property, No 27. We later bought it to become our new home, which it is for me to this day.

The move brought more tension. Sands was insecure, more so when around my family. They meant well but that pioneering, albeit somewhat domineering, streak was often too much in our delicate situation.

I commuted each week to Fothergill. Sands was bedridden, looked after by the wonderful Suzie who had joined us in Harare to help her with the children and housekeeping. The girls were placed in the first schools we could find at short notice. One took Neen as a weekly boarder, the other two were at different day schools as Sands and I travelled the medical treadmill.

The team was broken up. Everyone was as miserable as a hearse driver with no coffin.

Ten-year-old Neen's teacher phoned. 'There's something wrong with your child, Mr Fynn. She won't talk to anyone, makes no friends, and is very unhappy.' Our composed, self-confident Neen, leader of the 'Fothergill Pirates', our Island news reporter, regaler of stories to strangers and friends alike . . .

It took a decade for her to get over this turmoil and regain her self-esteem and confidence.

Eight-year old Cathy's teacher phoned. 'We think she should go to a remedial school.' She was behaving oddly. She didn't like to wear her uniform and when told to put it back on, would wear it back to front. They reported how she would get up from her desk in the middle of lessons, walk to the back of the classroom, open her lunch box and have a picnic right there, not caring that nobody joined her. She became an out and out rebel, uncooperative, bunking school and home, refusing to go back when she turned sixteen.

Our ever-helpful Cath, always cleaning and tidying, the easy-going family comic and happy fisher-girl, the most content with life . . .

Years of her life to recover, too.

Little Rach was at the same school as Cath. As ever, she went along with whatever and wherever her big sister led. Everything okay. I couldn't get any other answer out of her for years, besides 'I dunno!' Her trust in her sisters was her security. Parents always away, travelling to distant lands, looking for medical solutions, in some drama or another, our children staying with *our* friends, not *theirs*. And little peace even when we were home, much controversy between Mum and Dad. She succumbed to anorexia when she got to University, having valiantly covered up all her stress for these years.

Dad tried to run around being the everything to everybody. Unsuccessfully, irrationally, and irascible in his dreadful aloneness. Sands desperately tried to be the homemaker, wonderfully creative with her sowing, cooking and loving her children in her few bouts of energy in between the long depressing sick spells, which dominated more and more of her life.

I recalled our life on the island, when the only time we used a vehicle was when we climbed onto one of our beat-up old Land-Rovers to head down a track, with the sun on our backs and a fresh breeze in our faces, the only traffic being elephants, buffalo and impala, the only noise a fish eagle's cries, a lion's roar, a trumpet or a hippo's chortle.

It was very hard for all of us.

Chapter 36

Deferred Hope

'Who amongst us has not lied?' asked the Honourable President Mugabe in his statement to the nation. 'Yesterday you were with your girlfriend and you told your wife you were with the President. Should you get nine months for that?' He was defending his Ministers over the latest corruption scandal.

The importation of new cars had been banned for a year. Only those from the state owned Willowvale Motors factory were to be made available to the public. Which meant only to those well connected. They would then sell them on at several times the registered purchase price.

Known as the 'Willowgate' scandal, Ministers, MPs and army officers were all guilty. And were granted a presidential pardon.

The only one who lost his job was Geoffrey Nyarota, editor of *The Chronicle*, who exposed the scandal.

Zimbabwean Independence euphoria was beginning to wear thin.

The Matabele were cruelly and shamefully repaid for their dominance of a hundred years earlier. In 1983 the government let loose the 5th Brigade, specially trained by Koreans at Inyanga Barracks, when an estimated 20,000 tribes people were murdered in cold blood. The operation was named 'Gukurahundi'—Shona for 'the rain that blows away the chaff before the spring rains'.

We heard terrible stories. The inhabitants of whole villages burnt alive in their huts, hundreds of bodies thrown down disused mineshafts. The few survivors spared to dance and sing praises to ZANU-PF, the ruling party, on the mass graves of their dead.

The Ndebele leader, Joshua Nkomo, had fled for his life and was in exile in London. His ZIPRA fighters who had been integrated into the new Zimbabwean army found themselves victimized and many had deserted, taking their weapons with them.

Mugabe had promised land, jobs, water and electricity to everyone. Ten years on, little had changed, other than for the ruling elite—*Wabenzi (*a name relating to the Mercedes Benz cars they drove*).* Wealthy beyond expected means, with posh houses, the latest of everything, cars that would make a Californian blush, Swiss bank accounts, their children at the most expensive overseas schools, often using scholarships awarded for use by the underprivileged, they were legend with lavish entertainment.

The new ZANU-PF headquarters was a gleaming concrete and black glass multi-storey office block, paid for by the Chinese Communist party. Mugabe's motorcade, his long bullet and mine-proof Mercedes with tinted windows, siren screaming outriders, army bodyguard, ambulance, and the inevitable Special Branch, careered its way through town and country. All other road users had to pull off or risk being shot at.

While 30,000 ex-combatants from the war went unemployed, the army chief made a fortune on kickbacks from defence contracts, opening hotels, supermarket chains and farms—his estate was valued at $9million. George Orwell's *Animal Farm* couldn't have been more apt.

Whites were castigated for the colonial burdens they had imposed, and for owning too much land, much of which was legally purchased post-independence with a government certificate of 'no interest'. The imbalance of land development, as opposed to distribution, was clear to all, and offers were made by commercial farmers to sell farms for resettlement to the newly developing black farmers, and to help them run them. Government baulked at the market price, in spite of considerable 'Aid' money available for this purpose. This was diverted for more attractive purchases which enriched the *wabenzi* in the style they were rapidly becoming accustomed to.

Mugabe was awarded honorary degrees, including the 'Africa Prize' for 'Contributions to the Sustainable End to Hunger', and an honorary knighthood from Great Britain's Queen. He was later to say he also had a degree in violence.

On Fothergill, Sands was feeling that the safari operation, its workload, and maybe my obsession with it, was largely responsible for her condition. She wanted out.

Then she had a dream where she saw us living in the mountains of Nyanga, on the Mozambique border. Exciting—I'd always yearned to live there from the time that little boy was holidaying in Uncle Dr Robert's cottage.

Her dream showed us by a lake, running a family camp. I thought I knew where it was. Our friend Dave Wheeler had a chunk of land next to the Stables dairy farm where we'd spent many happy family holidays. It looked onto a trout dam in the valley. It fitted perfectly into Sands' vision and Dave agreed we should build a camp there.

It was a great reprieve. Filled with new energy and enthusiasm I planned and prepared for the mountain camp. We sold a part of the safari business to our former staff and colleagues on a soft deal, monies to be advanced when available, and I went into action on Nyanga.

We found a place for the children in a lovely private school on the outskirts of Mutare, our nearest town. My brother–in-law Davey, the now owner of our old family cottage, made it available for a base while I built the new home.

I was thrilled. Good swap for the hot old Zambezi valley.

Then Sands had back-track syndrome. Too isolated, no medical care, would she cope? Her specialist advised against it. I couldn't believe the turnaround. Where had her faith gone?

Poor Sands—unsympathetic husband response, again. We asked the elders of our church to advise. They all solemnly agreed that Sands' misgivings were founded, and advised me to pursue the Harare based plan I had previously initiated at Mazvikadei dam just outside Harare.

I was devastated and thought life, and the whole lot of them, 'sucked'.

The book of Proverbs in 12:12 says 'Hope deferred makes the heart grow cold . . .' Mine was very cold and confused.

Home in Harare was not a happy one. Sands' condition deteriorated to the extent that she lived at the end of an oxygen tube. Not dissimilar to a hospital at visiting hours, a constant stream of friends and councillors came and went—our bedroom centre stage—the girls when home were glued to the TV that was always on, feeling they had a bit of catching up to do.

All anathema to me, I would retire into my office and think about new camp designs and their activities, household shopping, looking at organisational charts for where I should be and when.

I would dream about game walks, aeroplanes, boats, the wide open spaces and its wildlife, the haunting cries of fish eagles and the terrorising trumpeting of elephants—the motivating fuel to my engine for so long—now all gone. Camp building was now an hour and a half's drive away compared with my stroll through the Mopane on Fothergill. And groans all round at home if I wanted to do anything but watch the dreaded box. Life and all my exciting plans for bringing up my plucky little team had just been switched off. Like we did with 'the box' last thing at night.

And these, my children, loving coming out with dad on a walk or a game drive, the highlight being opening the tea box to see what biscuits Mum or Buhnu had slipped in. There was always the chance of finding an orphaned animal—we once loaded a buffalo calf after seeing its mother taken down by lion. They then became camp pets, and we all knew that tamed wild animals invariably become an accident waiting to happen, so we'd have to cart them back into the bush, vowing we wouldn't do it again. Until the next time.

Now this gutsy little team of adventurers simply wanted to stay home and watch TV!

Sands' horrendous home background had seriously dented her security. She had told me how her drunken dad locked her, aged 6, out of their house for the whole night, threatening through the window with a kitchen knife if she tried to enter. And for all the love and devotion the orphanage nuns gave, nothing could substitute for real loving parents.

Her previous marriage had been disappointing, and then, to meet this way-out, off the wall, ridiculously ambitious, going for broke, make it but don't fake it, here's the shovel, 'start digging now' kind of guy, who just didn't give a hoot what anybody thought—in whom understanding, compassion and cherishing were still a long way down the line . . . and now all this . . . bitter pills to swallow.

Thankfully, she had found a deep faith in Jesus, and would stand with Him to her dying day. But we couldn't talk to each other. Deep down, at gut level—couldn't empathise in the battle we knew the other was fighting—our personal needs, passions and pride inhibiting the support and love for each other we each looked for more than anything else in the world.

It was tough beyond our ability to handle, and we were going under.

Chapter 37

Church vs Sunday Roast

'We need a camp, Rob.'

'Okay, I can do that. Camps are my thing.' Aren't they? I wasn't sure what *was* any more.

David and Janet of Scripture Union had been faithful friends through this trying time, attending and counselling us both. They too suggested that I build the camp to replace the loss of Long Island, on the site I'd found by the new Mazvikadei dam near Banket, 100kms from Harare.

'Just get on with it, Rob' was a good message for me to pick up on.

Ian and Sally Barrat who donated the site were a long time farming family, as down to earth as you could find. Ian's philosophy, 'I've never seen a trailer behind a hearse', prompted their wonderful generosity. Funds to build the camp were raised by friends from within our ailing country and from around the world. We called it Sanganayi Creek, Sanganayi being Shona for 'Let's meet together'.

I designed structures built from poles and local farm bricks, under thatch, to accommodate up to 300 kids, expandable to 600. Assault courses, canoeing and sailing, tennis, soccer and rugby fields, horse riding, an abseiling tower with 'foofy' slide (rolling sling on long suspended wire cable), and the wild surrounds of African bush offered campers a challenging world of activities. It became host to virtually every major school in the country on Christian leadership and environmental courses.

Mazvikadei & Sanganayi Creek

'You missed sports day, Dad', Cath was telling me.

'Oohh, nooo. I'm so sorry.' I *never* missed sports days.

The toll on my family was not good. I allowed myself to be carried away in Sanganayi where the buzz of camp life made it easier to forget the depression and difficulties at home. Sands could not join me and, shamefully, it looked acceptable for Rob to be out there.

'Do not worry about your life, what you will eat or drink; or about your body, or what you will wear . . . but seek first His kingdom, and His righteousness, and all these things will be given to you as well' was a scripture I'd read from Matthew 6:25-33.

It was a fine excuse not to pay attention to my own income, trusting in God to supply. In the absence of our Fothergill income, now taken over by a government hotel group, I had invested in a ranch in the lowveld, five hour's drive away in the southern part of Zimbabwe, that I looked to for my future security. I did not spend anything like the time such an investment required, to find I'd been badly 'ripped off' by my partner/manager and former owner. Now, there was no income.

'What's with all this then, God?' I wondered belligerently, with sick wife who needed considerable sums for her medication and treatment, and children to put through their schooling and university.

Not surprisingly, there was no discernible answer. I had neatly missed the scriptures that urge us to attend to our family's needs before charity or business demands (1 Timothy 3:5).

Sanganayi was doing okay. But Rob and his home were not. And that time of rest and recuperation after the years of slogging to establish Fothergill I'd so looked forward to, had been catapulted into space. Sanganayi was a tough enough call, and now, our family future security slashed—TAB—That's Africa Baby—Time to move out and earn a living again.

'No thanks. Got that T-shirt!' was my first reaction when I heard about some islands for sale on the Zambian side of Lake Kariba. The seller, Commander Jonathan RN, was a persistent man. A retired British Military type who travelled the world picking up opportunities through contacts in the Foreign Office, buying well and selling better. I flew up with my ex-fighter pilot brother–in-law Richy to take a look.

Not permitted to cross the border, I studied the islands in the deep blue waters far below. They were remote, 150kms from both the dam wall and our Fothergill end of the lake, right on the border between Zimbabwe and Zambia. At this point, only a few hundred metres separated the two countries. Not much happened up here. On the Zim side—inaccessible bush, hunting and odd subsistence farmers, a Zimbabwean ferry passing once a month, if that. On the Zambian side—I had no idea. It sure looked pretty barren.

Chete Island was the largest of the group, and the biggest island on the Lake, forming one side of the spectacular Chete Gorge. 'Ambush alley' during the war.

But it looked fabulous. I felt a stirring within I knew only too well.

I contacted Commander Jonathan.

'Excellent, I'll come up and escort you down for a closer look.' He sounded far too keen. I should have known.

'I'll bring my boat so that we can get around on the Lake,' I told him and arranged to drive up with Mike La Grange in his Land Cruiser.

Mike had been in National Parks and on the pioneering game-capture teams, and knew well how to assess the potential carrying capacity of these islands, which had been severely poached over the years.

Jonathan waxed on about how easy it would be to develop the islands for tourism. I was wary, having no misconceptions about the huge amount of energy and finance required to get such a project off the ground. I'd done it four times before and had a good idea of what was required.

Our first stop was Lusaka, the capital city of Zambia, to check out the legality and reality of the leases. The stark and broken down city was not inspiring compared with our beautifully treed, well-planned Harare, thanks to the old city fathers in both capitals with their very different outlooks. Lusaka has, as with the whole Zambian economy, hugely improved since then.

Our meeting with the Permanent Secretary from the Ministry of Lands was rudely interrupted. 'There is somebody in your car!'

Within twenty minutes of arriving we were galloping down the stairs, the lift out of order, to chase some thieves who had broken into Mike's Land Cruiser.

I was getting the drift. The leases were so vaguely worded it was quite unclear as to what we could or couldn't do. The Secretary was giving little away. I wondered how much it was going to cost before he budged.

Concerned, but able to see a few chinks of light, we headed for the Islands.

The mainland town closest to Chete is Sinazongwe, a fascinating relic of the early administration. It had been developed as the major fishing port for the newly formed Lake Kariba in the '60s. The plan then was to teach the Tonga who had been displaced from their ancestral home in the Zambezi valley how to fish in the new lake.

Kapenta (*Limnothrissa miodon*), or Lake Tanganyika sardine, named from where they were introduced in 1967 by a farsighted fisheries officer, were flown in to the specially built airstrip at Sinazongwe in a Douglas DC3 Dakota. This effort was to grow into the biggest fishing industry on Kariba, producing 30,000 tons per annum. For those who knew how.

The harbour boasted the only inland lighthouse in Central Africa and the biggest slipway on the lake, a fish processing plant and ice-maker that were state of the art. All built on Aid funds. It had the finest access on the entire Zambian Lake shore, tarred road, electricity supply and Zambia's only coal mine nearby. The country's largest irrigation scheme, with 24 centre pivots watering 100 hectares, was installed on 'The Farm'.

'Why is so little of the irrigation system operating?' I asked the South Africans who had won the tender to run 'The Farm', noticing three quarters of the sprinklers not working.

'Aagh, man, some is stolen, and some is the sodic soils, hey. An Aid company sets it up for KK to grow wheat. But they's neverr done theirr homework on the soils, ne? Now salts is coming up from allus water going on. Yous jez sommer gotta rest ze soil for years, man, even generrations.'

Aah well, at least Sinazongwe had electricity, thanks to the scheme.

These were unheard of facilities in Zambia back then, let alone along its neglected lakeshore. Thirty years of President Kaunda's socialism had ravished the country's economy, bringing development to a standstill.

During the Zimbabwean liberation war, Sinazongwe had been used to ferry guerrillas across the lake. The Rhodesians retaliated by blowing up every boat in the harbour. No one has been willing or able to replace them since.

We arrived to a ghost town. All facilities abandoned and pillaged, empty corrugated iron sheds standing derelict, silted up harbour, non-functional lighthouse darkly guarding the harbour mouth, cattle grazing the shoreline. Dugout canoes paddled by with their nets to catch the few remaining fish.

But it had an extraordinary wild beauty in its abandonment. Large stretches of water overhung by huge riverine trees and palms looked across to blue distant hills, fisherman worked their nets in the dugouts, goats and cattle bells clanked to the shouts of herd boys, women cackled over their washing on the shore, all giving it a haunting timelessness of an Africa that never really changes. I loved it. This was a future tourist destination.

'You think so, Rob?' Mike was looking at me sideways.

'Absolutely. This will be the new Kariba tourist town of Zambia, and out there, the new Matuse.'

It could be a biggie, and visionary developer Rob was jumping out of his box again.

We launched our little boat on the huge slipway and headed across the lake with Parks game scouts as our guides and policemen.

'Kudu!' they pointed to a herd of impala as we arrived.

Mistaking the rutting roar of impala, one of them cautioned about the dangers of meeting those 'lion' on foot (they do sound very similar to the uninitiated). More aware of how useful and experienced our guides would be, none of whom had ventured thus far before, we pulled out maps and went looking for campsites.

'Kudu!' whispered Mike.

'Wow! Now, he's a beauty!" I was impressed. A beautiful specimen stood proud on the edge of the gorge, surveying his territory.

We were in *mopane* scrub, with spectacular views in every direction. But little sign of game. We watched a strange looking almost camel-like elephant breeding herd with high stomachs and long legs, probably so evolved thanks to the scarcity of food and their highly tuned survival instincts in this rocky, poacher's terrain. They'd be good runners. Lion and elephant bulls would apparently swim across from the Zimbabwe side for a change of scenery—we couldn't think why else they'd be doing it.

Kaunda's Zambia had not planned National Parks or protected areas along the entire length of Kariba's shore. The game and fish had been virtually eradicated over the years by the villagers desperately eking out a living in this forsaken and barren land. Chete Island was better off, being more difficult to poach thanks to the 17km of rough water reaching across to the mainland.

I envisaged setting up a National Park status and reintroducing game. The potential was exciting, elevated by its remoteness.

Chief Sinazongwe was first on the list of visits. His clean swept village was known as 'The Palace'. All chief's villages are called such in Zambia, I guessed thanks to some wag of a District Commissioner in colonial days. The dusty winding track that led there would be impassable in the rains. I noted to make sure of completing my business here before they broke.

A cardboard notice written in charcoal and wired to a tree announced that visiting hours with the chief were to be from 1000 to 1200. I found him in his office, a small brick building with frameless open door and windows, furnished with an old school desk, two hard backed chairs and an antique typewriter, files in a box on the floor. He came out to sit under a big shady fig tree in a homemade chair resembling a throne, his waiting audience on low planks supported by bricks patiently stalwart. The secretary at his side, in off-white shirt and tie, poised ballpoint above school exercise book.

My offering of a bag of mealie-meal lay at the foot of the tree, noticed but unacknowledged. He asked me where my directors were. Disconcerted that I'd arrived alone, he proceeded to inform me of the protocol and a history of the area, ensuring I was aware how it had developed in his lifetime. This was no rural backwater, he was at pains to point out. No bones about it, though, times were tough. All contributions would be welcome.

'When I was a boy, Mr Fynn, the elephants would raid our crops year after year.' He waved his hand at the stunted drought ridden mealie fields surrounding The Palace. 'Today, we never see one.'

Sinazongwe eco progress.

He established his documentation and financial requirements, duplicates of those I'd just been instructed to submit to the Ministry of Lands and National Parks in Lusaka.

'Don't worry about what *they* say, I approve everything first, and then you see *them*.' The antithesis of what the Ministry had me understand.

My request to give Chete Island some protected status in the absence of any Parks along this lakeshore was met with mixed acquiescence. Did this Zimbabwean think he was the big deal around here?

There was no question that its location was good with the substantial tourist hub of Victoria Falls only a couple of hours driving, or 20 minutes flying, away. And my plans were ambitious. Restock and build safari camps on all three islands and a resort hotel in Sinazongwe. Going for big with a corresponding marketing and promotional clout made sense. Small would simply leave it the little ghost town with its nondescript islands 'somewhere out there' that it was. We needed to make our mark to be noticed.

I just had to find another burst of energy and a lot of cash to get it rolling. The thrill of seeing the potential in a new unknown and uncharted site was always the stuff of stimulation for me.

But this would be my last. And biggest.

'Good morning, I'd like to introduce the black rhino breeding programme we're planning to establish on the islands. It has a lesser poaching threat than any other in Zambia, and has the backing of both South Africa and Zimbabwe, the two most prominent current Rhino breeding countries. The project would give us something very unique here in Sinazongwe to attract visitors.'

At a meeting attended by the chief, member of parliament, town councillors and other interested ministries from Lusaka, I enthused about the island's potential, our plans to import game, and explained how essential was a marketing strategy to establish this new Zambian lake safari destination.

'When will you open the hotel, Mr Fynn?'

No one looked excited about stopping the poaching, which was their convenient meat supply, or re-introducing the countrywide extinct rhino, with its attendant policing programme. The hotel bar was far more interesting. I tried to focus on the core development I believed necessary to kick this project into gear—developing the islands. A hotel on its own in ghost town Sinazongwe was not a big attraction.

All they wanted to know was what was in it for them. And were still apparently touchy about a Zimbabwean developing an island far from their shores but a mere stone's throw from his. Could he be trying to steal it?

The smug look on their faces told me that nothing would happen here anyway until they were a lot richer themselves, and they knew I had more money than sense—otherwise why would I be here? I had seen that look too many times before.

I left for the long drive home, wearied by the 'same old, same old', but surprised and excited by the beauty and tourist potential of the place.

I psyched myself up to give developing this wilderness one last big shove.

'But why do you want a lighthouse, Mr Fynn?' The Council works foreman remonstrated at my insistence on power right down to the tip of the harbour peninsula. 'There is no traffic after dark.' Indeed, there was no traffic at all.

'There is going to be traffic when we have finished, believe me, and it will look good. And it will add to the ambience, help to put us on the map,' I enthused, offering to pay for materials. He wasn't sure what ambience was, and knew Sinazongwe was already on his map.

I saw the lighthouse as a symbolic beacon of hope in the sea of despair the local displaced and marginalised Tonga had fallen into. All the promises given had been broken when they were forced to move out of their beautiful traditional homes along the Zambezi

River banks, where the annual flood revived their lands, producing spectacular crops. And all the game and fish they could ever ask for. They now lived in abject poverty with little hope of change.

'This is nothing unusual for us!' They argued with the DC (District Commissioner) back in 1955, who had been given the job to move them from their traditional homes before the rising waters of the dam.

'The river floods every year,' they reminded him.

'But it will be much higher and it won't go down this time,' he told them.

'How can that be?'

He tried to explain about the damming of the great river, at Kariwa (Kariba).

'On top of Nyaminyami's home? These *Muzungu* (white men) are truly crazy!'

They were very unhappy to be asked to leave their grand ancestral home. And nobody could build on top of Nyaminyami, their river god. Clearly the DC was unreliable.

They were finally taken out in government transport at gunpoint.

Thirty five years down the line, the promises of new fishing grounds, tourist development, jobs, and electricity in every hut were as empty as the harbour.

I was keen to get something going and show the people we were serious. It was their best chance to get back on the economic treadmill.

Importing interesting game onto the Islands was feasible, their survival guaranteed by their distance from the mainland and its virulent poachers that plagued the Zambian shoreline with its minimal controls.

In spite of the benefits such a project would bring to the region, I was only too aware of how empty stomachs come first in this harsh land. Survival in Africa depends on those who help themselves. The benevolent charities and concerned respect for the conservation of our planet are luxuries of the first world, ill afforded here unless organised and paid for. Survival comes first. From senior politicians and businessman, always with huge extended families depending on them, to the poor little family eking out subsistence in a hut, there is a bottomless pit that can absorb every resource and new initiative unless carefully thought out controls and measures are put into place.

'I think it's a mad idea, Jonathan, but I'm going to give it a crack. What's your bottom line?'

A gut decision made, I struck a deal and broke the exciting news to the family. Sands found it difficult to comprehend.

'How on earth . . . ?'

Good question.

My grand, hugely optimistic plan needed a US$ 2 million start up. I approached some big financers to come on board. In the meantime we needed to get sailing, and some small but plucky investors took their chances.

'Do you think dhows would work on this lake?' I ventured.

'Don't see why not. A tricky matter to get them here, tho,' Ben Freeth mused. He explained how they fall to pieces when transported.

He and his wife Laura were to manage the operation out of Sinazongwe. Ben's father was a senior officer with the British Army, training Zimbabwe's new army, pulled together from the widely divergent military who had recently been fighting each other. A formidable task.

Ben had the resourceful and tenacious outlook typical of that upbringing, with a deep Godly faith. He had been the British ski jumping champion, had mounted several expeditions into remote parts of Africa, and spent the last few years building dhows on the Tanzanian coast. We liked the idea of having dhows plying our tourists and provisions back and forth across the Lake.

Luara's family farmed in Zimbabwe. They both loved the remoteness of Sinazongwe, with its one rural store, even more rural hospital, and four churches. The missionaries had done their job well in Zambia, assisting in forming a religious nation with English spoken in every corner.

We were keen to develop the company's relations with the community.

Ben recounted his first attempt.

'I quietly slipped into one of the churches on a Sunday morning. Instantly noticed, an interpreter was appointed for my benefit. After the usual songs of praise and worship, taking an hour or so, a preacher leaped into action, which with the interpretation that he patiently waited for after each statement, took another hour.

'I knew it wouldn't be an in and out affair, the benches were hard, and having appreciated the sermon, I was quite happy it was drawing to a close. However, another preacher then jumped up to the lectern [,] and delivered a second sermon, again patiently translated, the congregation clearly relishing every moment, for another hour.

'I was becoming a little fretful, knowing Laura was preparing Sunday roast, but certainly couldn't walk out. To my horror, a third preacher took the podium. By the time it was all over, and the introductions, small talk and tea had been served, it was four o'clock in the afternoon!'

He didn't enrol into the congregation, in spite of pressing invitations.

Having done a grand job for a year, he moved where his heart really was, to work with the embattled farmers in Zimbabwe, based out on the family farm. Their courageous stand against the iniquitous farm invasions were an inspiration to the pursuit for justice, at dear cost, themselves close to losing their lives and their beautiful self-built thatch houses burned to the ground while their hugely productive farm was taken for Government ministers. Today, their most productive fruit farm simply hosts a subsistence existence for the occupiers.

Laura's father and mother have since died of their wounds and broken hearts following severe beatings by the Minister's men for their non-compliance, and Ben, similarly treated but survived, works for the plight of displaced farm workers. A recent film, '*Mugabe and the White African*', nominated for a British Academy of Film and Television Arts (BAFTA, 2009) award, tells the story, and is now in book form by Zebra press of Random House Struik.

Chapter 38

Is that You, God?

I felt like I was launching a new country. And funding it. We needed to have Sinazongwe declared an entry point into Zambia, so that international guests could fly or boat directly in. This innovation seemed to necessitate the participation of almost every ministry in the government. Suspicions about a Zimbabwean directing the project right on their border intensified. There had been disputes about ownership of the island in the past. Perhaps we weren't flattering the various administrative and political figures sufficiently?

I spent more time in government offices in Lusaka than I had ever, anywhere, in my life, trying to persuade lethargic, cynical politicians and civil servants why I wanted to spend vast sums of my money and time improving their land.

'The Secretary is playing golf with the Minister,' the bored receptionist explained to me.

'What?!' I'd just driven from Harare, setting out at 0400 with usual loaded trailer, to be in time for a crucial 1200 meeting to discuss why the Sinazongwe council were blocking our safari camp construction, insisting we build a hotel in the town first.

'Maybe you can see him tomorrow, Mr Fynn? Come at 0800 hours,' the receptionist suggested. My patience was tested to astronomic levels.

Sinazongwe peninsular & slipway

Chete Island Lodge & 'Gache Gache'

My tactic then would be to sit in his waiting room, talking to his receptionist and secretary, badgering her to pester him till he saw me. This could take days.

Agreements were as fluid as the sticky tar on the roads. Each understanding reached could simply be forgotten about, or changed after I left. And there I would be, back in Lusaka, thrashing it out again.

Finance raising was equally precarious. The Zambian economy had not turned at this stage, and collapsing Zimbabwe was effecting regional investment decisions.

'We'd like to see our money back in eighteen months, Mr Fynn. Can you do it?' Having previously been happy with three years.

I could do anything. Fiddling with the proposed budget programme, to show a positive return in the time stipulated, was becoming second nature. I'd learned how easy it was to produce required financial projections. You simply changed a few parameters in the programme, and . . . Hey Presto!

The whole picture improved to the new constraints. It didn't seem to matter how unrealistic they were, unlikely anybody would pick that up, as long as the end result looked good. Did the whole world work on this basis? A huge bubble waiting to be pricked? This was in 1998, before a glimmer of the world recession.

There always seemed to be another project that would return the financial institution's money faster than mine. Never mind the social, national or cultural benefits pertaining to the projects.

'Gee, thanks Sands.' She was trying to be helpful at home, although pretty sick, valiantly trying to get her head around stuff.

'No, sorry . . . he was the Permanent Secretary, but he's now Assistant Director . . . no, that's the member of parliament . . . yes, sometimes he acts as the chairman in the Council, but he's not really . . . well, they did say they would, but now they've actually . . . . yeah, I know, but the tax law has changed again and . . . [!]'

It was an administrative nightmare, and she did her best to unravel it in all the letters and the proposal she was attempting to type. Why was I even asking her to? Sinazongwe and Lusaka were simply different planets she knew nothing about.

Our office was next to the bedroom at home, through necessity if Sands was involved, where good intentioned employees, trying to help patiently, worked with her. For me, they only increased the imposition and intrusion into our home. The absence of privacy in our innermost sanctuary was one of the hardest for me to stomach.

I moved from one fire to another, never putting any out. Too much of a one-man band, everybody looking to me for direction and initiative, I felt like I was trying to run the space race, alone. Despondent and exhausted, I began, for the first time in my life, to experience deep despair.

Then God spoke to me. Crazy as this may sound.

Never have I heard Him so surely before, or since.

My routine was to spend two weeks in Harare on promotional, administrative and purchasing detail, then head for Zambia for two weeks, loaded to the gunnels with materials of all descriptions, everything being half the price in Zimbabwe.

I would arrive at the border with this staggering cargo, pulling a trailer, making out I was on a camping trip, goods carefully loaded for best concealment. Nerve-wracking bluffing my way through customs officials, somewhat taken aback by my camping consumption, was draining in the extreme.

'You drink much brandy, huh?'

'Yeah, well . . . why don't you have one while we're about it?'

Amazingly, I always got through unscathed. And always thanked God who seemed understanding of my smuggling.

The duties levied were substantial. And the time and paperwork to clear goods, and the hours more to organise it all in inefficient government offices would depress me beyond what I could take any more, so I just didn't.

The island development moved slowly. Local carpenters, plumbers and builders knew as much about their trade as my housemaid. Except they didn't dress as nicely.

'What do you mean, I have to reapply because he's got the same land on his lease as I have?!' I ask the clerk.

'Aaah, it's a problem, Sah.'

'You're telling me!'

I was in the registry office in Choma, the government administrative centre for the area, two hours' drive from the Lake, to find a lodge site leased to another party slap bang in the middle of one of our Islands. The process of drawing up my leases had cost me a small fortune in time and money, including finding, transporting and paying a government surveyor to draw up maps and place beacons.

'How could this be?' I raged. How could the same surveyor have issued such maps—he certainly had not set foot there with this other party? The clerk mumbled something about 'not being the one'.

Fuming, I headed straight back to Sinazongwe to have a showdown. Take it to court, if needs be. I didn't even want to think about the time and paperwork that it would entail.

It was the week before Easter, everybody winding down, my 'gals' were coming home from University in Cape Town. I didn't want to miss a day of their break. But nor was I going to take this lying down.

The Chief and Council chairman looked hurt and uncomfortable, agreeing to convene and discuss the situation in two days' time. Thursday morning, after which there would be time for me to make the twelve-hour drive home.

Come the day, I was packed and ready to go. Walking briskly up the gravel road to the council office, I enjoyed the village atmosphere. Few vehicles drove the rocky streets, quaintly named after Zambian liberation heroes in handwritten signs nailed to trees. I passed two black mambas entwined next to the track, mating or fighting I wasn't sure. Just glad they weren't interested in me.

The Chief and Council Chairman were nowhere to be found. Situation normal. I waited patiently. Two hours later I discovered that the chairman had gone to Lusaka, and the chief was at a funeral.

I was given a guide to bump and scrape our way for miles through bush tracks to the funeral. On finally reaching the mournful gathering, trying begrudgingly to show respect for the occasion, I insisted on seeing the chief for an explanation. He reluctantly drew me aside, offered his apologies, explained there was nothing he could do out here, and assured me we would meet on Tuesday after the holiday weekend—five days away.

At a very low ebb, I limped back to Sinazongwe. Nearly a week of enforced wait, missing this precious time with my girls. No food, and no workers at the base. Nothing to be done but sit. Which I am extremely bad at.

I was beginning to feel seriously ill, not surprisingly. I remembered Murray's family, who owned the cottage we stayed in at Sinazongwe, were coming down for the weekend. At least they'd bring food.

They didn't arrive, nor could I care any longer. I was very sick. Treating myself for malaria, I dropped out of the world. All next day I lay there, alone, pouring sweat, in a delirious coma. By evening, the treatment was beginning to work and I knew I wasn't going to die. Very week and feeble, I sat out in the evening sun looking across the water, just appreciating being able to appreciate again. I managed to have a crackly conversation with Sands and the girls at home on our HF radio, and went to bed, determining to find some food in the local market tomorrow.

Well into the night, I woke with a start. I sat up in bed, clearly having heard someone call my name. After a while, hearing nothing more, I lay back, feeling much recuperated from the fever, my mind whirring about all there was to do.

Then I clearly heard the voice again, not so much with my ear as with my mind.

'Why don't you just give it to him?'

Somehow I knew exactly who 'him' was, and Who was talking.

'What do you mean, 'Give it to him.' He stole it from me!'

'So . . . didn't I say 'Give him your shirt as well, if he takes your coat.' I listened, aghast, recognising the words from 'The Beatitudes' of Matthew's Gospel, Chapter 6. I remember thinking when I was reading them. 'Oh, c'mon, God. Get real! How can anyone live up to this?'

'Yes, Lord, You did,' I replied, still in amazement that this conversation was taking place, receiving the rebuke and determining to live these teachings better as I listened to this gentle, loving, understanding voice..

'And if he strikes your cheek, turn the other also. If he forces you to walk one mile, go the other, too.' This was a reference to the hated custom in biblical times when Roman soldiers would require passers-by to carry their bundle for the next mile. I knew He was also referring to my commitment in walking with Him, which was abysmal.

'Yes, Lord.' I was ashamed at my complacent obstinacy and disregard for the biblical admonitions I knew so well and always had excuses why I couldn't comply.

'Don't you also know that I can bless you abundantly, as you give and bless others? Can I not give you more than you could ever yearn for?'

As He talked, recalling His Holy Scriptures, although I knew I was being reprimanded, the love and compassion with which He spoke overwhelmed me. I lay there, hanging on every word, aching with every part of me to serve and be right before Him. Beginning to weep with heartrending sobs, I felt a huge release of all the hurt, anger, disappointment, frustration and exhaustion that had so consumed me.

And knew that on my part, all I had to do was be obedient to his bidding. Gutted for all I had let Him down, calling myself a Christian, yet deceiving border officials, being hard on my workers, not loving my wife or being as responsible to my family as I should . . . and so much else. I poured out my repentance, tears streaming down my face, my whole being aching with remorse.

Then I lay there, in huge and absolute peace. I felt so forgiven, invigorated, sensing deep down that as I let it all go, trusting Him, He would take me, and all I was trying to do, into another dimension, where the steep, hard uphill would become a gentle, happy downhill.

I didn't sleep again that night. Blessed out of my socks, filled with an excitement, love and peace whose quality I'd never experienced quite like before, or since. I just drank it in, feeling like I had been transformed from the grub of a restricting cocoon into a beautiful butterfly.

As soon as it was light, I jumped up, amazed how beautiful the early morning sun was on the trees, how blue the water looked, how sweet the melody of the bird-calls, filled with an astonishing energy and deep appreciation to be so alive and well.

I drove off to find the Chief and tell him what had happened. He listened, wide eyed, a big smile on his face, even though I had arrived way before appointment time.

'So you heard God speaking to you, Mr Fynn?' he grinned, visibly trying to work out whether I was the new Sinazongwe prophet, or just plain crazy.

'There won't be a court case, Chief. That guy can have that piece of land. I have enough for what I need. I'll go over to Zebra Island today and find another campsite to replace the one I am losing.' I was so confident that dropping the matter was right and was reminded during the long night that there was a site on the other side of the island I'd hardly looked at. It might even be better. The Chief was happy. It let him off the hook. He gave me one of his officials to accompany me, in spite of it being the Easter holiday.

Sure enough, the new campsite was far superior to the one I was losing. It had a deeper harbour, faced the morning rather than evening sun, making it cooler, and was more spacious and appropriate in every way. I marvelled, knowing that I would not have discovered all that had this not happened.

I spent the day sketching plans for the new site and rehashing our paperwork for the re-allocation of the land. I left these with the Chief, asking him to ratify the plan with Council next week. And headed for home, high in spirits and filled with an energy and enthusiasm I hadn't known for years.

Now all would imagine that this was the turning point, and everything would change and run smoothly and happily ever after. But it wasn't.

How did I miss the big one back there? Not taking my side of the bargain seriously enough? Obstinately resisting fundamental change in my approach to life? Unprepared to risk all in 'It's You, God, nothing of me, whatever happens'? Or was I in a malarial coma?

I believe it really was Him speaking, and have no doubt I failed to accept the gentle rebuke and do something permanently, strongly and positively, about those weak old life patterns, in assured faith that He in turn would do His part. I felt so sorry for myself, and tested beyond what I could handle. In fact, I think my obstinate pride in refusing to do it His way was what I could not handle. Too many shortcuts.

The project got tougher; my relationship with Sands got harder; the finances never came through. And my energy dissipated till I could hardly get out of bed in the morning.

I tried being straight at the border for one trip, and spent a whole day sorting the export papers in Harare, and another arguing with Zambian customs officials and paying lots of duty I thought I couldn't afford. I didn't do that again, efficiently, but emotionally, crossing in old smuggler style.

Nobody else, other than God, I'm sure, noticed my downhill slide. Maybe they just didn't know enough about how much I was dealing, or not dealing, with? I'm sure Sands did, but didn't know how to talk about it, as I didn't know how to listen. I only knew I could no longer walk the line. And how utterly tired I was.

Too much stress, too many demands, disappointments and ensuing bad judgements, for too long—a recipe for disaster.

Which duly struck.

Back on the trail, life in Africa continued to challenge, and thankfully amuse. I borrowed a double-axle trailer, designed to carry a rhino, from Mike Le Grange. Heavily loaded with goods to be smuggled, going up was no problem. Returning empty, it stood firmly on its double axle 30cms above the tow hitch on my truck. I had to tie it down with wire. Not such a good plan for the long haul home.

As I left Sinazongwe, I passed through the 'fish' boom, where every vehicle was checked for carrying fish, on which a tax was levied. There stood three women, babies on their backs, baskets of fish at their feet, asking for a lift to Lusaka.

I often carried people when I was travelling empty. I asked two of the ladies if they wouldn't mind riding in the trailer, to which they readily agreed, together with all their heavy fish baskets. This would put some weight in the front and make the trailer more secure on the tow hitch. I thought it better, just in case, if the third lady would ride in the back of the truck, with all the children. It is a common practice for people to ride in open trucks in this part of the world.

Everything went well up the escarpment until we hit a stretch of road recently done up by the Chinese, leaving a wave-like surface that one rode over like being on a calm rolling sea. The trailer didn't like this, bucking as we dropped over the crests, putting strain on the wired-down hitch. I was contemplating what I should do about it when I heard a 'twang'. I saw in my rear-view mirror the trailer swerving sharply from side to side, clearly off the hitch and now only held by the safety chain.

Another 'twang'. Louder. And bigger jerk.

To my horror, the trailer rode up alongside me, at 80kph, firmly and stably running down the wrong side of the road, two women hanging on to the front rail, screaming.

I tried to hold on to the half-ton of free runner with one hand, driving with the other, desperately hoping no traffic would appear from the other direction.

Suddenly the trailer veered off the road, ramped a storm drain, side walled a termite mound, tried turning over but resolutely continued, careering through the bush miraculously missing massive trees in its path. Finally, the hitch dug in to another termite mound, huge chassis reared in the air, all four wheels on the skyline, like a dinosaur trying to somersault, then in slow motion it fell over. I skidded to a halt in the storm drain.

Groans came from the grass. That was good—somebody was still alive. We found the ladies, grass, sticks and fish stuck in their hair and everywhere else one can imagine, and the trailer still in one piece, but upside down, wheels spinning.

'Aaaahh, sorry *maningi!* (very much)' Lymon, my assistant, was muttering, collecting up the fish and the ladies.

'Looks like you need some help, Rob?' A voice calls from the road.

'Willem Lublinkof!'

Willem, a nearby farmer whom I hadn't seen since Fothergill days, was passing and had stopped to see what was going on.

With his land cruiser and winch, we soon got the trailer back on its wheels and onto the road. He made the excellent suggestion of unbolting the front axle, which immediately solved the high tow-hitch problem.

'Now why didn't I think of that?' I asked Willem, and myself.

'I've had this happen before, Rob, that's how I know.' There wasn't much Willem hadn't had happen before.

We resumed our trek, a little worse for wear but thankful to be in one piece, mindful of the Bejing conference being held at the time on women's rights—and dear Mr A who'd stayed off disaster again and brought along good Willem.

Chapter 39

Adrift

An old friend, Dr Stewart Jamieson, born in Bulawayo, now a well-respected surgeon in charge of the lung and heart division of the University Hospital in San Diego, California, booked on a Safari to Chete Island. Stewart's sister, Margie, had married my good Navy buddy, Richard Goodfellow.

I laid on something special for him and his family party. Not least of which was a storm that blew our boats out to sea, leaving us stranded on our little island camp. We risked our lives to retrieve them swimming through crocodile waters, Stewart with me all the way.

'How is Sandy?' he asked when we were in a more peaceful mood.

'Not too good, Stewart.' We discussed her condition at length. He listening carefully and then explained how he had developed an operation for those who appeared to suffer from asthma but never improved. These may have an 'emboli' problem, where, described in very simplistic layman terms, small clots of blood were breaking out from the heart and imploding on the lungs, giving a symptom similar to asthma, but wasn't. His new operation involved removing the lung and heart, giving them a good 'service', and putting them back with filters that would ensure the condition could not recur. A biggie.

He offered to come to Harare and see her. Returning thereafter to San Diego for further consultations with his colleagues, he informed us his hospital was prepared to offer the op at half price, US$500,000.

'Would we like to book?' Stewart asked.

We explained our predicament. Our Zimbabwean medical aid society would not even scratch the surface of this charge.

After further consultations, he came back to us.

'The Hospital has agreed to take Sandy on as a charitable case. Can you get here?' Californian generosity.

It was Sands' call. She bravely looked at it as a 'do it, be healed and become a new person, at the risk of dying in the process, but no in betweens, please!' Simply carrying on was not an option.

Poor Sands carried the brunt of the decision-making. It was all I could do, in my disabled state of mind, to organise and delegate my responsibilities on Chete Island for the indeterminate time we would be away.

Donations came in from friends all over the world. The Zimbabwean State Lottery assisted with air tickets, including one for a physician to accompany us. Till now, Sands could not travel further than the Chisipite shops, five minutes down the road, attached to an oxygen bottle. We were talking of a thirty six hour journey, halfway round the world.

Ambulance and medics met our epic flight on the runway in San Diego. The next week was spent under intensive tests, culminating in a microscopic camera inserted into her main artery, through the heart, and also into the lung.

The hospital had a special wing for family to stay, like a self-catering mini motel. Cath arrived from London to join us; we were all conscious that this might be our last time together.

The tension mounted. Tests showed anomalies. The hospital routine encouraged prospective patients for the big op to take the weekend off after the week's tests, coming back for a final prognosis and decision on the Monday. Stewart kindly lent us his car and cottage in the mountains.

'What set you two off into such an argumentative relationship? Where did all the anger I see in you both come from?' Cath asked in the car. 'Surely it wasn't always like this?'

'Good question, Cath.' And a hard one to answer.

I was still finding everything very difficult to assimilate, feeling pathetically numb and like I was on another planet most of the time. I couldn't begin to handle the deep discussion needed. Full blown clinical depression running rampant—undiagnosed and unchecked

'No, it's not the condition we suspected. I'm afraid the operation won't help. It seems it's a case of chronic asthma after all,' the Hospital informed us on Monday morning.

Sand's reaction was more positive than mine. She was so mad, she determined to chuck out doctors, medicines and hospitals as a complete failure to humanity.

'I never want to see another medical anything again, I'll go it with God!' And flushed all her pills down the toilet.

I approved, although reeling, unable to think clearly about anything.

Sands was persuaded by the hospital counsellors to spend time with the fantastic 'rehab' unit, who talked her onto some great medication, inspiring her to exercise and thus strengthen her lungs, indeed her entire body.

An email arrived from my sister, Ness, back in Harare. She'd been fighting breast cancer and was in remission when we left. It had returned with a vengeance. Time was limited. She insisted we didn't rush back, and that we should take a break before coming home.

We visited family and friends in the USA. Sands seemed to be doing well as we drove across California. No oxygen, no special facilities. A new experience for both of us.

But I was being eaten up. Why had it taken her so long to simply decide to be well again? How could she allow our relationship and our family to go through such misery, during which we lost the precious and irredeemable growing up years of our children, our unique and amazing home, life and business, and the very core of our togetherness when all she needed was this decision to chuck the sickness aside?

I was gutted with the bitter waste of it all, and simply could not recover myself

'And You, God, what were You doing all this time? Couldn't You hear us? Couldn't you see the devastation this was causing? How come You couldn't do something, or say something clearly and audible?'

In my imperceptive state, all I could see was 'poor me'—blaming God, Sandy, anybody and anything, but myself.

Dear, oh dear.

Unable to shake off this cancerous reaction, nor talk to her about it without exploding, I festered. All the counselling and attention was on Sands, for obvious reasons. My huge problem just remained bottled up inside me.

In hindsight, although it is possible that Sands' sickness was a desperate cry for more love and compassion from me, to be put higher on my priorities, I also know how much more sensitivity I should have shown towards her plight, and less towards my own. How I wish I could replay it all and deal better.

I only found out later that a part of my condition was severe clinical depression, which untreated and not recognised left me perplexed and bewildered about what was happening to me. It was a frightening place to be, where I was unable to talk to anybody about it. What a drag on poor Sands when she needed somebody so different?

We flew home, and weeks later we buried our Ness.

I was numb. So numb, I wasn't sure my heart was pumping any more. Brother–in–law Davey and his family stood magnificently steadfast in their grieving for their irreplaceable wonderful wife and Mum, and my loving understanding friend and sister.

Back in the fray, the massive problem of my Islands in Zambia still plagued my very soul. Nothing was coming together. Politicians and civil servants were more obtuse than ever, greedier, and cared less. Financiers wanted faster turnarounds, bigger profits, more security—leaving me high and dry attempting to continue this huge development with no backing.

Sands' health had reverted, now so damaged by the drugs she had been fed for so long, her situation ever more complicated, back on mounds of medication and treatment by doctors in Harare. Home, hope, the future, life—just everything, sucked.

Before I too went under, I knew I had to make a big break, far from this graceless existence, marriage and exacting bottomless pit of a business, to none of which had I anymore of anything left to give.

Like that helpless state under the elephant, I knew how, where and what, but simply had no energy or initiative to do it. I couldn't even talk to God, nor thought it would help anyway. I felt hopelessly abandoned.

Heading for the momentous millennium Christmas and New Year to celebrate the eclipse of the phenomenal twentieth century, we were to meet with the extended family at my brother Mike's home in Peitermaritzburg, South Africa. I had already determined I wasn't going back to Chete Island, although hadn't spoken to anybody about what I was going to do, other than my brother-in-law, Richy, who'd sold a mine and was about as 'bucksed up' as he'd ever been.

The family knew I was struggling. We had all been through 'stuff' together, and Richy had kindly said if there was anything he could do, to let him know. I asked him if he'd bankroll Rach's last year at university, and me to go on the Cape to Rio yacht race that was leaving Cape Town that January. To be paid back out of the profits from the Chete operation which I was so sure were to come. With or without me. Not hesitating, remembering the good times we'd all enjoyed back in those Fothergill days, he simply patted me on the back.

'Pay-back time, Robbie. Where and when do you want it?'

Thank God, and Richy. I started to plan as seriously as I could with my gummed up heart and head. I contacted my friend and genius craftsman, Tony Turner, a fine Zimbabwean boat builder who'd made half the best looking craft on the Lake and was now racing his yard built yacht on the Cape to Rio. He promised to look out for a place for me on one of the boats.

Sands was unhappy, questioning my sanity, with good reason. I just knew if I didn't do something drastic to get away from the stress zone, I would drop off the edge. Remove, restore, refresh, and return.

Brother Mike observed my anxious, peculiar behaviour after a few days in their home. Knowing me well enough to understand this was uncharacteristic, he made a kind and considerate suggestion.

'Rob, old bro, would you have a chat with my friend, a psychiatrist?'

I was relieved at the thought of finding somebody who might release me from this mental torture and was appreciative of his concern.

After half an hour's questioning, the Doc diagnosed me as chronically clinically depressed and reckoned if I didn't get treatment, I would commit suicide within six months. That got me listening. At last I knew now what was behind my crazed state of mind.

He advised against my going on the Cape to Rio race, fearing I'd be a liability to the crew. I believed he was mistaken and couldn't imagine a better treatment. But the die was cast, and I simply didn't have the energy or focus to argue my case.

I limped home, referred to another psychologist and psychiatrist, who interestingly reckoned the yacht race would have done much good, and further discerned that I'd allowed too much of my life to be dictated by circumstances, people, even my faith, and I needed to get control of it again. I was warned it would be a long slow recovery. I realise today that the only One I should have let take control, I hadn't.

My partners in the Zambian project were intolerant. I requested that I take unpaid leave for six months. They responded with a boardroom coup, reducing my shareholding to an ineffective minority, and fired me. I lost everything, even my gumption to fight back.

Sands and I separated, no longer able to bear tearing each other apart. The bitter pill of failure and self-imposed loneliness had taken its toll.

Chapter 40

Those Flying Machines

'Can you still fly, Rob?' Colin asked me.

'I reckon.'

I wasn't sure, but longed to be good at something again.

Friend Tony returned from the Rio race, and put me in touch with his friend, Colin, who was building kit Tiger Moths on a farm in Karoi. His dream was to run 'Out of Africa' safaris across Zimbabwe, in self—fly kit Tigers, with a support mother-ship, the amazing Lockheed Air Cam. Right up my street.

I found great solace in building these aeroplanes, working quietly with my hands and learning a new skill in the peace of the hangar on his farm. Deeply therapeutic, it did more for me than any pill or psychiatrists. I loved being able to concentrate on the creative task and be part of progress again, rare commodities in my life for some time.

On top of that, I met the gorgeous Megan. In the throes of a divorce, she would visit a girlfriend on the farm next door. We fell madly in love. How good it was to feel alive once more and be crazy, in a good way.

Colin asked me to test pilot his planes. I was the only one in the team with a valid pilot's licence. As I soared the skies in those magnificent flying machines, so did my soul. A little scary, their not having had anything like enough research in their design—it was wonderfully exhilarating and just what I needed.

Typical of the entrepreneurship in the farming community, this venture was Colin's plan to survive Mugabe madness. On his maiden flight, with a real test pilot at the controls, their first plane only just remained in flying mode with full power on throughout. Anything less sent it into a perilous dive. The descent to land was controlled solely by gently varying the power setting off full throttle. Landing over halfway down the strip, the brakes collapsed and the plane careered off the end of the runway into the surrounding grasslands. Thankfully it only suffered minor damage, nobody was hurt, and runway was extended for future possibilities.

After straightening out these quirks as best we could, it was decided to take the planes down for a promotional photographic session in the scenic surrounds of my old hunting ground, the Matuse and Fothergill.

I had three engine failures in a week in the 'Tiger Moth'. I'd never experienced one in my previous twenty five year flying career. The first was coming in over the fiord-like Sanyati Gorge towards the lake when the engine abruptly cut, without any warning, at 8000 feet, giving, I thought, lots of time to attempt restarting—which totally failed. I had the choice of landing in water or on a rocky shoreline.

A fascinated group assembled in a camp below to watch the fun. Frantic switch and fuel manipulation in the cockpit finally coaxed the engine into life at 300 feet above the waves. I skimmed past over the campers heads to their cheers and victory salutes, to land soon afterwards on an emergency strip I knew of, used by Parks in their anti-poaching patrols.

These 80% scale kit Tiger Moths, powered by Suzuki jeep engines, with no backup systems or previous aero application, were toys in comparison to the real thing. They clearly needed some serious analytical researching before 'client' pilots could fly them on safari across the African wilds. We could not find the problem that caused this failure until after two more, with narrow escapes, had occurred, we simply had to sit on the ground until we did.

After removing and examining every component of the engine, and finding no fault, it turned out to be the simplest matter of removing a rubber seal at the rear of the engine compartment which then allowed an escape of the hot air from the exhaust box that had previously been vaporising the fuel in certain conditions.

The Air Cam, however, also built from a kit, which was to be used to carry the *katundu* for the fleet on safari, was an extraordinary aeroplane. It looked like a WWI bomber, or flying canoe, sporting an open cockpit protruding three metres from the overhead wing with an all-round view for the pilot and passenger sitting in line behind him.

Designed and built as a camera platform for National Geographic to use over jungles, with its twin 100hp engines it could take off and land in 50 metres. It would even take off on one engine, allowing a 'get home' performance on that single engine from just about anywhere. Hanging in the air at its slowest, 25mph, it could boost up to 100mph. It really was a magnificent flying machine.

'What about building and selling Air Cams, Colin?' I tentatively suggested as it dawned on us that the 'Tigers' were not what we had expected them to be.

'Mmm, let's look at it. Work out a marketing strategy, Rob.'

The possibility of manufacturing this superb camera platform aircraft to replace costly helicopters for aerial surveillance in our flying orientated land was an exciting thought.

Our friend and widely respected aviator, Air Vice-Marshal Ian Harvey, the only white man left in the Zimbabwe Air Force, with more hours on Alouette helicopters than any in the world, offered to lay on a promotional day for us. We were to show off the aircraft to the army, air force, police and National Parks, ranchers, safari operators, and anyone else who was interested.

'We have to do the practice, Colin. We can't arrive to do the routine for the first time tomorrow?' I was insisting on the last afternoon before the big day, having hassled him about it all week without effect.

He had been very distracted with war vets, Mugabe's hit squads invading farms, threatening him with the appropriation of his. I understood, but nevertheless, the show had to go on. In the last light of the evening, in horribly unsuitable gusty conditions, I took off, Colin standing on the airstrip to observe.

Building 80% scale Tiger Moths

Maasie, Rob & Colin with Air Cam

The first manoeuvre I planned was to fly past the spectators into wind on one engine, at lowest possible speed. In anything of a headwind, the plane would almost appear to hover. Then I was to return, both engines fired up, at full speed roaring past the crowd. A dramatic contrast and impressive start to the air show.

Flying past Colin on one engine, I noticed the airspeed varying between 20 and 40 knots. These were indeed gusty conditions. Conscious of the failing light and little time left to complete the programme, I turned sooner and lower than I should have. At the same time, starting up the other engine. Classic pilot error. Too busy, too low, too slow.

I hit wind-shear and dropped 150 feet straight into the ground. I went in with wing and nose down, engines screaming as I tried to pull out of the dive, strangely imagining this a video that could be rewound and replayed differently. The reality was the ghastly sight of the ground coming up very fast and then the noise of an aeroplane breaking up around me. And dust, pain, and the agony of knowing it was all over.

I cut the roaring engines, switched everything off and started to climb out in the deathly silence, with the help of many black hands. But no Colin.

'Baas and Madam, they drove out,' I learned from the staff as I staggered across the field and collapsed on the floor in the dark empty house. My back was very sore, and blood was coming from my neck. I crawled to the phone and called the local nurse. She came round within minutes, stitched up the gash and didn't think I had any broken bones. She was harried and hurried, on her way to a farmer who'd been beaten up by lawless thugs.

'Get a proper check-up soon as you can, your back doesn't look too good—it's already black and blue from bruising.' She rushed away, leaving me with painkillers.

Colin's maxim was that with God in control, no insurance was needed. I realised he simply could not handle the blow of what had happened and had gone to the neighbours to pray. He arrived back an hour or so later, apologising. As I did to him.

The "Out of Africa" dream Tiger Moth

The
Zambezi
River

Victoria
Falls
Bridge

What do you say when you've just written off a man's life dream? We hugged, forgiving each other, emotionally strained and shattered.

Strangely, that night Sands phoned for the first time since I'd been on the farm. In the moment of confusion, I asked her to meet me next morning in Harare for the medical check-up. I was due to go with Megan to the mountain family hideaway cottage in Nyanga after the flight display, and my guess is that it would have sealed our future.

The doctor found three crushed vertebrae discs, which have partially healed under rigorous physiotherapy and diligent exercising. I have never been able to speak to Colin since, him declining to meet or talk about it. An apocalyptic loss, adding to the ghastly general mahem, *typique* of so much in crazed Zimbabwe.

In February 2000, Mugabe called the nation's first referendum to ratify his new constitution, primarily designed to protect him and his party *ad infinitum*. It was rejected and he was shocked by the realisation that serious opposition had grown, coordinated through the new MDC (Movement for Democratic Change) party.

This party and their courageous trade union leader, Morgan Tvsangirai, stood resolute in the face of brutal and relentless persecution. Mugabe's ruthless and radical steps now focused on attacking MDC's strongest supporters, the predominantly white industrial manufacturing sector and commercial farming community.

Two thirds of the country's GDP was supported by these sectors. Obsessed by holding power to himself, Mugabe unleashed a political monster, the so-called war veterans. Hired thugs, many far too young to have fought in the liberation struggle, these supposed ex-combatants were let loose on the farmers with free rein to 'help themselves', the more brutally the better. The lawless inhuman campaign was launched under the pretence of land redistribution.

Large groups, armed with traditional weapons, knives, knobkerries and axes, camped on farmer's doorsteps, commandeering whatever equipment, crops or livestock they fancied. They unsparingly abused the farm labour force to ensure the new understanding that they were to serve the 'war vets' from here on, hefty termination packages demanded for them by the 'vets' and backed by government, from their former employers.

By 2005, there were an estimated 30 farms left intact. Out of 4000 of the most productive in Africa. The Zimbabwe dollar crumbled beyond recognition, inflation running to hundreds of millions percent. The IMF described it as the fastest declining economy recorded in the world for any country not at war.

The majority of the farms taken were handed to the 'Chefs' and their cronies, who treated them as weekend retreats. The few farm cooperatives failed through lack of support, technical knowledge and subsidies from government. The former black farm workers, 350,000 of them, supporting family members estimated at 3 million, a quarter of the country's population, were mercilessly hounded, tortured, their women raped and their homes destroyed. Farm compounds were turned into 're-education' centres, occupants forced to sing 'Chimurenga' (War against whites) songs and chant slogans throughout the night. Lists of MDC supporters would be read out and the individuals whipped and beaten, frequently to their death.

On most commercial farms, workers had been provided with schools, clinics and recreation centres. They and their families would have land and would have been provided for to their dying day. Today, they walk the roads and townships. Most who were re-employed by the 'new' farmers ran away due to lack of facilities and sub economic wages.

Our farming friends were traumatised and scattered across the Globe, starting afresh, empty handed after their life's work, as were the state coffers and granaries.

Mugabe's 'land reform', ostensibly to put to rights colonial wrongs and to recover land for the millions evicted by invading colonisers, might sound plausible. A few thousand whites occupied all the best land whilst millions of blacks were crowded into the infertile and valueless remainder, so the government propaganda went.

Seems powerful enough. But these emotional and sweeping excuses are seriously flawed.

When the country was first colonised, no millions existed. It was sparsely populated with no shortage of land. The British colonisers initiated a land policy intended to protect traditional tribal systems and allow new developers security of title. Medicines, better food and crops, effective pest control and an end to tribal conflicts allowed the formerly static population to soar.

Far from dispossessing millions of indigenous people, the development process ushered in by colonisation can honestly claim to have led to the millions coming into existence. These new social and economic developments created one of the best-educated populations and most advanced economies in third world Africa.

Disparities between the qualities of land in different areas in Zimbabwe today are real and important, but the processes that led to the differences are carefully neglected in Mugabe's attempts to justify his actions.

Land bought by the new commercial farmers was developed using funds raised with their title deeds as collateral. Since Zimbabwe's Independence, an agreement of 'no interest' had to be signed by the Mugabe government before any change of ownership was approved. Farming is high-risk business where only the best prosper.

The commercial farmer's land improved due to the methodical process of development and good husbandry. Crucial support for this came from funding made possible by the land's collateral value, which stemmed directly from property rights and the security of tenure policy.

The same advantages were not available in the areas occupied by traditional farmers. Collective land tenure rights were so deeply embedded in culture and traditions that neither individual tenure nor use of the land as collateral was possible. Neither was the concept of individual ownership acceptable to the tribal chiefs, for whom the allocation of land was the foundation of their traditional authority.

But for the rapid population growth, these areas could have remained moderately productive. Unfortunately, the population growth was gravely incompatible with traditional farming methods. The more exacting demands and financial requirements of better farming could not be met. Space was no longer available to continue with the shifting cultivation practices of the past and soon the damage suffered by the ecologically fragile soils became a serious issue.

This lack of foresight and efforts to address the pending ruin was a grave blunder by all.

The traditional communal farming areas make up 42 percent of the total area of Zimbabwe, about the same as the area of England. Mugabe dismissed them as barren, overcrowded and beyond recovery. This was the basis for his claim that the better-managed areas held by commercial farmers should be confiscated and given to politically selected beneficiaries in a process he described as land reform.

However, it was really the communal lands that should have been the targets of painfully needed land reforms and access to resources for needed transformation. By choosing to dispossess the owners of the successful large-scale farms and to allocate their land to non-farming party supporters and several hundred thousand small-scale peasant farmers, the less successful and ecologically damaging farming systems have been transferred into the formerly productive areas.

Our principal industry has been nationalised and handed over to the unskilled, destroying hundreds of thousands of jobs, which had formerly made up 30% of the total formal income. Also disappeared is a high proportion of our export revenues and the hundreds of manufacturing companies established to support the farmers.

Compounding the problem is the fact that the land, a valuable former resource to the owner and the country, is allocated free to people who do not become the new legal owners. As the land will not be transferable and the new occupant will have no title deed, the property is essentially valueless, and clearly deteriorates from its former developed state.

In other words, all of Zimbabwe's most productive land now has most of the characteristics of communal land. And as it will be farmed under the same constraints, the land will soon exhibit the same effects that such constraints cause. Declines in fertility, severe soil erosion and general degradation.

Statements claiming that 5000 whites occupied 80% of the land and 12 million blacks crowded into the remaining 20% have been repeated so often that they are now taken as fact.

The nearest interpretation that was fact in that statement is that of the land that could be owned by individuals, known as commercial farming land, the whites owned most of it. That is because the Europeans were able and prepared to invest, and insisted on title

371

deeds for the properties they were offered to occupy. The amount of farmland that was under this form of ownership was a little more than a quarter of the total land farmed in Zimbabwe, around 10,3 million hectares.

The communal areas plus the resettlement areas plus the tenant schemes, the Development Trust of Zimbabwe lands and the small-scale farming areas totalled 57% of the farmland in the country, a total of 22 million hectares (220,000 sq km).

This same 22 million hectares are dismissed as unimportant, or, more usually, completely left out of the descriptions of land distribution. Why spoil a 'good' argument with cold, hard facts?

This 220 000 sq km is a considerable area—2,6 times the size of Austria, 2,5 times the size of Portugal, 1,7 times the size of Greece and 5 times the size of Denmark. It is bigger than the whole of Denmark, Belgium, the Netherlands and Portugal combined, where the total population of those countries is 41 million, while Zimbabwe's communal areas support a population of about 8 million.

The claims of overcrowding would have best been dealt with by careful studies of land management systems and the application of more capital and knowledge-intensive cultivation techniques. Simply authorising the theft of the country's better-managed land will prove, and is proving, to be a bad solution.

Chapter 41

Veterans of Violence

Peter Cunningham, David and Janet's son, offered me the job of running 'Dollar Block', a game ranch in Matabeleland. An Indonesian co-investor, and Mugabe ally, allowed him a degree of protection from the seizures. He had managed with sheer tenacity, deep faith and some help from his friend to continue operating in the country's devastating agricultural and economic collapse.

Dollar Block is 60,000 acres of prime hunting and game country. He offered me a generous share in its ownership, a great opportunity. The safari camp looked over beautiful African savannah, giraffe heads sticking above the acacia, antelope roaming under them, lions roaring from a nearby breeding programme in their big enclosures.

Controversy always surrounds such ventures—suspicion of canned hunting, cruelty in caging wild animals, some valid, most certainly not in this case. It was an exemplary breeding programme set up in conjunction with the well-known Andy Connolly's Antelope Park for the restocking of lion into areas where they had been decimated. Some politically motivated vandals had opened the doors to the lions on one occasion, predictably causing havoc in the area. Nobody was eaten other than some unfortunate goats. In the fracas of their recapture by the Zimbabwe National Parks team, four lions were killed, and two more died under poorly administered tranquilising drugs.

Hunting and game ranching is a favourite target for the world's 'bunny huggers', as some animal rights groups are known amongst conservationists. They regard hunting as barbaric, conveniently oblivious to its part in wild animal management and its contribution to the sustainable economics of wilderness areas. The Wildlife and National Parks of old Rhodesia, one of the foremost in wildlife conservation research, used controlled hunting and culling as an essential tool in their management techniques and economic success.

A few months after arriving, I was working in my office early one morning, all game scouts out of camp on patrol, no guests in house, when I noticed a movement out of the corner of my eye in the grass outside my window. Looking closer, I was taken aback to see a man crouching in the bush. I opened the door to investigate to find a group of some two hundred villagers who had stealthily approached down the back road without detection.

I closed the door and made for the radio or telephone to raise the alarm. They rushed the office and within seconds I was surrounded by a sea of shouting tribesmen, dressed in traditional war gear, carrying spears, axes and knobkerries, a strong smell of alcohol and *dagga (marijuana)* filling the air.

'Now it's your turn, White man. We are going to burn you.'

'Wait up, guys, this is doing nobody any good.' In return for which I receive a hefty slap.

'Shut your mouth, White man.'

This group of 'war veterans', no more than three of them eligible by age to be considered one, had established themselves on the top third of the ranch some months earlier, causing havoc to our game protection and hunting programmes. A few weeks ago, they had started a fire that nearly burned out the entire estate. We had fought it for days, back burning from firebreaks and roads to halt its advance. Some of their huts had been endangered in our countermeasures. Now they were here to exact their revenge by burning the lodge. They handcuffed me and tied my feet with a rope, the other end of which was thrown over a big tree. It looked like I was about to be lynched.

'Let's talk about this, men,' I tried to open dialogue.

'Keep quiet, White man.' Punctuated with a kick in the ribs.

They were hyped-up, nervous and agitated—bloodshot eyes and flared nostrils. Not good. Punches and boots continued to reinforce their authority—repeated questions about why I was on their land. Having rifled our gun cabinet, they toted our weapons with 'guards' posted in an aggressive and undisciplined manner.

A messenger arrived. The leaders were required at another venue for a meeting. This was clearly a well orchestrated offensive with other operations involved. The leadership and with their armed bodyguards jumped into my truck, shouting instructions as they raced off, grinding and crashing gears.

The remnant of youngsters and women left behind milled around, not quite sure what to do with 'White man' handcuffed and tied by his legs to a tree. An occasional macho youth would poke a finger up my nose and assail me with highly charged political questions. If I attempted to answer I would be told to hold my tongue, and get another kick or well-aimed spittle.

Four hours later, police arrived, which didn't always auger well in our upside down society. They sometimes were the bad guys. I watched apprehensively for the next move.

'Sorry about this, Mr Fynn,' an officer politely approached me.

'Good to see you, Sergeant. Thank you for coming.'

Happily, I knew these officers well and had established good working relations with them in the past. They removed the tight handcuffs which had been biting painfully into my swollen wrists.

I was driven back to the workshops and administrative offices on the farm, where Peter had now arrived from Bulawayo, together with police chiefs and political dignitaries. A protracted meeting ensued, where accusations were levelled towards me and my ranch management for attempting to burn them off their land, harassing their hunting operations and their dogs with our game scouts, and generally being uncooperative in their aspirations to occupy the ranch. Finally, it was agreed the matter would be handled in the district governor's office in a few weeks' time, and the meeting was dispersed, inconclusively.

'We need to be taken home,' the 200 strong crowd who'd wanted to burn the lodge and string me up were demanding.

Scraping together every tractor and vehicle we had, they departed down the road past the safari camp, while we continued chatting for a while longer with Peter and the Police Chief. An hour later, I headed for home, having fixed two punctures incurred by my abductors. As I approached the safari camp I was surprised to see our tractors parked in the yard, people all around in the bush.

I then spotted my game scouts lying in a heap in the yard. They'd been ambushed on their return from their day's patrol and were badly hurt. I rushed in and literally threw the wounded men into the back of the truck with the assistance of the cook. Shouts rose from the surrounding crowd who were running towards us. I drove straight at them. They dived aside in surprise with exclamations and orders for me to stop, throwing rocks as I sped past.

Driving straight to the local hospital, I left the scouts for medical attention and went on to the police camp. On our return with the police several hours later, we found our camp deserted and ransacked. Tractors and vehicles had been commandeered and driven off. Collecting our traumatised drivers, we headed for a night's rest in a safer place.

Scouring the surrounding village area with police over the next couple of days, we found our vehicles and firearms, but no camp or personal kit. Our scouts were in hospital for weeks with broken limbs and serious internal injuries.

Only the ranch management turned up for the arranged meeting with the Governor, where Peter described the foreign currency being earned by the Dollar Block operation and the necessity for anti-poaching activities.

'We are Africans, Mr Cunningham, you must remember.' The Governor of the Province explained. 'We don't need your foreign currency, your hunters, or even your fuel. If necessary, we can go back to living in our huts in the bush.'

Quite. From a man who drove the latest Mercedes and 4x4, lived in a mansion, flew abroad wherever and whenever he wished, shopping with precious foreign currency exchanged at official rates (paying around one thousandth of its true value with worthless Z$), much of it on government expense allowances and external bank accounts in place to keep his family for generations.

It was wretched to see our simple traditional village people being so duped by these power and wealth hungry hypocritical politicians.

The Zimbabwe we loved was being drastically manipulated and changed.

None of this did much for my depression. I was sinking back into that awful indecisive, 'this ain't going nowhere' syndrome.

Sands made a brave move to head, with her daughter Jo and family, to New Zealand. We drew up a settlement, which gave her a start in NZ, but left me penniless, but at least with my home, albeit very rundown. Although the severing was a relief in a way, out of each other's hair, it was admitting huge failure.

Also needing to get away from the stress zone in Zimbabwe, I raised a loan and headed out with a ticket to Palma de Majorca, Australia, and New Zealand—to find my precious scattered children and resolve the unfinished issues with Sands. Fifty dollars in my pocket to show for the thirty years of hard work, it was daunting, and wonderfully freeing.

My beautiful daughters were working in exotic spots—what a treat it was to arrive in these havens of peace after all the turmoil back home. They had tossed their crumbs onto the waters when they finished their degrees in Cape Town and found their niches after fierce skirmishes to survive in the big bad world.

Neen, artist and English scholar, found a job as hostess in the Mediterranean yacht world. Cath, trained in architecture and interior décor, after a tough spell trying to be a secretary in London, joined her. Rach, an English graduate, taught in Taiwan for a while and then also succumbed to the adventure of seagoing life. 'The Fothergill Pirates' were united again on the French Riviera.

Cath was the first to find her man, Scott Elliott, an Australian from Perth. She was in Antibes, between yachts, staying in a campsite, as always with her bongo drum. Also passionate about bongo drumming, Scotty heard the African beat coming from the other side of the campsite one evening. He headed across to find this dishy bird on her termite scarred Zimbabwean bongo. Kneeling beside her, he picked up the beat, which took them long into the night. And on into the rest of their lives.

I was on my way with a pile of wedding presents to Perth, including three large Zambezi Tonga drums. Harare checked—in, fifty kilos overweight.

'African wedding in Australia,' I explained.

Brother-in-law Davey had dropped me at the airport with a worried look on his face.

'Never travel with more than you can carry, Rob!'

Smiling at his concern, and wisdom, I stubbornly pushed my two trolleys through the departure door. The Zimbabwean ticketing staff kindly swallowed my story.

Next problem was diverting en route to Palma de Majorca, where I was to spend a month with Neen and Rach before heading onto Perth. Dubai International was not as generous over my tale. Pushing the trolley loads around the airport, three African bongo drums blocking my forward vision, I discovered my fifty dollars would not even cover four weeks in 'left luggage' for the excess.

After several hours of exasperated amazed uniformed officials who could hardly believe what I was asking, I spotted a gaggle of air hostesses coming in from their flight.

'Might as well . . . Nothing to lose . . . And you've got to do something, Rob!'

I approached them.

They patiently listened, amused in a compassionate kind of way. One petite figure asked me if she understood correctly. I confirmed she did. Staff in the United Arab Emirates airline, she looked again at the drums, tin warthog with spiky tail sticking out of its wrapping and all the boxes tied together with rope. And laughed.

'What's that?' she asked, pointing at the warthog's tail.

I explained.

'What's a warthog?' she laughed again.

After listening to my story, embellished a little further by admitting to being a safari guide, she asked:

'Just wait right here, I'll be back.'

'Thank you,' I replied with great feeling.

A little desperately wondering how I could be so foolishly naïve and optimistic, I waited, obediently standing there in the huge arrivals hall, masses of people walking past curiously looking at my pile of luggage, for twenty minutes.

'How silly of me to think she'd come back!' I was beginning to think. 'And what now?'

Then, down the glitzy passage she waltzed, giggling away. Leading me to an outside door, her little car was parked and waiting.

'No bombs?' she laughed again.

We filled the whole of the inside of her little Renault 4 with my goods, exchanged email addresses, and the date I was booked to fly back, and parted company.

'See you in four weeks,' Maha called, still laughing.

'Unpack the warthog and have a look at it,' I called back.

I sighed with relief, wondered again about my sanity, and marvelled at this Muslim angel.

Arriving in Palma after the mammoth journey across the airline routes of Africa and Europe, exhausted, but hugely looking forward to meeting with my 'gals', not the best of correspondents and whom I had hardly seen or heard of since they'd left Africa, I found the airport emptied from the last, late night flight I had just arrived on. No sign of anybody to meet me.

I managed to track down Neen's mobile number in one of my bags.

'Daaad!' Lots of party noise in the background. 'You're where? . . . oh my gosh! We didn't know . . . well . . . Daaad . . .' (Chatter between Neen and Rach).

'Dad, if you can get a taxi to . . .' more chatter . . . 'Ask him to drop you at the Turk's Head restaurant.'

'Where's that?' I had absolutely no idea of the geography of this city.

'Uuumm . . . . or . . . . maybe the harbour . . . no, okay, tell you what, just ask him to drop you at the Cathedral, and we'll find you there,' she shouts above the music. 'So exciting, Dad, see you just now.'

I staggered out, hoping there'd still be a taxi in the now very empty airport, relishing the thought of a quiet cathedral to recover in while I waited.

Amazingly, we found each other. It was so good to meet again, forgive the bad times, remember the good, deeply appreciating our family bond. A wonderfully restoring time.

'Do you know about rudders?' the harassed owner working on his burned out yacht asked.

'Sure, what's the problem?' I quickly learned that whatever I was asked about when job hunting, always to respond positively. The docks were a good place to look for work—which I needed to pay my way around here—and soon found.

Daughters, friends and father met at the end of each day, quaffing kioja and enjoying delicious, different Mediterranean fare.

Six weeks of heaven, apart from a dose of malaria that came with me (much to the consternation of the local hospital).

Too quickly it was time to move on.

Back in Dubai, Maha faithfully kept her commitment, and received a soapstone sculpture of a Zimbabwe bird as thanks.

Excess luggage now paid for from wages earned on the Palma docks, I arrived to Australia's intolerant wood and animal skin policy—Tonga drums top of their anathema.

Decontaminated and deloused, I received a wonderful welcome from Cath, Scotty, and my first granddaughter, Noa, and the dogs.

Their home is something of a permanent building site, with Scotty's skills and Cath's artistic decorating flair constantly on the go. They had decided to postpone the wedding for a year till they could do it 'properly'. Penniless Dad didn't feel so good about that, but their generous understanding made it clear. 'No worries, Dad.'

A month of their big-hearted hospitality and lovely family Christmas meant it was time to meet Sands in New Zealand.

**Fothergill
Pirates
over the
years**

Chapter 42

A Far Off Land

This was the hard bit. Sands and I each had a lot to work through about where we went from here. Meeting me in Wellington, a year and a half down the line from our separation, she drove through the mountain pass in her little car connecting the sea port to the farming valley of Masterton where she lived, looking after Jo and Gary's home.

The scenery was awesome, and blustery winds knocked us as she drove the mountain roads, describing living in NZ as like being on a ship with weather rolling off the sea and changing hourly.

Just like a doughty little ship in a storm, Sands' capacity to absorb all that had happened between us was commendable, and she now focused on our reconciliation. I was still hung up with that depression and was far from ready to live as husband and wife again. The old chains clanked in the background. Yet I so much wanted for us to be understanding friends.

The little farming town of Masterton lay in a wide valley with a river meandering through snow-capped mountains on the one side, low hills on the other, the sea just beyond both. Several of our displaced Zimbabwean farmers had settled in this beautiful spot and it was where Jo and Gary had decided to live—a fitting and peaceful place for Sands and I to spend time together.

We headed off in her car to explore NZ, and our hearts. The beauty and grandeur of New Zealand helped our gentle sounding of each other. A prestigious world class sailing event, The America's Cup, was on in Auckland. The glitter and glamour of the event added to the healing experience of being on holiday together, probably the first we had ever had truly to ourselves.

But the million dollar question hovered permanently between us. Could we, or not? As ever, we couldn't really talk about it either.

After a lovely month of meandering, I had not resolved the agony of my broken marriage, nor felt good about heading back so empty in spirit, to an emptier Zimbabwe. It was with a heavy heart that I was flying back via Perth on the long return leg of my three-month excursion ticket.

The awful washing machine was churning again.

'You what, Daad?' Cath was wholly exasperated.

'I'm going back to NZ,' I said. Having just arrived in Perth for a three day stopover on the way home, I had decided on the plane journey over that I would have to return and sort things out better.

Easier said than done. With no money nor plan. I mused about ferrying a boat or an aeroplane to Auckland—I might just as well have been volunteering for the space programme. Fantastic ideas whirled around in my mind. Cath and Scottie were supportive, but didn't need this on top of their very full life in starting the new family home.

Two good old Zimbabwean friends, Rory and Roshine McArthy, offered to stand my ticket back to NZ, in lieu of a bunch of unsellable stone sculptures I'd brought over and left with them to get rid of.

'We love you, my Dad. Just hang in on the blue days, the silver ones are coming. Take care and look after yourself. We're always here for you. Love, Cath.'

Her special message inside the front cover of BTG's book, 'Blue Days', an hilarious collection of animal photos with ingeniously apt captions, was a heart-warming gift as she saw me off a week later to who knew where or what.

I arrived for the finals of The America's Cup, with ten dollars in my pocket, enough for the airport bus into town, donated by Scotty's brother Dan on my way through Sydney. Who's Who in the sailing world were in port. I was convinced I'd find a job working on a yacht. Never mind where it took me.

The competition was stiff. Jobs hovered, and fell. A few small ones kept the wolf from the door. I wore my soles out walking the wharfs and shipyards. The city was in magnificent carnival mode in honour of the sailors, and I pretended I had just arrived from Zimbabwe to watch the racing, enjoying the generous New Zealand hospitality in the festive dockside cafes. At the end of the day I would head back to my backpacker lodge which was holding my passport until I paid the bill.

It was like a weird dream. On the other side of the world, with no money, no job, no work permit, no return ticket, not knowing a soul, other than Sands, whom no ways could I contact in this forlorn situation.

Good planning, Rob!

And then The America's Cup was over. NZ lost it—to fame and big money. Huge disappointment gripped the country while the glamorous sailing world sailed away. And the buzz in the town and docks with it. Demolition squads removed the special paraphernalia that had been set up along the waterfront. All went quiet, and Auckland got on with its normal sober life again.

And I still had no job.

'You're a delinquent, Rob. This is the kind of thing you do when you're eighteen. You are now fifty five!' I could not believe myself.

It was the craziest thing I'd ever done, and that was really saying something.

'Naaa, sorry 'ol timer, nothin' gaoin' t'daiy.'

'Okay, see ya tomorrow.'

I lined up with the hobos and professional skivers at the Auckland labour exchange, waiting my turn to be picked for cleaning up on a building site, or digging trenches, whatever was going. Some days I'd be there for hours to get half a day's work. The bosses picked the younger guys first, reckoning they'd be stronger—and less professional at skiving. Sitting on the pavement, alone, after everybody had left, I would remember Fothergill, the thriving business *I had owned*, with boats and aeroplanes and sixty odd staff, the African Bush, my beautiful home and lovely young wife, my special and now scattered children . . . and would quietly weep.

How had it come to this? What happened, God? Or are you just a big myth? Did I really miss the mark that badly back there?

I'd pitch up again the next day.

'Fothergill Bushmen don't cry,' I would tell myself. 'Just make it, man. You've gotta do something. Anything.'

I landed one day on a site right on the waterfront, where I could have watched the The America's Cup racing while I worked, with a superb view over the Hauraki Gulf.

'You're not the usual kind we get from the Labour Exchange?' The South African engineer in charge had noticed me struggling with a large jackhammer next to a Maori whose forearms were the size of my thighs. Discovering my background and experience, he took me on as a regular to assist him. On labourer's wages. It was a win/win for us both. For me, the luxury of a daily job to go to was exquisite. I was sailing again, in every sense, and came to love this harbour city.

. I would race back after work, throw off boots and overalls, jump into my sailing gear, and turn up to crew in the 'rum' race that one of the yacht clubs would run most evenings. A great apartment looking over the Harbour Bridge was generously offered me to look after by one of the sailing crowd.

'Haiy, Zimbao, where you bin?' old John would ask if I missed one of the races.

'Gettin' on with life,' I'd tell him, smiling.

He'd smile back, happy to see me, no need for any more questions.

'Zimbao' was climbing back into the land of the living.

Absolutely on my own, something I couldn't handle a short while back in those ghastly depressed days, I was strong and resilient again. I had no responsibilities to anyone in the world, no one around me having a clue who I was, and those who knew me hadn't a clue where I was. I hardly knew myself. But was slowly finding out—and that Mr Angel hadn't abandoned me after all.

A marvellously freeing four months, but winter was looming, and it was time to move. I'd earned enough not to be a burden on anyone. I'd been in touch with Sands, and Nick Crozier, a Zimbabwean doctor who saw the light earlier than most and had kindly helped to settle many of our refugee farmers in Masterton, and me on my first trip. A little surprised, they okay'd me to come back down there. I found a job as an assistant 'chippy' (carpenter), seeing Sands here and there—no pressures, no time limits, no decision-making. Just free to be as we were.

A new experience was tying white frosted steel in building foundations at—4°C in the early morning.

'Gloves? Only for softies, Zimbao!'

'Hey, Kiwi, just 'cause you keep warm going to bed with sheep!' We joked and enjoyed the camaraderie in the hardness.

I soon found myself wandering the Masterton aerodrome, a huge grassed airfield with the feel of a WWII bomber base. A great variety of aviation activity hummed, whistled and roared overhead. Vintage aeroplanes, gliders, skydivers, helicopter training and the inevitable 'ag' flyers.

A young and progressive owner of a busy aircraft maintenance business took me on as a 'spanner boy'. Those silver days of Cath's were rolling in.

Much of New Zealand's pastures are in the hills where, tractor access being difficult, fertilizing the grazing is done by 'ag airies'. This spectacular feat is accomplished from airstrips dotted around on the sides of hills that most people would think twice about walking up. The technique is to land in a climbing attitude, keeping the power on so that gravity wouldn't play its embarrassing role if the aeroplane dropped too low in speed on the landing run up the steep gradient.

As the plane rises over the brow at the top of the strip, the pilot cuts his throttle, does a smart 'U' turn, and waits for a ton of fertilizer to drop into the open hopper behind his cockpit—from a specially made front-end loader, also acting as the fuel tanker. This loader/ tanker tows in a trailer of 'fert' for each day's operation in the early hours of the morning.

The plane would then power down the precipitous runway, now assisted by gravity, stagger off with its heavy load, drop and return to reload within 8-10 minutes. This process is repeated throughout the day, at the end of which the plane lands back at Masterton, invariably with a few 'probs'. A heavy landing, knocking a sheep, corrosion damage from 'fert' on the structure, and once, following a fuel miscalculation and forced landing on the side of another hill.

Mountains of New Zealand's North Island – and landing up a mountainside

"Av 'er ready boiy seven, Mait,' the parting shot as a pilot swaggered out the hangar after a few beers. We'd work through to get it sorted, on overtime. I'd always thought nothing touched a navy pilot, but these NZ 'ag' flyers were something else.

And what a joy it was to be back amongst aeroplanes. There was the odd chance to join a ferry trip or a test flight, even some gliding. I spent five blissful months through into the NZ summer, soaking in this delightfully uncomplicated enthusiastic world of aviation, deeply enjoying my relaxed and stress free life. Good companionship, banter and stories over 'smoko' (tea break), and just being again a valued part of a team. As good a tonic as I could have found. My paint shop boss, Forest, had a typically wry comment for tricky situations.

'Alwaiys three soides to the story, Zimboa.'

'Yeah. Right, Forest.'

So true.

Sands and I came to a comfortable place where we could enjoy each other's company, and although romantic love didn't rekindle, we could be friends again, and move on. She was well loved and nicely busy in caring for Jo's home, and the NZ health service was dealing with her medical problems admirably.

My temporary tourist immigration permit ran out.

It was time to go home, with a big thank you to New Zealand.

I flew back via Bali, taking the first holiday on my own that I could remember since university days. How good it was just paying my way again and being able to enjoy the adventure. Depression completely over. Rob was Rob once more.

I remembered Michael Cassidy, a good friend and leader of African Adventure Missions in Natal RSA, saying back in those difficult times. 'Take a holiday from God, Rob.' I was a bit perplexed at the time, but understood more now. Moving away from the intensity helped find oneself, and new perspectives.

I've quietly got on with life in Zim since, slowly working back into the safari industry and enjoying being a guide again. So much happened, and didn't, in those years behind. The wisdom of hindsight fits some of the pieces together, but can do nothing for the insensibilities and tragic losses.

That we tried, and mostly had a good time doing it, is unquestionable. Understandings gel out of the great learning curve of life, though many questions remain unanswered. Nothing can change the past, but we sure can the future.

The painful school of suffering and adversity, much as we hate, offers immeasurable gain that nothing else can achieve. And the consequences of choices are accountably clear. In being able to laugh more and deeper now than ever before, I am totally persuaded of the essentiality in seeking The Kingdom, although a little wary of religious fundamentalists with their personal hotlines to heaven.

I sincerely respect those who are in the spiritual frontline, having seen something of the exacting demands and responsibilities it brings. And have huge respect and compassion for those enquiring through the myth of His very existence, which I know well, and so deeply hope they too discover the magnificent truth.

One of the wealthiest and wisest men of the old world, King Solomon, who wrote the book of Proverbs in the Bible, exhibiting a wisdom rock solid today, wrote in the book of Ecclesiastes, in 950 BC.

'There is a time for everything.

A time to be born and a time to die, a time to plant and a time to uproot . . .

There is nothing better for man than to enjoy his work.

But who can tell him what will happen under the sun after he is gone?

Give generously, for your gifts will return to you later.

It is a wonderful thing to be alive.

Fear God and keep his commandments.'

This King, son of the great King David, who had everything any man could dream of, pursuing every pleasure and observation life had to offer. His stable held 12,000 horses and 1,400 chariots, his household 1000 wives and concubines (I Kings 9-11). The absence of TV and internet did not seem to bother him.

He was compelled to admit that only God could satisfy the order in the universe he studied so diligently. And that the elusive value of life he'd sought all his days would come from not "under the sun", but "above the sun".

Together with many in today's world, I used to shun this quaint old stuff in the light of modern science and technology. Some of our eminent scientists have this to say.

'This most beautiful system of the sun, planets and comets could only proceed from the counsel and dominion of an intelligent and powerful Being.' Sir Isaac Newton.

'A common sense interpretation of the facts suggests that a super intellect has monkeyed with physics, as well as with chemistry and biology, and that there are no blind forces worth speaking about in nature.' Sir Fred Hoyle, Royal Astrophysicist.

'The world is too complicated in all its parts and interconnections to be due to chance alone. The existence of life with all its order . . . is simply too well put together." Alan Sandage, Cosmologist and winner of the Crawford Astronomy Prize.

'If the universe had not been made with the most exacting precision we could never have come into existence.' John O'Keefe, NASA Astronomer.

They've all been around the science and space world a good deal more than most of us, with intellects that leave more of us even further behind. I find these modern observations interestingly akin to Solomon's. The deep thinkers appear unaffected by time. None of this, of course, can be proved. It's what we know as Faith. We'll find out in time—hopefully not too late.

'He has given us new birth into a living hope through the resurrection of Jesus Christ . . . and into an inheritance that can never spoil.' (Peter 1). We can choose to believe and trust. Or not. And face the consequences.

I might have missed Him back there, but I know that the author of the beginning and the end, and everything in between, hasn't missed me, or any one of us for that matter. In this age of Grace, He is indeed the God of second chances.

Chapter 43

The Agony and the Ecstasy

Back home, a political time bomb waited my arrival.

In 2008, an election, after Mugabe's 27th year in power, voted Morgan Tsangirai as President, and MDC as the majority party in parliament, in spite of gross rigging. After delaying the results for a month, Mugabe allowed MDC their majority in parliament, but maintained the presidential results were too close to be decisive. Having patently lost, he called, illegally, for a re-run. Unlimited power rests with the President's office, engineered so by himself, and he wasn't letting go of it.

A systematic campaign of brutal retribution was wreaked on all who had voted for the opposition in the recent election, the ruling party having carefully designed the polling stations to show that up. Tsvangirai withdrew from the presidential election re-run to save his party members from further torturous intimidation.

The man who had it in his power to call an end to this dissoluteness and had supported Mugabe for all his years, the South African President, Thabo Mbeki, now brokered a deal of sharing government in 2009 in such a manner that simply plunged our country back into the hands of the former ruling party.

Tsvangirai was persuaded to accept this power sharing agreement as a powerless Prime Minister, tasked with re-establishing the ailing economy. Cunningly, the newly legalised President Mugabe now had new money coming into his formerly totally empty government coffers. There was always huge surplus in his private ones.

The people were desperately unhappy. 85 percent unemployment, the Zimdollar worthless, municipal and government amenities virtually unserviceable. Strikes and go slows from state health workers, doctors, teachers, civil servants, and mutinies in the armed forces were ruthlessly crushed.

90 percent of our population lived in abject poverty, statistically categorised as starving by the UN's World Health Organisation. Urban parents could no longer afford to send children to school. The people grew weaker, and lost hope. Cholera stalked the land. Many died in silence. Whole families who had been existing on roots and bark were found dead in their rural huts, starved to death. Only the party prospered, grossly and inhumanely.

The biggest, most irrefutable and unstoppable opposition to the Mugabe regime was the failing economy. The country was on the verge of collapse, kept afloat only through the external contributions of the diaspora and the few mining ventures still functioning, and now a large cache of diamonds, understood to be the biggest new field in the world, its income siphoned off by the 'Chefs'. The catastrophic brain drain left few behind with initiative to combat the mega machine. More than a third of our population were refugees.

Our pariah state is an embarrassment to the continent, hampering development of the entire SADC region, a federation of southern African states that seek a united strength by aiming for cross border resource distribution and trading ties. Zimbabwe sits plumb in its centre, key to the region's successful growth. All surrounding former despotic regimes have crumbled out of office in the last decade. Yet Mugabe was extraordinarily supported by this body, receiving standing ovations when he appeared at their public meetings. The Octogenarian flourishes, celebrating his birthdays in lavish jocular fashion, financed by donations from company and party supporters.

The former opposition party, MDC, elected to lead parliament, battle on, determined to straighten things out, but undermined at every step by the old ZANU-PF guard who fear losing their lavish lifestyle, and being made accountable for the past. Inevitably, some MDC parliamentarians are attracted by the gravy train. Corruption and lawlessness preside.

The only certainty is that all this and these will pass. How and when, and what will be left, are questions one shrinks from answering.

Most black Africans live under conditions we Europeans would give up on after a week. After a month we'd be committed to an asylum. Used and abused shamelessly by ruthless selfish politicians, they continue to smile, shrugging their shoulders.

'It's in God's hands', I hear so often. Sometimes I wish they'd take it into their own hands, but know they'd be mowed down instantly if they tried. And they're just too plain good natured to do that anyway.

A most frustrating, unfathomable, unreliable, patient, obstinate, willing, smiley, wonderful people. I love them to bits, and wouldn't choose to live anywhere else in the world.

We never know what tomorrow brings. I ended a season as a bush camp manager in Zambia's Luangwa valley, arriving back in Harare with an assortment of *kutundu*, including my laptop holding this story and my hard earned dollars in its case. While talking twenty to the dozen and loading into my friend Janet's car, we drove off, leaving the laptop in the rear basket of the trolley in the car park.

Only later that evening did I discover the loss. Frantic phone calls to security established they hadn't blown up any small black suitcases, but nor did they know of one being recovered. I went straight out there, praying like I hadn't for a long time. I half expected I might find Mr Angel standing there with his hand on the trolley, making it invisible until I got there.

No Angel, but a little man, doing his security job, told me he'd found it and handed it to the police charge office. Very thankful he'd found it, although aware that the US$, if still there, might now be a problem. It was illegal to hold without special currency permission at the time. At least I knew the laptop was intact. Unimaginable in starving Zimbabwe.

On presenting myself to claim my property, I was informed the officer in charge would like to see me before I collected it. Not unexpectedly, he would only be available next morning.

I drove out to the airport again next day, to find a large bellied man in plain clothes introducing himself as the officer in charge. He grumbled about having to come all the way out here to see me on a Sunday morning. I responded how equally irritating it was for me.

Following the grizzly bear across the car park to his office, I launched my plan to save my currency.

'I am so impressed with your security measures here, Inspector,' I told him, 'I phoned my friend, the Air Marshal, this morning, to congratulate him on the levels of efficiency the Harare International airport has reached. He thanked me and asked me to be sure to phone him back if there were any delays in recovering my property . . . which I'm sure there won't be, will there, Inspector?'

The Air Marshal was the mastermind behind the *Gukurahundi* in Matabeleland, striking fear into most hearts at the mention of his name. I don't know him from a bar of soap. An unfair strategy, but I was desperate.

The bear looked at me without saying a word. I followed him into his office where he opened his safe, pulled out my laptop and a brown envelope with my cash, asking me to check if everything was in order. I did, and it was, to the last note. I signed his book to that effect. Three minutes later, I was tipping the security man who found it and climbing into my car and on my way home.

That's a Zimbabwean miracle.

And then another. Suzie is our maid in our home in Glen Lorne. She helped Sands in the house and with our children, and became part of our family. Suzie Fynn she calls herself. Stalwartly looking after Sands through her sickness, when she left for NZ, Sue transferred her caring skills to ageing Maasie (born 1915).

With deep concern I heard of Sue falling seriously ill while I was working in Kariba. She had been taken to a rural mission hospital where the care was more reliable than in the city. Her family then removed her to their village home, as is the custom in the face of impending death, to tend to her themselves.

I went to find her, down the old Domboshowa Road, passing the typical rural towns with their dusty yards and streets, barest of non-stocked shops, never ending hair and beauty parlours, and beer halls, wondering how Sue could be faring in this forsaken backwater.

The scenery was magnificent. Winding roads through big old granite hills, huge balancing boulders, like some giant had been building 'domino' castles with them, breath-taking views down valleys towards shimmering distant Mozambique, laden 'mohohobo' trees with groups of women all selling the same sweet fruit in the same place, mobbing each unwary customer who dared stop, and children and goats and donkey carts and cattle and bicycles staggering under unbelievable loads, and old cars and trucks under even more unbelievable loads, belching black smoke.

Wonderful timeless rural Africa.

I parked the car by the roadside and walked down a track I'd been directed to. A one roomed bare brick hut, roofed in corrugated tin, came into view. No running water, no shade, no windows. Family were gathered. Faithful mother, and aunt whose house it was; father, who had not been seen for many years; sisters who had gone their own way and not kept in touch; brothers who worked and had little time or energy for much else beyond surviving. They had heard, brought a little food, and were there to watch her die.

She was lying inside the dark room, so thin I could see the shape of her bones, utterly lacking in energy, even to smile. Sue was all but gone, gradually subsiding into the bottomless hole.

I was horrified, and upset that nobody seemed there to help her recovery. I found out she had TB. And discovered there was a clinic close by, within wheelbarrow distance, the only way she could get there. I went to see them.

Amazed, I found one of the few hospitals in the country, run by a Roman Catholic Mission who specialised in TB. Although so isolated, everything was beautifully clean and cared for. The doctor assured me that they had the drugs to treat Sue, with which she could recover, as long as she dutifully followed their advice and attended their clinic.

I made arrangements to cover the costs and took the good news back to the family. They received it in the pathetic manner of overwhelmed poor people, as though I had brought certain salvation. I wasn't so certain, but was humbled and deeply grateful I could do something in the pitiful circumstances. I left her with provision, promising to be back. Her appreciation of my going out to see her was heart wrenching. I assured her of her value and future security, but wasn't so sure I'd see her again.

I heard reports, back in Kariba, that she was getting better. That could mean anything considering the condition I'd last seen her. Sitting up in bed and drinking a glass of water would be an improvement. So I was looking forward to seeing how she was on my next visit to Harare.

I gathered she'd moved back to her mother's village, and I set off, taking with me, as a guide, 13 year old Mercy who used to look after Sue's child. She still stayed at our home and went to the local mission school.

'Allounde nexty corner, Baasy, lasty housey," Mercy was saying in her newly learned English.

'Okay.Thank you, I'm slowing down.'

She and her little friend, Mauline, giggle in the back seat, delighted that we've made the journey in an hour compared to half a day on the bus.

A little cluster of huts snuggled into the big msasa trees on the side of the road. We stepped out into a clean swept yard, where a toothless old lady, immediately on greeting us, patted her stomach and rolled her eyes.

'Sugar, Baas. Salt, Baas. Eeeeh, nzara (hunger) Baas!'

We gave her some of the kapenta I'd brought for Sue, and locked the car securely as Mauline advised in her excellent Grade 7 English.

'I don't think we can trust this old woman.'

Looking over our shoulders at the old lady checking her kapenta, and to make sure she wasn't fiddling with car door locks, we headed for the hills and Sue's village, the girls leading.

In the heart of rural Africa, no roads or piped water, no electricity, just lush bush and rocky 'kopjes', and baboons, and little villages, strategically placed for proximity to a stream, or just because that's where the chief put them. We walked down paths, along bare fields waiting for rain, amongst giant trees towering in spring bloom, their new leaves a shiny copper, through dry riverbeds, up long hot hills, passing small groups of friendly smiley people, with their dogs and chickens and goats and cattle, who asked how we were, exchanged greetings, and nodded they knew we were going to visit our friend. And on and on in the midday sun, feeling so good to be African.

At last, a little village of three huts and a maize coop on a distant hilltop came in to view. Mercy and Mauline, beginning to claim how tired and hot they were, shouted with glee.

'There they are!'

We saw a woman in a big hat working in the field. From a long way off, Sue saw us coming, dropped everything, and ran down the hill crying

'Heloooooooooooooo Baaaaaaaaaaaas', laughing and weeping, which by this time I was too.

We literally fell into each other's arms. Picking up the bag of kapenta and goodies we'd bought, we trekked the last few hundred yards, greeted like returning heroes by old 'Gogo', Sue's mum, her elderly new husband, and little four-year-old Blessing, Sue's child.

Sitting under the mango tree on polished pieces of tree trunk, together with a goat and small puppy, we chatted about everybody and everything back home, laughed over stories of how No 27 survived a recent break-in by some 'Tsotsis' (bad guys), and how Janet living in the old house had received a hit in the head by flying glass from a ball bearing fired through the window by catapult, and thought she'd been shot, but was okay, and how the little community had responded and beat them off, and how appreciative Sue was of the loving letters from Neen and Rach and Cath that had found their way from France and Australia to this remote little spot. A moment never to be forgotten.

The old smiley Sue, fully recovered, strong and healthy again. It happened to be my birthday. I could not have had a better present. What a privilege to play this little part in the continuing unfolding drama of our country.

Sands died in New Zealand on 20 June 2012. She spent her last five years tenderly cared for by the Bethlehem Home staff in Tauranga, and Jo faithfully visiting. Sands' health deteriorated to such an extent that the very professional medical world of New Zealand simply did not know where to turn. Her pain and suffering were hard to bear, mostly of course for her, but also for all who cared for and loved her.

Rob, Maasie & Suzie

Cath, Scotty & Noa

Grandpa, Neen & Guilly, Rach & Olly – and children

We all visited when we could, but Jo and her little family bore the brunt of the daily burden, with grace and fortitude. I had just been over two months before, sensing the end was near. Then we were given a week's notice by the doctors that she was on the last lap. It was extraordinary to contemplate where she would be at the end of that short time. She knew, and had a great peace in it all.

The girls scrambled from across the world, Neen and Rach arriving last after two days of airport's and flying, carrying Rach's ten month old baby, Yael. It was the eve of Sand's last composed day. She was in a coma for the rest of that night and next day, with all the girls united and around her, being given a room next door in the home.

Neen had struggled to come to terms with the whole saga of Sands' ill health ever since she'd been a little girl, holding her Mum responsible for messing up her life and family—illogical, but real. She desperately needed to come to terms with that and find peace with Sands before she died—but those few hours at the end of a long and wearying flight, with all the trauma and emotion of the gathering, were not the best time for that.

In the early hours of the following morning, Sands having been in coma for thirty six hours, Neen was woken with an urge to be with her Mum. She got up and sat by Sands' bed, holding her hand. She was overcome by an enormous spiritual and emotional sense of forgiveness and love flowing between her and her Mum, totally cleansing and releasing her from all the confusion and resentment that had dogged all those years. And then Sands died, holding Neen's hand.

She called the others, and they spent an hour or more in the deepest prayer and sense of the Lord in their midst that any of them had ever experienced. It was a life changing time, from which all of them have retained the wondrous knowledge of knowing that they had met the almighty, all-loving God, and that their Mum is with Jesus now, running and laughing and as beautiful as ever, and that each of them will be there with her one day. As I know, too.

The 'jewel' has become seriously flawed, and clearly huge change must lie ahead. We await an election in 2013, hoping and praying for truth and reconciliation to win through. As strange and unlikely as the God driven destiny that brought my family to make this land their home all those centuries ago, that brought this story to happen, we live in faith that a new wind will blow through the land and bring better times.

I work the safari seasons in our National Parks, where I love every minute of every day, walking amongst the elephants, introducing visitors to this harsh, balanced, beautiful African Bush. The off season break from guiding brings me home where I finish this writing on my veranda, fix old cars, and help out where I can in the battered country I love and am so much a part of.

Back in that timeless wilderness, I walked the banks of the Zambezi River in the Lower Zambezi National Park of Zambia, following lion spoor. The 'Parks' scout was nose to the ground. I cautioned my clients, 'we're close, very close, they could be anywhere. Keep right behind me. And don't sneeze now.'

As we dropped down a steep trail to the river, on the Nkalangi Channel that we often canoed and on which I knew every ripple, we were watched by two old hippo bulls called Mugabe and Mbeki, the former as he obstinately held his position, quick to attack and make life as uncomfortable as he possibly could, the latter as he always slid off and avoided confrontation. The lions broke cover with a grunt from a dense thorn bush just metres away and bounded into the water, pursued by two big crocs which just missed catching them as they made the island 30 metres across the channel.

We all live to enjoy another adventure-filled day in Africa's wilds, where it's never over till it's over.

The story is still on, as are the players. And where there's life there's hope. And where hope there's life.

And Angels in thorn bushes.

Always to be there . . . ?

17248893R00246

Printed in Great Britain
by Amazon